CLIFFORD ODETS:
Playwright-Poet

by
HAROLD CANTOR

The Scarecrow Press, Inc.
Metuchen, N.J. & London
1978

Library of Congress Cataloging in Publication Data

Cantor, Harold, 1926–
   Clifford Odets, playwright–poet.

   Bibliography: p.
   Includes index.
   1. Odets, Clifford, 1906–1963—Criticism and
interpretation.
PS3529.D46Z6   812'.5'4   77-27284
ISBN 0-8108-1107-3

To Elaine, in gratitude
for her editorial help,
understanding and love

CONTENTS

ACKNOWLEDGMENTS

It is impossible to acknowledge all the help I received in writing this study, but special mention must be made of: Alfred A. Knopf, Inc., who permitted me to quote extensively from The Fervent Years by Harold Clurman; Paul Warshow, for permission to cite his father's essay in The Immediate Experience by Robert Warshow; Michael J. Mendelsohn, who allowed me to quote from his two-part interview with Odets published in Theatre Arts; Arthur Wagner, for permission to quote from his seminal article, "How a Playwright Triumphs."

I am also indebted to the librarians, Alice Griffith and Harry Tarlin, and the library staff at Mohawk Valley Community College, Utica College and Hamilton College. I owe special thanks to three generous individuals--Emanuel Mussman, Carleton Wood and Sheldon N. Grebstein--and to Anita Bartelotte, who typed the final draft. To my children, Carla and Richard, who became fervent Odetsians and discussed the plays with me, I owe the insights and understandings of a generation not my own.

For permission to quote extracts from the plays of Clifford Odets, I am deeply grateful to Harold Freedman Brandt & Brandt, Inc., who are the author's agents for the following plays:

INTRODUCTION

This recent critical estimate of Odets represents what is perhaps the standard view: "Although his work transcends the social problems of the 1930's and yields characters of wider psychological and social validity, Odets' plays, particularly the early ones, reflect an attachment to his times which precludes true universality."[1] My intention in this study is precisely to correct what I believe to be a mistaken and simplistic view.

Not only is Odets regarded as inextricably bound up with a vanished era, but his three post-Depression plays are often dismissed as "superficial" and a departure from his former "socially significant drama." I have been quoting Allan Lewis who, reviewing Odets' work in 1965, summarized as follows: "Odets betrayed his own talents. He was a sensitive man who believed in a better world to come, but he was unable to sustain that belief under difficult and changing social conditions. He was a lonely writer, but too weak to become a great one."[2] The ad hominem bias of such a statement is, unfortunately, typical of too much Odets criticism.

Though he has always been recognized as an influential playwright--who made contributions to the development of such later writers as Tennessee Williams, Arthur Miller, Paddy Chayevsky, William Gibson and Lorraine Hansberry-- his plays are nevertheless regarded as museum pieces. His critical standing among literary scholars has been touched by condescension and distorted by biographical and political factors which detract from his genuine literary achievements. Despite much recent "rescue work" by authors I shall later cite, the charges persist that he was in several respects a failure: that he was a brilliant flash-in-the-pan who "sold out" to Hollywood; that he lost his sense of purpose when the Marxian dialectic became meaningless to him; that his plays are often flawed by naiveté, crudeness, and sentimentality.[3]

1

There is some truth in all of these assertions, but I think they obscure larger and more significant truths. Odets is the paradigmatic spokesman for the Jewish middle class in the Thirties in drama. Further, he became a poetic play- wright and myth-maker for middle-class ethics and aspira- tions and the dilemmas they produce. Despite their flaws, his best plays achieve a depth and complexity, especially in their idiomatic and idiosyncratic use of language, that lift them out of the category of social realism into the realm of evocative parables and allegories in dramatic form, indeed, constructs which I shall later describe as "poetic."

While I cannot claim that these insights are original, they have not been demonstrated in any systematic way else- where, nor have their implications been fully explored. I propose to examine Odets' plays as a unified body of work without following in direct sequence the chronological order in which they were written. Surprisingly, to my knowledge no such attempt has been made before. [4] In doing so, I shall draw upon the pioneering work of several scholars who have done much to defend the reputation of a playwright I would rank with O'Neill, Miller, Williams, and Albee as one of the five best this country has produced.

Since Odets' death in 1963, three full-length books on him have appeared. Before them we had only R. Baird Shu- man's 1962 volume in the Twayne American Authors series, a work handicapped by its facile identification of Odets with the proletarian writers of the Thirties and its insistence that he wrote only social problem plays. Shuman even read so- cial significance into The Country Girl, Odets' most atypical and psychologically inward play.

In 1968, Edward Murray published Clifford Odets: The Thirties and After, a competent critical study which offered detailed analyses of eight of Odets' plays, with spe- cial attention to structure, character, language, and theme. Professor Murray's approach is similar to my own but, like Shuman, he works from a chronological methodology. He makes a dubious critical judgment when he dismisses Para- dise Lost in the same breath as Till the Day I Die as plays "neither of which ... can add any luster to Odets' reputa- tion." [5] Since both Harold Clurman and Odets considered Paradise Lost as the playwright's most profound play, an evaluation supported by its highly successful television pre- sentation in 1972, Murray's failure to analyze the play is surprising.

Shortly after Murray's work, Michael J. Mendelsohn in 1969 published Clifford Odets: Humane Dramatist, a work that is eminently sane and balanced in its critical judgments. Colonel Mendelsohn had the advantage of a personal interview and correspondence with Odets and he was able to provide new information about Odets' theories on playwriting, as well as useful accounts of his Hollywood and television work. But as Walter J. Meserve, in the 1969 volume of American Literary Scholarship, pointed out, "... because of the brevity of the book the analyses of the plays are not as full as one might wish."6 Once again the approach was chronological: 1) The Early Plays: Written in Anger, 2) The Middle Plays: In Moderation, 3) The Post-War Plays: In Maturity. Unfortunately, like most neat categorizations, this scheme also has loopholes: for example, the post-war The Big Knife was surely written in anger, and it can be argued that Odets was never more mature as an artist than when he wrote Awake and Sing!

The most recent book on Odets, Gerald Weales' Clifford Odets: Playwright, is probably the most comprehensive in its attention to all of Odets' writing (including his two unproduced plays, movie and TV scripts), as well as in its attempt to reconstruct from newspaper interviews, reviews, and memoirs a biographical account of his life. Until the long-awaited full-length biography appears by Odets' friend, Dr. Margaret Brenman-Gibson, Weales' bio-critical study will remain the most reliable source. Weales' efforts make it unnecessary to consult the shooting scripts and unpublished material since he concludes that they are ephemera that can add little to Odets' reputation as a dramatist. However, although he struggles valiantly against what he calls the "failed-dramatist cliché," Weales' commitment to a strictly sequential or evolutionary approach suggests implicit conclusions his words often belie: that is, the critical scenario for Odets remains essentially unchanged--rising star in the middle Thirties and setting sun in the Fifties--as each play is trotted up for review, examined (often perceptively) in the context of its time, then dismissed as Weales moves his newspaper-morgue Odets-figure to the next cycle.

While such an approach to Odets is tempting, I have adopted a more formalistic approach. With it have come certain advantages: 1) It has permitted me to assess the major themes and preoccupations of the playwright without labeling him "a child of the Thirties"; 2) While I have considered the biographical material, I have not allowed gossip

column chitchat and newspaper reviews to influence unduly
my estimate of what I take to be a unified oeuvre of twenty
years; 3) I have subordinated questions of Odets' intentions
and the reception of his plays, and his growth and/or failure
in Hollywood, to an attempt to see his plays as a whole; 4) I
have searched for the "figure in the carpet," the recurrent
themes, characters, and devices of language which comprise
the uniqueness of an Odets play and which permit a dramatist concerned with the texture of the social environment
nevertheless to create prose-poetry, to use the environment
as material for the composition of "a world elsewhere."

Although a major purpose of this study is to separate
the art of Odets from the distortions and improper emphases
of the legend which surrounds him, it would be folly to ignore the fact that his work has passed into history--much of
it non-literary. For example, there are segments devoted
to Waiting for Lefty in all the standard social histories on
the 1930's: one finds them in such works as Arthur Schles-
inger's The Politics of Upheaval (part of The Age of Roosevelt) and in Irving Bernstein's account of the worker and the
trade union movement, The Turbulent Years. Epigraphs
from Odets' plays preface such highly personalized memoirs
as Alfred Kazin's Starting Out in the Thirties and Murray
Kempton's Part of Our Time. To attempt to extricate the
socially committed playwright from his setting, to totally ignore the ferment of political events and cultural trends which
impinged on his work would be a blunder.

It is precisely because Odets does epitomize for so
many the Depression era that he has been not only underrated but valued for the wrong reasons. Just as his plays
were once political footballs kicked around by Stalinist and
anti-Communist critics, so today his reputation is caught on
the perilous tide which has floated the New Critics (and their
aristocratic biases) out to sea and returned the Radical Left
to the shore. Where formerly his work was damned for its
crudeness and sentimentality, he is now likely to be dismissed as irrelevant and nostalgic by the barbaric avatars
of Marcuse and Roszak.

Yet there are everywhere signs that he is enjoying
a healthy revival: Awake and Sing! and Paradise Lost en-
joyed excellent productions on the Hollywood Playhouse syn-
dicated by the National Educational Network in 1971-72;
Awake and Sing! was presented off-Broadway in 1972 and
again in 1977 and received fine critical notices; in 1973 the

newly organized Labor Theater, sponsored by 13 New York City labor unions, staged Waiting for Lefty; in 1974 the Hallmark Hall of Fame Theater presented a video version of The Country Girl starring Jason Robards and Shirley Knight; in my own area, a new repertory group, the Syracuse Stage, selected Lefty for its debut in 1974, and both audience and critics received it with warmth and enthusiasm. (It was particularly interesting to note that the excited applause at the performance I attended came from an audience comprised of many young people.)

I cite these recent productions--and there have been others in different parts of the country--to suggest that since the Seventies regards Clifford Odets with increasing respect, the time has arrived for a reconsideration of his plays.

I stated earlier that Odets is valued for the wrong reasons. An instance of this must surely be the general failure of criticism to acknowledge his influence on Jewish-American writers. Jews in American fiction have received extensive attention lately, but one finds no reference to Odets in Sol Liptzin's The Jew in American Literature, and Allan Guttman's The Jewish Writer in America affords him only a bare mention. The same cursory treatment prevails in Irving Malin's Jews and Americans, Robert Alter's After the Tradition, and Max Schulz's Radical Sophistication. While these last three works concentrate on the novel, and literary critics are somewhat finicky about mixing genres, Alfred Kazin has attested to the tremendous liberating effect the appearance of Odets' recognizable and believable Jewish characters had on his generation. [7] Many of the dilemmas and the foibles of the characters of Bellow, Malamud, and Roth are foreshadowed in Odets' plays, not to mention those of a direct descendant, Arthur Miller. Indeed, without Odets, the Jewish Renaissance of the Fifties and Sixties might have been retarded; at the very least, one feels compelled to cry out that "Attention must be paid!" to such a playwright.

But I do not wish to convey the impression that this study is primarily concerned with Odets' place in literary history. My major emphasis is focused on the richness of language and dramatic excitement of the plays themselves. I should like to inquire why so many people refer to the "honest ring" of his plays and the "Odetsian line" with fondness and affection; and so I have quoted liberally from the plays and analyzed his dialogue to fully answer this question.

The other hallmarks of Odets' plays are their emotional intensity and narrative urgency. Like any neo-romantic (and I use the word advisedly), Odets took large risks; he demands nothing less from his audience than its complete emotional involvement in the dramas he presents. Where he fails, it is usually because he forces his lyrical emotions into forms and constructions that are unable to contain them. Mordecai Gorelik, who was the stage designer for several of his plays, said in 1940: "Odets has never been able to strike a balance between his amazing intuitive grasp of the American scene and the oversimplified patterns into which he forces his materials."[8]

Yet even the weakest of his plays have compensations and, although there are dull moments, there is no Odets play without moving scenes and arresting characterizations to redeem it. I can still remember the rising excitement with which I read my first Odets dialogue (Act I of Rocket to the Moon) in the bulging, green-bound Whit Burnett anthology, This Is My Best. Re-reading the plays after many years, I can still respond to their vitality and enthusiasm. If to some of today's affluent generation "the Depression is old newsreels and the term, 'soup line,' and Grapes of Wrath with Henry Fonda looking sincere and downcast,"[9] many can see themselves, slightly transformed, in the brawling, quarrelsome atmosphere of an Odets family drama, and identify with his young lovers struggling to find a place for themselves and resolve an uncertain future. My students respond to the idealism of his attitudes, though most of them regard Marx as a bearded old fogey studied in Economics I. The more sophisticated repeat the cycle of their parents and, knowingly puffing on their political and philosophical cigars, approach Odets through a hazy ideological smokescreen. Let us blow away the smoke by first approaching him in his political-cultural context. Hence, we begin with that young playwright living through one of history's most terrifying nightmares.

NOTES

[1]McGraw-Hill Encyclopedia of World Drama (New York, 1972), 3, 341.

[2]Allan Lewis, American Plays and Playwrights of the Contemporary Theatre (New York, 1965), p. 113.

[3]The charge that Odets sold out to Hollywood is made in almost all discussions of his work, though mitigating circumstances are often cited. It may be epitomized in a dubious epigram by Odets' friend, Oscar Levant: "... everything he was against, in the beginning of his career, he wound up doing himself." The Memoirs of an Amnesiac (New York, 1965), p. 188. The ebb in vitality of Odets' post-Depression plays is traced to his loss of political commitment. "Once the Marxist metaphor had lost its validity, once the substructure of the Marxist dialectic no longer sufficed, Odets was deprived of the structural framework upon which he had consciously or unconsciously built." Gerald Rabkin, Drama and Commitment (Bloomington, 1964), p. 203. The charges of crudeness, sentimentality and naivete are usually made in connection with specific plays and are not unmixed with praise. Therefore they should not be quoted out of context. However, for a sampling of criticism unusually sensitive to "crudities" in Odets' work, see Joseph Wood Krutch, The American Drama Since 1918, rev. ed. (New York, 1957), pp. 265-77.

[4]There are six dissertations on Odets listed in James Woodress, Dissertations in American Literature, 1891-1966 (Durham, 1968). Two of these are the original versions of Shuman's and Mendelsohn's books. I have examined abstracts of the others, and all are organized along chronological lines. Three additional dissertations on Odets' plays, written since 1966, are described in Dissertation Abstracts. Since they are in the fields of Mass Communication, Psychology, and Political Science, none is directly relevant to my study.

[5]Edward Murray, Clifford Odets: The Thirties and After (New York, 1968), p. vi.

[6]Walter J. Meserve, "Drama," in American Literary Scholarship, 1969, ed. J. Albert Robbins (Durham, 1971), p. 298.

[7]Alfred Kazin, Starting Out in the Thirties (Boston, 1965), pp. 80-81. I quote some of his reactions in my chapter on dialogue.

[8]Mordecai Gorelik, New Theatres for Old (New York, 1962), p. 242.

[9]Studs Terkel, Hard Times (New York, 1970), p. 24.

CHAPTER I

ODETS AND THE THIRTIES

>I know about the 1930's.   I'm
>a child of sorrow.
>   --Ben, Paradise Lost

     In 1929, when Black Thursday struck on October 24th
and burst the speculative bubble on Wall Street, Clifford
Odets was a twenty-three year old bit actor who was playing
a non-speaking role as one of the robots in the Theater
Guild's Broadway production of Karel Capek's R.U.R.   Six
years and six months later he was the most prodigious playwright on the literary horizon, the author of three plays running concurrently on Broadway--Awake and Sing! and the
double bill, Waiting for Lefty and Till The Day I Die--the
sought-after subject for newspaper interviews and magazine
profiles, a spokesman for his radical generation, "Revolution's Number One Boy."[1]

     The process by which he achieved success, while by
no means accidental, was the result of the convergence of an
unusual temperament with the force of circumstance.   But his
situation as an artist was not without irony.   The play he
claimed he had written in three nights in a hotel room in
Boston, Waiting for Lefty, and co-directed with Sanford Meis-
ner for the New Theater League, had captured the attention
and admiration of its audience and was soon to have even
greater impact in 32 productions across the nation.[2]   For
contrast, Awake and Sing!--the play he had struggled with for
over two years and which expressed his deepest convictions
and inner contradictions--had been produced reluctantly and
was received by the critics with only moderate enthusiasm.[3]

     The disparity in the reception of his plays can be
largely explained by briefly surveying the mood and temper
of the period, the emotional substratum that made Lefty not
so much a play as a theatrical event that was to symbolize
an entire generation's impulse toward social protest.

8

Within a few months of the stock market crash, national unemployment began to soar. The figure climbed steadily until it peaked in March 1933, at 15 or 16 million. [4] These statistics merely outline a panorama of industrial paralysis: idle factories, lay-offs, wage cuts and shortened work weeks. Concomitantly, there was individual despair: homeless men arrested for vagrancy, Americans applying for jobs in the Soviet Union rather than stay to sleep in the park or come home to the hungry faces in the tin and cardboard shanty towns sardonically dubbed "Hoovervilles." There was a sense of general breakdown of the once-celebrated free enterprise system. "In 1931 and 1932 talk of social revolution became common. Surely, thought thousands of people, the dispossessed and the hungry will revolt against the government and the economic system that had brought them to their desperate situation."[5] But there was no revolt. That it did not come in the violent form many had anticipated was partly due to the inertia and innate conservatism of the American working man, but, to a greater extent, it was forestalled by the election of Franklin D. Roosevelt, who, once in office, vigorously set to work a series of pragmatic reforms. For a time it looked as though the efforts of FDR and his brain-trusters had succeeded. Unemployment during the spring and summer months of 1933 had a sudden fall of three or four million.

But not all Americans welcomed the advent of FDR and not all applauded what they saw as marginal efforts at reform. To Edmund Wilson, who had traveled to Washington for Roosevelt's inauguration, the phrases of his speech seemed "shadowy," with the "suggestion, itself rather vague, of a possible dictatorship."[6] Where the moneyed class feared that Roosevelt was a turncoat Communist, the Left distrusted him as a potential "man on horseback." In the election of 1932, Wilson had been among the 100,000 who had voted for the Communist Party candidate, William Z. Foster. Along with him, presumably, so did the 52 other artists and intellectuals who had, in September 1932, published an "open letter" to writers, artists and professional men denouncing the two major parties as "hopelessly corrupt," rejecting the Socialists as a do-nothing party, and pledging their support to the Communists. [7] Among them, and later involved with the League of Professional Writers and signers of the pamphlet "Culture and Crisis," were such luminaries as Waldo Frank, Lincoln Steffens, Granville Hicks, Sherwood Anderson, John Dos Passos, and Michael Gold. [8] No simplistic explanation can account for the conversion of so many writers

and thinkers of such diverse backgrounds. But Malcolm Cowley, who had recorded in his Exiles Return the evolution of
the Twenties' expatriates into Communist sympathizers and
party members, offers some cogent reasons for the extraordinary appeal of Communism to the American intellectual
at this juncture in time and history.

> [A] search for opinions, consistent ones if possible,
> goes a long way toward explaining the popularity of
> Marxism in the 1930's, particularly among review-
> ers, commentators and foreign correspondents.
> The secure world of their childhood had fallen apart.
> They were looking for a scheme of values, a direc-
> tion, a skeleton key that would unlock almost any
> sort of political or literary situation (and help them
> to write a cogent page). Marxism, in a more or
> less rudimentary form, was the key that many of
> them found. Uncompromisingly materialistic as it
> purported to be, it served the same unifying pur-
> pose for writers of the depression years that Emer-
> son's uncompromising idealism had served for the
> New England rebels of an earlier time. [9]

The times seemed apocalyptic; and Leslie Fiedler has
traced a nihilistic undercurrent in the left-wing movement
emerging in the novels of Nathanael West and Henry Roth,
and even James Gould Cozzens.[10] "The urge to destroy is
a creative urge," said Mikhail Bakunin, the nineteenth-cen-
tury anarchist. The Thirties' intellectuals could accept this
dictum; indeed, it was mouthed by James T. Farrell at the
YMCA in New York City to his cohorts, whom he considered
Philistines engaged in useless commerce.[11]

But what of those young men, the fledgling artists and
writers, whose years of early manhood were the period of
1925-1935? To most of them, the books and articles of earlier writers such as Lincoln Steffens and Waldo Frank offered
hope and a program for action that appealed to youth's natural optimism.

This appeal was doubly strong for such Jewish intellectuals as Clifford Odets and Alfred Kazin, who had grown
up in the Jewish enclaves of the Bronx and Brooklyn, where
their immigrant parents were undergoing the painful process
of acculturation, still sprinkling their conversations with Yiddishisms and making trips to the "pushcart" markets and
kosher butchers. For them we may conjecture that Marxism

represented a double escape--first, from the hardships of the
Depression and, second, from the confining Old World culture
of the ghetto. Alfred Kazin has recorded in A Walker in the
City[12] how, as a young boy, he would look longingly at the
mysterious towers of Manhattan, not physically visible from
New Lots Avenue but symbolically visible, the hub of intellectual freedom and ferment to which all the streets led. Marxism enabled Kazin to follow those streets: he picked it up
not only from the unemployed cutters and striking fur-industry
workers on Pitkin Avenue, but from books in the library and,
later, as a student at City College. [13]

Kazin's path was that of the scholar and literary reviewer. Odets, impatient with studies, had left Morris High
School in the Bronx in November 1923, at the age of seven-
teen. Here, his parents--Louis Odets, Russian immigrant
and journeyman printer, and Pearl Geisinger Odets, Austrian-
born--had moved from Philadelphia when Clifford was two,
and had struggled "up" until they could actually move into
"one of the three elevator buildings"[14] that the borough
boasted. But the view from the Grand Concourse could not
have been very different for Odets than that from New Lots
Avenue for Kazin. He, too, had literary inclinations and
joined the school literary magazine but, in addition, he acted
in school plays, and a former teacher remembers his joy
when he won a declamation contest. [15] His path was to be
the theater (even though he proved to be an indifferent actor),
and his youthful struggles are identified with bit parts and odd
jobs with the usual nondescript organizations: the Drawing
Room Players, Harry Kemp's Poet's Theater in the East Vil-
lage, and Mae Desmond and her players in repertory in Philadelphia. He also tried his hand at radio announcing for a
small station in the Bronx and took a job as an early disc
jockey at another radio station in New York (where he wrote
two radio scripts, in one of which he performed). In 1929,
he had "arrived" on Broadway as an understudy for Spencer
Tracy (who never missed a performance), and as the voice-
less robot in R. U. R. [16]

These formative years are spottily documented by play-
bills and retrospective reminiscences. [17] Though undoubtedly
these experiences helped Odets learn his craft and gave him
his theatrical know-how, they provide no clue to his inner
education, his spiritual and emotional ordeal. He may have
been the "ordinary middle-class boy, unconsciously ambitious,
but with a kind of purity and unselfishness," he described to
John McCarten, [18] but he could not have been unaffected by

his parents' struggles and by the misery he saw later in the Depression. In 1952, he told the HUAC Committee that his mother had worked in a stocking factory at the age of eleven and died "a broken woman and an old woman at the age of forty-eight," and proudly stated, "I did not learn my hatred of poverty, sir, out of Communism."[19] Undoubtedly, he was exaggerating, for he had told a Time reporter that he was a worker's son only until the age of 12.[20] It had taken only ten years for his father to prosper in the Bronx; in Franklinesque fashion, Louis Odets bought out the owner of a printing shop and, in 1927, he moved the family (Odets had two younger sisters) to the fashionable Oak Lane section of Philadelphia.

Clifford, therefore, could sympathize with the poor and seedy residents of the Bronx enclave ("I saw people evicted, I saw rent parties, I knew a girl who stayed in the park every day ... ")[21] even while he himself experienced the security of Jewish middle-class life. But he clashed with his father over his future; when he revealed his plans to be a poet and an actor, his father violently objected and urged the more practical occupation of advertising copywriter. Odets twice related that when he demurred, his father smashed his typewriter, but it is not clear from Odets' biographical sources whether this incident occurred just after he left high school or when he was already in stock theater. What is clear is that he grew up in a charged emotional atmosphere. Odets told Seymour Peck of The New York Times: "My mother was a strange and nunlike woman who had to live with two brawling, trigger-tempered men in the house--my father and myself. She couldn't take it, with that nunlike quality."[22] Mendelsohn believes that Odets' rebelliousness "is surprising, especially when viewed in the light of the traditional Jewish pattern of close family ties,"[23] but surely such a father-son conflict is quite common among immigrant families, where the father has built up the business the hard way, and the son strikes out into the creative world so alien to his parents' experience.

We can only conjecture how much this family environment affected the youthful Odets, and there would be no need for psychoanalytical speculation if not for Odets' statement to Arthur Wagner in a 1961 interview:

> It's surprising how very important a small satisfaction [his own room at the Group's summer quarters] can be in the life of one who is moving

away from what I can only call illness to some
kind of health or strength. (You must remember ... that before I was twenty-five I had tried
to commit suicide three times: once I stopped it
myself and twice my life was saved by perfect
strangers.)[24]

Still later, he was to tell Mendelsohn that his early attempts
at writing "were very painful attempts to not only find my
identity--not only to locate myself--but to write down the
nature of neurotic illness, to try to come to some clear,
objective sense of myself and my inability to handle and deal
with life. "[25]

Those early works, which he called "sad affairs" and
falsely claimed to have burned, were part of an introspective
process by which neophyte writers reveal more about their
ambitions and self-doubts than about their genuine talent.
Significantly, this material includes a play about some tor-
tuously windy intellectuals in Philadelphia, a novel about
Beethoven, and a play about a violinist who loses his hand--
all prefigurations of themes that were later to be important.
But these works do not yet speak in Odets' characteristic
voice. This man-youth, always at war with himself, was
trying to find his place in a competitive, chaotic society,
carrying with him "an internal injury"[26] about which we can
only guess. When Harold Clurman first met Odets, he described him as a "peculiar duck" and "a strange young man"
with a tendency "to nurse his own oddities, combined with a
shadowy life he seemed to be leading and an occasional sally
into highly charged but vague verbiage in the form of letters
and sundry pieces of writing.... "[27]

From such interviews and reminiscences, a picture
emerges resembling that of Odets' favorite actor, John Garfield (né Jules Garfinkel): a cocky, confident, yet vulnerable
young man, internally sensitive, externally tough, creative
and on the make, striding along with his hat at a jaunty angle
and a wisecrack on his lips. Perhaps this is only a com-
posite of a Thirties' movie hero (a stereotype which Odets
helped create), but it is corroborated by the impression the
young Alfred Kazin had of "a proud and conscious sense of
physical 'vitality, ' a flourish of dangerous experience that I
saw in the sharp faces of James T. Farrell and Robert Cant-
well, of Clifford Odets and Elia Kazan. "[28]

Despite Odets' pose of confidence, his sense of per-

sonal isolation was relieved when he joined the Group Theater
in 1931; that experience had a wholly salutory effect on him,
as it did for so many others.   Founded by three dissident
young theater people--Harold Clurman, Lee Strasberg, and
Cheryl Crawford--as an offshoot of the Theater Guild, the
Group Theater offered its members a collective experience,
a respite from the dog-eat-dog economics of Broadway; above
all, it offered an aesthetic and social ideal of wholeness and
a sense of purpose.   Though it was critical of American in-
stitutions and perceived itself as a radical agent for social
change, the Group was neither Communistic (only four or
five were card-carrying members) nor massively unified in
any political attitude.   To the contrary, its strife-torn ten-
year history is a record of individualistic differences among
its members, who were by no means convinced that "art was
a weapon" in the narrow, doctrinaire sense.   Yet it is significant that when Clurman sought a new play with which to
begin rehearsing his still-to-be-born company, the script he
secured was Waldo Frank's.   Indeed, that novelist was later
invited to address the company, which he did in these terms:
"The one method whereby the new society may slowly and
laboriously be created is a new alliance in place of the alliance of the intellectuals with the money class, an alliance of
the men of mind, of vision, the artists, with the People, consciously working toward this creative end. "[29]

Clurman himself was capable of similar generalities:
"We must help one another find our common ground; we must
build our house on it, arrange it as a dwelling place for the
whole family of decent humanity.   For life, though it be individual to the end, cannot be lived except in terms of people
together, sure and strong in their togetherness" (p. 28).
Nevertheless, perhaps ingenuously, Clurman was surprised
by the political controversy injected into Group discussions,
and by the demand of some of the actors for direct propaganda in drama.   Wisely, he fought to keep the Group from
being typed as "revolutionary, " while, in his talks he emphasized Art and People in capital letters without subscribing to
a specific political orientation.   So, too, he insisted that the
Group not be narrowly insular and that it draw its actors
from widely different backgrounds (page 58).   On the whole
he succeeded, but it remains nonetheless true that two of
the Group's three directors and many of its leading actors--
Luther and Stella Adler, Lee J. Cobb, Morris Carnovsky,
John Garfield--were Jewish.

For Odets, who had attended the earliest meetings,

the Group was a receptive communal home in which he for-
mulated a sense of his own identity.   Here he found warm,
responsive idealists, who strengthened his own humanistic
impulses, and a healing optimism.   Here, too, he picked up
political ideas, tried them on for size and discarded them.
For three years, he acted in bit parts for various Group pro-
ductions--House of Connelly, 1931--, Night Over Taos, Men
in White, his own Waiting for Lefty, with an occasional outside job for the Guild--and he accompanied the Group each
summer to the hotel or camp where it was rehearsing.   More
than the benefits of the acting classes conducted by the Stanis-
lavski disciple Lee Strasberg, for whom he had the greatest
respect but with whom he differed, he appreciated the com-
panionship and the camaraderie--whether he was staying at
the Group's "poorhouse" apartment in New York or enjoying
the talk on warm summer nights at Dover Furnace or Brook-
field Center.   Above all, there was his friendship with Harold
Clurman, who became his older brother.

Clurman gave him sound advice about his early writing,
diverted him from unconstructive, narcissistic introspection,
urged him "to stand up straight and see the world more ob-
jectively, " and later to "write about the people he had met
and observed the past few years" (p. 88).   When it became
apparent that he was "into" something with the first draft of
Awake and Sing! (then called I've Got the Blues), Clurman,
despite his reservations about the play, encouraged him, arranged for its trial rehearsal at Green Mansions in the Adi-
rondacks, and later even invited Odets to share his apartment.
In the winter of 1933, when the Group's fortunes seemed at
a very low ebb, the two men roamed the streets together and
"could smell the depression in the air. "   Clurman reminisces:

> In my disconsolate meanderings from place to place
> I found Clifford Odets constantly by my side.   I
> cannot remember how this came about, for, as I
> have said, his personality, though peculiar enough,
> had not strongly impressed itself on my conscious-
> ness.   We began to see each other nightly, and
> with hungry hearts wandered aimlessly through sad
> centers of impoverished night life.   We would drop
> in at some cheap restaurant and over a meager
> meal make dreams of both our past and future.
> We would see a movie on a side street, pick up
> more friends, who, whether working or not, seemed
> equally at odds with the now consumptive city.   We
> listened to queer conversations on street corners,

> visited byways we had never suspected before.
> There grew between us a feeling akin to that which
> is supposed to exist between hoboes in their jungles,
> and we were strangely attracted to people and
> places that might be described as hangdog, ratty,
> and low.
>
> ....
>
> Odets seemed to share a peculiar sense of gloomy
> fatality, one might almost say an appetite for the
> broken and rundown, together with a bursting love
> for the beauty immanent in people, a burning belief
> in the day when this beauty would actually shape
> the external world. These two apparently contra-
> dictory impulses kept him in a perpetual boil that
> to the indifferent eye might look like either a stiff
> passivity or a hectic fever. (pp. 107-9)

It is in this context that one must assess the decisive
step that Odets took in 1934 when he joined the Communist
Party. Frustrated by his efforts to get Awake and Sing! produced by the Group, he decided to make a commitment, which
Clurman subsequently summarized from their talks:

> ... He wanted comradeship; he wanted to belong to
> the largest possible group of humble, struggling
> men prepared to make a great common effort to
> build a better world. Without this, life for him
> would be lonely and hopeless. In the Group Theatre
> he had found kindred spirits, intellectual stimula-
> tion. But we were artists. Now he felt the need
> to share his destiny with the lowliest worker, with
> those who really stood in the midst of life. (p. 133)

Later, Odets would explain his motivation to the HUAC Committee somewhat differently:

> I believe at that time there were perhaps 15 or 16
> million unemployed people in the United States, and
> I myself was living on 10 cents a day. Therefore,
> I was interested in any idea which might suggest
> how as an actor I could function as a working actor
> who could make a living at a craft he had chosen
> for his life's work. These were the early days of
> the New Deal, and I don't think that one has to
> describe them. They were horrendous days that
> none of us would like to go through again.

On this basis there was a great deal of talk about

amelioration of conditions, about how should one
live, by what values should one work for, and in
line with this there was a great deal of talk about
Marxist values. One read literature; there were
a lot of penny and 2-cent and 5-cent pamphlets. I
read them along with a lot of other people, and
finally joined the Communist Party, in the belief,
in the honest and real belief, that this was some
way out of the dilemma in which we found ourselves. 30

   We do not know if he acted impulsively or after long
deliberation. Certainly he could not have made any deep
study of Marxism for, other than the pamphlets he mentions,
Odets' reading had been minimal. The authors he grew up
on were those who appealed to his romantic idealism, Victor
Hugo and Ralph Waldo Emerson and, we infer (from his later
play The Big Knife, and its partly autobiographical hero,
Charlie Castle), Jack London, Upton Sinclair, and Ibsen. 31

   But decisions of this kind, though they may seem
hasty or superficial, are never without psychological importance. A novel of this period by V. F. Calverton, The Man
Inside (1936), demonstrates that its titular hero, "terrified
and energized by his fear of annihilation, " can only function
in an increasingly chaotic world "by de-individualizing himself, by dissolving himself in the matrix of the race."32
Some such motive--given the probability of Odets' neurotic
bent--may explain his having joined an activist party at this
point of his career. On the other hand, we may be dealing
here only with a young man's impatient and spontaneous ges-
ture--similar to an incident that Clurman narrates when, after
a performance of Hauptmann's The Weavers, Odets applauded
suddenly when a radical speaker "urged strong political action
against the terror of the crisis, the unemployment, hunger,
destitution of the day. "33

   Whatever the pressure upon him, Odets was a Communist for only a short period of eight months, before the restraints of political directives began to gall. He quit the
Party in 1935, but it was during his brief harmony with it
that he wrote his propaganda piece, Waiting for Lefty, in
response to a contest initiated in the New Masses. 34 Though
it is generally regarded as the most successful piece of agitprop writing in American drama, Waiting for Lefty differs
appreciably from the proletarian dramas of the period such
as Dimitroff of the New Theater League and Newsboy of the

Workers' Laboratory Theater.[35]   Gerald Rabkin has pointed
out that, though Lefty is in the agitprop tradition--"overtly
didactic in its affirmation of communist doctrine ... episodic
in structure, cartoon-like in its character delineation, directly
presentational in technique, and replete with slogan and political comment"--it skillfully uses the occasion of the taxi
strike for "a symbolic call to arms, a demonstration of unity
and achieved class consciousness."[36] Ostensibly, Waiting for
Lefty deals with the class struggle between the corrupt, bigoted, indifferent rich and the hungry, decent, exploited poor.
Viewed from a political perspective, its characters seem
close to caricatures and its premises naive.   But it avoids
abstract and blatant simplification by humanizing the conven-
tions it adopts.   What has never been sufficiently emphasized
is that the play is a middle-class playwright's attempt to
arouse a middle-class audience.   Three of its major characters are middle class: an actor, a young interne, and a lab
assistant.   Nor is the working class depicted as monolithically
pure; it contains villains and turncoats as well as heroes.
Most of the play's vignettes are miniature conversion dramas[37]
which analyze the Depression difficulties and capitalistic evils
found in a wide spectrum of society.   So disparate is the
cast of characters that John Howard Lawson, reviewing the
play for the New Masses, objected to Lefty's designation as
a proletarian drama and remarked: "One cannot reasonably
call these people 'stormbirds of the working class.'"[38]

Later, in my chapters on Odets' themes, characters,
and dialogue, I shall demonstrate that portions of Waiting for
Lefty are part of Odets' major achievement as a middle-class
poetic playwright; it is more than a propaganda piece, because
of the vitality of its language and its vivid, colloquial evocation of middle-class myths and attitudes.   These qualities,
together with its swift dramatic movement and emotional
urgency, are still capable of generating excitement in the
theater.[39]   Harold Clurman described its effect on its initial
audience: "... a shock of delighted recognition ... like a
tidal wave....   Deep laughter, hot assent, a kind of joyous
fervor seemed to sweep the audience toward the stage.   The
actors no longer performed; they were being carried along as
if by an exultancy of communication such as I had never witnessed in the theatre before....   It was the birth cry of the
'30's.   Our youth had found its voice."[40]

Such an event, like the Woodstock rock festival of the
1960's, cannot be explained simply in terms of the aesthetic
response of an audience to a work of art.   As Odets later
remarked:

> ... the opening and performance of the play were
> a cultural fact. You saw a cultural unit function-
> ing. From stage to theater and back and forth the
> identity was so complete ... that the actors didn't
> know whether they were acting and the audience
> didn't know whether they were sitting and watching
> it, or had changed positions.... The proscenium
> arch disappeared. That's the key phrase. Before
> and since, in the American theater people have
> tried to do that by theater in-the-round, theater
> this way, that way, but there, psychologically and
> emotionally, the proscenium arch dissolved away. 41

Like the youth who converged upon Woodstock, Odets'
contemporary audience had been preconditioned by a series
of political, economic, and cultural events to participate in
a communal, almost ritualistic experience. Granted that the
predominantly leftish audience at the old Civic Repertory
Theater on 14th Street would be disposed to applaud the play's
revolutionary "message," this still does not explain why, when
the play was moved to Broadway by the Group, middle-class
matrons and Scarsdale commuters would leap to their feet
and chant antiphonally in response to Agate's prodding--"Strike!
Strike! Strike!"--at the play's conclusion. 42 Odets instinc-
tively had used the taxi strike as a metaphor to harness all
the pent-up frustration and anger of the victims of the Depression, regardless of class; he had given them a theatrical out-
let for the prevailing social mood.

Spurred on by the critical acclaim given the new playwright, the Group finally produced a revised version of
Awake and Sing! This play, as well as Paradise Lost (which
was presented in the late fall), had not been forged at white
heat, but was the product of painstaking deliberation. Awake's
genesis can be traced to a note in Odets' diary of 1932:
"Here I am writing the Beethoven play, which when it is
finished may not even be about Beethoven. Why not write
something about the Greenberg family, something I know better, something that is closer to me?"43

Unlike Lefty, written by a man who had never driven
a cab or harangued members of a union, Awake and Sing!
and Paradise Lost (begun in 1934) are the products of intuitive understanding grounded in the experiential, and reveal
Odets the playwright operating at a mature artistic level.
Far better than Lefty, they sum up the ethos of the 1930's
if only because they contain the ambiguities, the tugs and

strains of what William Phillips called "a period of contradiction ... a time of sense and nonsense, idealism and cynicism, morality and immorality, disinterestedness and power drive ... when it was possible to believe simultaneously in democracy and dictatorship, in an anti-human abstraction called History, and in a moral idea of man usually regarded as unhistorical."44 Both plays contained insights into the then-as-now dominant middle class, insights that were new and remarkable in American drama. Indeed, they embody understandings which historians of the Thirties, such as Susman and Pells, 45 are only now articulating: namely, that the popular media (the detective story, self-help literature, radio, and the movies) had re-enforced essential American values in the middle class as well as the sluggish working class, and, despite the efforts of intellectuals to change the form of culture and the structure of society, the style of commitment led "not to revolution but to acquiescence."46 Ironically, these ground-breaking plays were received with critical obtuseness: Paradise Lost was almost universally damned, while Awake and Sing!, in its initial presentation, was praised largely for the artistry of the Group's ensemble acting--with restrained appreciation of the author's powerful dialogue and meticulous observation but rebukes for his craftsmanship and politics. 47

Obviously, these plays about the middle class were not without political bias and sloganeering. Especially in their endings, they had what Oscar Levant once characterized as "that inescapable Communist ending: Let there be light, or Let there be air or what have you."48 Even if one discounts the quip of the pianist-misanthrope, it is difficult to disentangle the activities of Odets the Party Propagandist and Odets the Artist during his annus mirabilis-- 1935. On the one hand he proceeded to follow the Party's "art is a weapon" theory and, when a companion piece was needed to pair with the Group's uptown production of Lefty, he turned out Till the Day I Die. It was another occasion piece written in three or four evenings, thematically inspired by a letter in the New Masses, 49 and with heroes who are German Communists mouthing party platitudes. Also, in July, he allowed himself to be used as the titular head of a delegation of writers and union officials who investigated the repressive Batista regime in Cuba, only to be unceremoniously incarcerated and shipped home. 50 This serio-comic episode succeeded only in angering Odets at the Cubans, at the Communist Party which had inveigled him into making the trip, and, one suspects, at himself. Though he did co-author an angry pamphlet, "Rifle Rule in Cuba,"51 with

Carleton Beals, this was his first and last attempt to editor-
ialize on a political subject.

Yet there are signs that even before breaking with the
Party shortly after the Cuban episode, Odets was chafing
under Party directives and restraints.

Some of the evidence may be the result of hindsight
but according to his own testimony, he sensed a real threat
to his artistic independence. This is what he told HUAC in
1952:

> ... They would have liked to have had me write
> what they would call ... "progressive plays."
> They would like me to write plays on what themes
> they would think would be burning issues of the
> day. I am sure, for instance, the Communist
> Party thought that the war in Spain was a burning
> issue of the day.... I didn't respect any person
> or any party or any group of people who would say
> to a young creative writer, "Go outside of your
> experience and write a play." I knew that as fum-
> bling as my beginnings were, and they certainly
> were, that I could only write out of my own ex-
> perience, out of my own incentive. I couldn't be
> given a theme and handle it. It was not my busi-
> ness. It meant to me, if I may say it this way,
> a loss of integrity. And so I persisted in going
> along on my own line and saying and writing what
> did come out of my true center. And whenever
> this happened, I got this violent opposition in that
> press and I became further disgusted and estranged
> from them. [52]

If this is true, as late as 1961 Odets was still ruefully re-
gretting the damage these pressures had done to his early
work:

> I am interested in investigating not so much why--
> I understand why--but how I tried to take some
> kind of real life I knew and tried to press it into
> an ideological mold. How, actually technically, I
> used to try many ways to make the materials of
> my plays say something that they really were not
> saying by tacking on a certain ideological posture.
> I think this did damage to the plays and the mater-
> ial, but I couldn't have done otherwise in that

period. It's the one thing that really disturbs me
about the early plays--that I would very easily,
very fluently and naturally, give an expression of
a certain kind of life, and then try to tell the audience what it meant. 53

Yet in the hectic Thirties he apparently had believed that the
issue of art vs. ideology could be solved by a paradox. As
he told a reporter during this period:

... all plays, just like all literature and drama,
are essentially propaganda of one sort or another.
A creative endeavor, from the Homeric sagas down
to the films of Maurice Chevalier, exists to re-
commend some specialized type or conduct of life.
My problem and business in the world is to present
truth dramatically, appealingly, entertainingly....
The presentation of truth without any editorializa-
tion is the most revolutionary thing in the world. 54

In reality, Odets was torn between two irreconcilable
drives: the compulsive belief that "new art works should
shoot bullets, "--a slogan he was still repeating in the Preface
to Six Plays in 1939--and the simultaneous need to develop at
his own pace and in his own way.   (Curiously, in that same
Preface, he states that his personal favorites are Paradise
Lost and Rocket to the Moon, though he admits the remaining four plays "are more immediately useful" [Odets' ital-
ics]. 55 Nevertheless, some inner warning signal kept him
from yielding to a strictly utilitarian theory of art, for he
seemed to realize that his best work sprang from his own
deepest experience. Conversely, his worst plays are far-
thest from his favorite middle-class milieu. For example,
the unproduced Cuban play (1938) and the strike drama, The
Silent Partner (of which he was so unreasonably proud), fit
squarely into Rideout's categories for proletarian art, but
are best left unpublished since they are lifeless and unconvincing except for an occasional character or scene. Among
the produced plays, Clash by Night (1941) and Till the Day
I Die (1935) are among his least interesting works, perhaps
because Odets knew no more about Staten Island working
people than he did about Germans. Hence he made a wise
decision to leave the Party, though not entirely his Marxist
orientation and revolutionary stance. "I have a great deal
of work to do, " he later said in reconstructing his feelings
at that point in his career; "I have enough to say out of my
own mind and heart, and I had better leave. "56

The summer of 1935 was a particularly appropriate time for the separation. Although in some respects the highwater mark for revolutionary literature, with the meeting of the First American Writers' Congress in mid-April, the publication of the anthology Proletarian Literature in the United States, and the formation of the League of American Writers, history was about to reverse itself. The Comintern had met that summer and had officially adopted the policy of the Popular Front against Fascism. Henceforth, for American Communists, this meant a rapprochement with Trotskyites and Progressives, support for the policies of the New Deal, a massive effort to organize the CIO, and a switch from class war to a less stringent opposition between the forces of "progress" and "reaction." Solidarity among the Left inevitably meant a temporary acceptance of the ongoing capitalistic system. As a series of aggressive acts abroad dominated the headlines from 1936-1941, Guernica and Hitler replaced Wall Street and the bankers as bogeyman terms for American Communists.

Walter Rideout has pointed out that this turnabout was "like a killing frost" for the proletarian novel. The radical writer ". . . could not emphasize the class divisions implicit in a strike, he could not document the disintegration of the middle class, he could not, as a convert to Communism, hurl defiance from a metaphysical barricade."[57] A few writers continued to write proletarian literature (Native Son and The Grapes of Wrath came at the end of the decade), but production dwindled to a mere trickle by 1941. By then there were too many waves of contradiction and muddied waters for the radical writer to swim through. How did one square one's conscience with the ignominy of the Moscow Purge Trials (Dos Passos and others cried "frame up"), the astonishing Nazi-Soviet Non-Aggression Pact of 1939, which made treachery a virtue in the name of expediency, and the growing certitude that the Party of peace was urging the United States to join in a capitalist war? Faced with this swirl of events, the radical writers began to withdraw from even the Popular Front organizations; recantations became commonplace; and Granville Hicks, who had occupied the mandarin chair of Communist criticism, resigned from the Party, stating: "Politics is no game for a man whose attention is mostly directed elsewhere."[58]

As for Odets, after 1935 his attention was directed mainly toward being a "man of the theater." His sensitivity to the political currents of the time had been amply demon-

strated. If Waiting for Lefty had summed up the impulse
toward revolutionary drama from 1930-1935 and transcended
it, Till the Day I Die, for all of its faults, had signaled an
early warning of the gangsterdom and sadism that was to
characterize the Nazi threat to humanity from 1935-1940.
From then on, he was concerned primarily with people, and
only indirectly with politics. Though he made some attempt
to organize the Hollywood screenwriters and allowed his
name to appear on People's Front organization stationery, he
did not follow Hellman and Sherwood in writing about the international crisis but remained rooted in middle-class domestic concerns. After all, the recession of 1937 had thrown
new millions out of work, and the breadlines had not disappeared. He, himself, was beginning the private struggle
of conscience which shuttled him between New York and Hollywood. He had left, after the poor reception of Paradise Lost,
to write his first screen play, The General Died At Dawn,
and had sent money back to keep the play running. In 1937,
with his first wife, Luise Rainer, he returned and wrote for
the Group its greatest hit, Golden Boy, and followed this in
1938 with Rocket to the Moon. By then there were signs of
strain within the Group among Odets, Clurman, and Strasberg, signs of dissolution in his married life, signs of a
growing awareness of the inevitability of world conflict, and
a concomitant world-weariness in his work. Though in Night
Music (1940), the last play Odets did for the Group, he still
belonged to the party of Hope and still championed the common man, there are hints that he was whistling in the dark.
Certainly Clash by Night (1941), produced under the aegis of
Billy Rose, closed the decade on a pessimistic note as, in
a highly symbolic scene, the principals enact a melodramatic
climax in a projection booth within sight and sound of the
meaningless shadows of the flickering screen.

    After the war, Odets returned to Broadway with three
striking dramas: The Big Knife (1949), The Country Girl
(1950), and The Flowering Peach (1954). Although each pursued Odets' characteristic themes, each also demonstrated
his capacity for growth and versatility of technique. Certainly these plays compel us to distrust the all-too-familiar
depiction of Odets as a prisoner of history and of the Thirties in particular. We find in each of these plays Odets reacting not merely to a momentary dilemma but revealing a
timeless concern with man's moral obligations and his capacity to surmount hostile external forces. This is not a
matter of politics, but rather of artistic vision. Nor is this
quest absent from the early plays, which have been too simplistically deemed "political" and "social" dramas.

Odets was not interested in the fierce dialectic of the Marxist literary men; the Gold-Wilder controversy and the Partisan Review-New Masses[59] disputes meant nothing to him. He was interested in the fates of people. His politics were those of a liberal humanitarian--muddled, foolishly inconsistent, but desperately sincere. If he acted as a literary seismograph for what Wilson called "The American Earthquake," he did so not as political propagandist but as an artist reacting to life. We must now step back from history and examine his plays for what is universal in them.

NOTES

[1]John McCarten, "Revolution's Number One Boy," New Yorker, 13 (22 January 1938), 21.

[2]R. Baird Shuman, Clifford Odets (New York, 1962), p. 27.

[3]"On the whole, the reviews were favorable but restrained, gravely welcoming a new young playwright into the circle of Broadway seriousness.... Awake had to make its own way, which it did, but it was not the way of commercial success." Gerald Weales, Clifford Odets: Playwright (New York, 1971), p. 60. See, for example, Stark Young, "Awake and Whistle at Least," New Republic, 82 (13 March 1935), 134.

[4]David A. Shannon, The Great Depression (Englewood Cliffs, 1960), p. 6.

[5]Shannon, p. x.

[6]Edmund Wilson, The American Earthquake (1958; rpt. Garden City, 1964), pp. 478-79.

[7]Daniel Aaron, Writers on the Left (New York, 1961), p. 196.

[8]Aaron, pp. 192-93.

[9]Malcolm Cowley, Think Back on Us ... (Carbondale, 1967), p. 387.

[10]Leslie Fiedler, Waiting for the End (New York, 1964), pp. 48-50; see also Fiedler, "The Two Memories:

Reflections on Writers and Writing in the Thirties," in Proletarian Writers of the Thirties, ed. David Madden (Carbondale, 1968), pp. 14-20.

[11]Murray Kempton, Part of Our Time (1955; rpt. New
York, 1967), pp. 115-16, 118.

[12]Alfred Kazin, A Walker in the City (1951; rpt. New
York, 1958), pp. 34-39.

[13]Alfred Kazin, Starting Out in the Thirties (Boston,
1965), pp. 3, 5-6.

[14]Weales, pp. 17-18.

[15]Weales, p. 19.

[16]See Weales, pp. 22-25; also Michael J. Mendelsohn,
Clifford Odets: Humane Dramatist (DeLand, 1969), pp. 2-3.

[17]There are five major sources: John McCarten,
"Revolution's Number One Boy," New Yorker, 13 (22 January
1938), 21-27; Seymour Peck, "An Angry Man from Hollywood,"
New York Times, (20 February 1949), Sec. 2, pp. 1, 3;
"Communist Infiltration of the Hollywood Motion-Picture Industry, Part I," House Committee on Un-American Activities, Hearings, May 19-21, 1952, pp. 3453-512; "How a
Playwright Triumphs" (Discussion with Arthur Wagner), Harper's, 233 (September 1966), 64-70; Michael J. Mendelsohn,
"Odets at Center Stage," Theatre Arts, 47 (May 1963), 16-
19, 74-76; (June 1963), 28-30, 78-80; Harold Clurman's
The Fervent Years (1945; rpt. New York, 1957) is still the
best source.

[18]McCarten, p. 22.

[19]HUAC, p. 3481.

[20]"White Hope," Time, 32 (5 December 1938), 45.

[21]Wagner, p. 66.

[22]Peck, p. 3.

[23]Mendelsohn, "Clifford Odets and the American
Family," Drama Survey, 3 (Fall 1963), 240.

[24]Wagner, p. 66.

[25]Mendelsohn, "Center Stage," (June 1963), 30.

[26]Clurman, p. 63.

[27]Clurman, p. 62.

[28]Kazin, Thirties, p. 12.

[29]Clurman, p. 73. From page 14 to 16, I follow Clurman's account of Odets' relationship with the Group Theater, and cite page references in the text.

[30]HUAC, p. 3456.

[31]See Joseph Mersand, The American Drama, 1930-1940 (New York, 1949), p. 63, and Mendelsohn, Clifford Odets, p. 5.

[32]Aaron, p. 33.

[33]Clurman, p. 108.

[34]Actually, Odets' play was not an official entry, but was later awarded the prize after it had been published in New Theatre. See Weales, pp. 35-36.

[35]Rabkin, pp. 171-73. See also Kazin, Thirties, pp. 81-82.

[36]Rabkin, p. 173.

[37]Walter Rideout, The Radical Novel in the United States, 1900-1954 (1956; rpt. Cambridge, 1965), p. 171. I am using the term "conversion drama" in the sense that Rideout employs it, as one of his five categories of proletarian fiction.

[38]John Howard Lawson, review of Lefty, New Masses, 2 July 1935, p. 35.

[39]"On the one hand, how corny a lot of it seems today.... On the other hand, how powerful parts of 'Waiting for Lefty' still are.... We watch, we listen, we are involved, we want to know what will happen next; and when the cabbies yell out their decision, we still feel like cheering." Dan Sullivan, review of Lefty, New York Times, 17 December 1967, p. 58.

[40]Clurman, pp. 138-39.

[41]Wagner, pp. 68-69.

[42]Shuman, Clifford Odets, p. 42.

[43]McCarten, p. 25.

[44]William Phillips, "What Happened in the 30's," Commentary, 34 (September 1962), 204.

[45]See Warren I. Susman, "The Thirties," in The Development of an American Culture, ed. Stanley Coben and Lorman Ratner (Englewood Cliffs, 1970), pp. 179-218. Also Richard H. Pells, Radical Visions and American Dreams (New York, 1973), passim.

[46]Susman, p. 214.

[47]See note 3 above. Also Clurman, p. 139, and Rabkin, p. 186.

[48]Levant, p. 189.

[49]There were other sources involved: a book by Karl Bellinger, Fatherland, published in March, 1935; and even the supposed "letter" in New Masses was a short story in letter form. See Weales, pp. 85-86, for a plausible explanation of Odets' sources.

[50]Weales, pp. 104-5. See also Aaron, pp. 303-4.

[51]Carleton Beals and Clifford Odets, "Rifle Rule in Cuba" (New York, 1935).

[52]HUAC, pp. 3476-7.

[53]Wagner, p. 73.

[54]Wilson Library Bulletin, 11 (February 1937), 374.

[55]Six Plays of Clifford Odets (New York, 1939), p. ix.

[56]HUAC, p. 3462.

[57]Rideout, p. 244.

[58]Rideout, p. 254.

[59]Aaron, pp. 300-1.

CHAPTER II

THEMES AND MOTIFS

1. The Family Trap

Marx said it: abolish such families!
--Jacob, Awake and Sing!

First and last, the terrain of Odets' plays is the
home of the American middle-class family, and the action
of those plays almost always arises from the family situation.
There is hardly a play in which domestic life does not figure;
even the homeless wanderers of Night Music face family conflicts in person or in memory, while the legendary travelers
aboard Noah's Ark in The Flowering Peach become trans-
figured in Odets' hands into biblical bourgeoisie. The family's dwelling place becomes a battlefield on which the recurring quarrels are fought between father and son, mother
and child, brother and brother, a combat that endlessly repeats itself even after the young have moved out and set up
homes of their own. Moreover, if we define themes as the
abstract concepts or "ideas" dominant in a work of any intention, it is clear that a major theme in Odets' plays is
that the middle-class family is a social trap from which the
individual must escape to achieve his human potential as a
member of the family of man. Yet this idea is consistently
refuted by Odets' simultaneous recognition that the family is
a viable source of tenderness, love and affection that can be
deserted only at the individual's peril. This theme, and the
ambivalence that accompanies it, is best dramatized in the
early Awake and Sing!, Paradise Lost, parts of Golden Boy,
and in Odets' last play, a kind of coda to his early work,
The Flowering Peach.

The Berger family in Awake and Sing! provides the
prototype of this theme, as they do for so much else that is
central to Odets' work. In their cluttered Bronx apartment,

30

they sing the blues as they sit down to supper in a familiar ritual of complaint. Ralph, the son, is stuck in a dead-end job as a clerk in a silk house on Fourth Avenue, drowning "in bolts of silk and velour" (III). Pinched on his sixteen dollars a week salary, he sleeps on a day bed in the front room and desperately wants to "be something" and to "get to first base" (I). Hennie, the daughter, as Odets tells us in his Preface Notes, "is fatalistic about being trapped, but will escape if possible. " But as the action unfolds she is forced to marry Sam Feinschreiber, whom she pities but does not love, to salvage her mother's sense of respectability and have a father for her illegitimate child. Life for Hennie, whom the family nicknames Beauty, becomes bestial--a weary round of diapers, dreariness, and sleepless nights in a hated marital bed.

If the young are trapped, so too are the old. Myron, the father, has been a haberdashery clerk for thirty years and is "heartbroken without being aware of it" (Preface Notes). Jacob, the grandfather, is a student of Marx and an advocate of revolution, but he is "a sentimental idealist with no power to turn ideal to action" (Preface Notes). He is an abject failure--"Every job he ever had he lost" (I)-- forced to depend on his children's bounty, and he is treated by Bessie, the mother, like a captious child. Furthermore, he is aware of his own deficiencies, recognizing that he is a talker not a doer, that he "had golden opportunities but drank instead a glass tea" (II, 2). In Act I he warns Ralph not to become enmeshed in a similar snare:

> RALPH: Life with my girl. Boy, I could sing about it! Her and me together--that's a new life!
> JACOB: Don't make a mistake! A new death!
> RALPH: What's the idea?
> JACOB: Me, I'm the idea! Once I had in my heart a dream, a vision, but came marriage and then you forget. Children come and you forget because--
> RALPH: Don't worry, Jake.
> JACOB: Remember, a woman insults a man's soul like no other thing in the whole world!

If all of the members of the family are trapped by "a struggle for life amidst petty conditions" (Preface Notes), it is this same fundamental activity which draws them together and makes them need one another. This ambivalence

is not so much a matter of conscious understanding on their
part; it is part of the very atmosphere in which they live.
At home, they are free to let off steam, to console each
other by hooting each other down; they live in a perpetual
frenzy of complaint or argument, but quick derision ("Quack!
Quack!") and anticipated attacks ("Another county heard
from!") are beneficial to the victim as well as to the attack-
er. Sarcasm in this play becomes a mode of familial affection. Yet they are not without moments of mutual love and
tenderness. Hennie is a loving daughter as she tries to
cheer her parents (and herself) by offering to treat them to
a night at the Yiddish theater. Jacob comforts the despairing Ralph with tears in his eyes when it seems as if Ralph
has lost his girl at the end of Act II, 1. Myron makes a
similar attempt in Act II, 2, in his usual ineffective fashion--
"It's an American father's duty to be his son's friend."

Even Bessie, the strong-willed and dominant mother
who embodies what Odets considers the ersatz values of
bourgeois respectability and pragmatism, is not without her
own style of family love. When Schlosser, the janitor,
makes an angry remark to Jacob about walking the dog in
the hallway, Bessie defends him indignantly: "Excuse me!
Please don't yell on an old man. He's got more brains in
his finger than you got--I don't know where. Did you ever
see--he should talk to you an old man?" (I). Bessie considers herself a realist, but she has been infected by the
American dream of success. All of the misery in the play
is fueled by her good intentions. It is her conviction that
"a woman who don't raise a family--a girl--should jump over-
board" (II, 1), and she dreams of the day when Ralph will
ride "up to the door in a big car with a chauffeur and a
radio" (II, 1), a success like his Uncle Morty. So she
tightens the trap around Ralph by opposing his love for
Blanche, and virtually strangles Hennie in a net of deceit.
All of her actions are justified in her eyes by her fear of
poverty and her sense of family loyalty. Even her rapacious
attempt to appropriate Jacob's insurance money is motivated
by her feeling that "It belongs for the whole family.... A
family needs for a rainy day" (III). But Odets cannot depict such a woman with mere contempt, and in Act III he
allows her more than a villain's measure of passion and
dignity as she defends her conduct:

> Ralphie, I worked too hard all my years to be
> treated like dirt. It's no law we should be stuck
> together like Siamese twins. Summer shoes you

didn't have, skates you never had, but I bought a
new dress every week. A lover I kept--Mr. Gi-
golo! Did I ever play a game of cards like Mrs.
Marcus? Or was Bessie Berger's children always
the cleanest on the block?! Here I'm not only the
mother, but also the father. The first two years
I worked in a stocking factory for six dollars
while Myron Berger went to law school. If I didn't
worry about the family who would? On the calendar
it's a different place, but here without a dollar you
don't look the world in the eye. Talk from now to
next year--this is life in America.

And a further touch of sympathy comes soon after as Bessie,
winding an alarm clock before going to bed, confesses to
Ralph that she, too, has been a prisoner all her life:

... I'll tell you a big secret: My whole life I
wanted to go away too, but with children a woman
stays home. A fire burned in my heart too, but
now it's too late. I'm no spring chicken. The
clock goes and Bessie goes. Only my machinery
can't be fixed. (III).

A similar pattern confronts the Gordon clan in Paradise Lost; although ensconced in Shakespeare Place in a
house of their own, they represent a higher bracket of the
middle class than the bourgeois Bergers. With the Katzes,
who rent upstairs, they have long lived on the proceeds of
a pocketbook manufacturing concern and have insulated themselves from the horrors of the Depression. Moreover, their
daughter, Pearl, is a dedicated pianist, while their older son,
Ben, is a star athlete whom they believe has a promising
future. But their "paradise" is an artificial one: it turns
rapidly to dust and ashes, as they lose their savings in the
bank crash and mortgage their house to keep the business
going. In this play Clara, the practical mother, is the
source of love and tenderness as she welcomes her guests
with the tag-line, "Take a piece of fruit," and proudly
boasts: "I raised my whole family on Grade A milk" (I).
Her husband, Leo, is an impractical, foolish dreamer who
"sits with artistic designs" (I) while Sam Katz runs the business, until Leo, awakening as from a deep sleep, gradually
realizes the gravity of his situation and that of the world
conflagration. The feeling of entrapment is imparted both
by dialogue and event: Pearl Gordon tells her boyfriend,
Felix, "No, I have no place to go, Felix. Where would I

go?" (I); Ben marries the silly, pleasure-loving Libby
Michaels and, unable to find work, gets sucked into the
rackets of his friend, Kewpie, and dies a gangland suicide;
Sam Katz confesses to his friend and partner why he doc-
tored the firm's books: "A man like me wants to stand on
a mountain. So instead he lays in a grave with dirt on his
face. Twenty-four hours a day he eats gall" (II). In the
play's most obvious bit of symbolic action, the younger son,
Julie, who dreams of a killing on Wall Street and follows the
stock market pages, lies dying of sleeping sickness, while
his mother reads to him from a book of biblical legends of
Moses' terrible anger at the worshipers of the Golden Calf.
Though Paradise Lost is a very different kind of play from
Awake and Sing!, it shares with the earlier work a vision
of a middle-class family facing extinction in an economic
holocaust (but in this play because of its own naiveté, in-
eptitude, and lack of social awareness), yet sustaining itself
by tenderness and mutual loyalty as the disintegration begins.

By the time he wrote Golden Boy (1937), Odets' interest had centered on the world outside the family; however,
the protagonist's home continues to figure importantly in the
play as a different sort of trap. Here we are given a sentimental and idealized version of middle-class family life whose
spokesman is Joe's father, a character so saintly, wise, and
folksy that he is hardly credible. The function of Joe's home
is to serve as polar opposite to the ruthless, competitive
fight world; it is characterized by the plaster busts of Mozart
and Beethoven and the cage of lovebirds that adorns the combination dining-living room where Mr. Bonaparte and his
skeptical Jewish friend, Mr. Carp, sip beer and, ·as the son-
in-law Siggie puts it, "slice philosophical salami" (II, 3). Joe
Bonaparte rebels against this "natural" background of wedded
bliss, music, and love (and adopts the "unnatural" competitive world of sports) because family life seems to him a
dead end. As the shrewdly pessimistic Mr. Carp remarks
of Joe's violin case: "It looks like a coffin for a baby" (I,
2). Though Joe's father benignly states, "Whatever you got
ina your nature to do isa not foolish" (I, 2), he is ambitious
for his son and is secretly convinced that Joe's "nature" is
to be a violin virtuoso. But Joe takes the way of the fist
instead of the fiddle because he is impatient for success:

> ... Every birthday I ever had I sat around. Now'sa
> time for standing. Poppa, I have to tell you--I
> don't like myself, past, present, and future. Do
> you know there are men who have wonderful things

from life? Do you think I like this feeling of no
possessions? Of learning about the world from
Carp's encyclopaedia.... You don't know what it
means to sit around here and watch the months go
ticking by! Do you think that's a life for a boy
my age? Tomorrow's my birthday! I change my
life! (I, 2)

Joe makes good on his promise but never loses his
affection for his father. When at the end the love-lined trap
proves to have been the better option, Mr. Bonaparte says
of his dead son: "Come, we bring a him home ... where
he belong..." (III, 3)

Japheth, in The Flowering Peach, has a loving attachment to both Esther, his mother, and Noah, especially the
latter with whom he shares deep affinities. Odets in his
Preface Notes to Scene 2, calls them "two outcasts in the
more competent and fluent world. " But Noah is a stubborn
traditionalist who insists on doing things his way--"Disrespect
to a father is disrespect to God!" (3)--and he orders his sons
about highhandedly. Noah and his troup of "assorted clowns
and acrobats" (2) become a comic equivalent of the earlier
bourgeois families, and the closed-in ark becomes a metaphor
for the family trap as quarrels erupt among the brothers,
wives, and parents. Japheth's quarrel, however, is mainly
with God. He feels compelled to protest against the cruelty
of the divine decree and states, "Someone, it seems to me,
would have to protest such an avenging, destructive God!"
(2). Despite his father's anger, when his conscience tells
him that he can work no longer for "this brutal God" (3),
he decides to leave his vital role in the construction process.
But he is only gone overnight and, after a tussle in the town,
returns to ask his father's blessing and explain: "The ark
can't be built without me. For your sake, Momma, and
Poppa's, that's why I came back--for the family, not for
God" (4).

Over and over, Odets' characters struggle with their
divided feelings toward their families. Sometimes, as in
Night Music, the conflict is expressed simplistically in
terms of the generation gap and rebellion against the ennui
of middle-class existence. Many a participant at Woodstock
or Watkins Glen might echo the credo of Fay, the fledgling
actress, as she refuses to return to "a secondhand life" and
confesses that she loves her parents but doesn't care for
their ideals. "Every relative I have tells me I'm a criminal.

But I think they're criminals. Because they don't live--because their alphabet's from A to B--because their lives are narrow, petty and small!" (I, 3). Fay, in this atypical comedy, does not return home, but often the more serious characters do: Ben Stark returns to "A life where every day is Monday" (I) in Rocket to the Moon; and Ernie Mott--in Odets' best screen play, None But the Lonely Heart--returns to the hated junk furniture shop, which will make him both victim and victimizer when he learns that his mother is dying of cancer.

How to break out of the family trap is a central concern of Odets'. In his plays he explored different ways of doing so: running away from bondage; social commitment; the search for independence and power; even death as a means of release. It is important to examine some of these attempts to understand how essential the break-out motif is to Odets' worldview. In Awake and Sing! there are three attempts to break out: Jacob's, Hennie and Moe's, and Ralph's. Jacob sees in Ralph "his new life" and a means of symbolic resurrection, and warns Bessie that rather than allow her to mold Ralph in her image he would die first, in this subtle foreshadowing of that event: "Bessie, some day you'll talk to me so fresh ... I'll leave the house for good!" (I). Presumably, his sense of outrage at Bessie's treatment of Ralph's girl friend, his humiliation when Bessie smashes his Caruso records, his desire to transcend his useless existence with some meaningful act of protest, his wish to give Ralph a chance to realize "the possibilities of life" (II, 1) with the proceeds of his insurance policy (an ironic motive in such an idealist)--all these motives contribute to his suicide in Act II, 2. There is, perhaps, an even more important motive for Jacob's sacrifice (not noticed by most critics) which I shall note in my section on the motif of treachery. Despite the critical bromide that Odets is a facile optimist, death as a way of breaking out of the existential trap occurs in Till the Day I Die, Awake and Sing!, Golden Boy, Clash by Night, and The Big Knife.

The break-out of Hennie and Moe, however, is more directly applicable to the family trap. Moe is a cynical hedonist who has lost a leg in the war and who believes "It's all a racket--from horse racing down" (II, 1). But his love for Hennie is genuine. He confesses that he, too, has struggled to escape a hellish environment, and he urges Hennie: "Make a break or spend the rest of your life in a coffin." The imagery in which he clothes his vision of their future

life is Edenic: "Come away. A certain place where it's
moonlight and roses. We'll lay down, count stars. Hear
the big ocean making noise. You lay under the trees. Champagne flows like--. " At this point a phone call from Sam
interrupts his lyrical appeal, but he continues relentlessly:
"... Paradise, you're on a big boat headed south. No more
pins and needles in your heart, no snake juice squirted in
your arm. The whole world's green grass and when you cry
it's because you're happy" (III).

Moralists have objected to Hennie's decision to leave
her husband and child, and have confused Ralph's approval
of her action with Odets'. [1] Hennie is swept along by her
passions, and decides to ignore the human cost and leave a
life founded on lies and hypocrisy in a desperate bid for happiness. We do not know whether her break-out will succeed
or not; it may be that her guilt about the vulnerable Sam
Feinschreiber or the thought of her child left to Bessie's
ministrations will bring her back. Odets has merely presented one of the possible options; in Axelrod's words, "The
doctor said it--cut off your leg to save your life!" (III)

But "breaking out" for many of Odets' characters
most often occurs at the moment when they become politically
aware and when, in a moment of flashing illumination like
St. Paul on the road to Damascus, they cast their lot with
the rest of mankind (e. g. , the working class) in the revolutionary struggle. This is particularly true in the early
plays, and Ralph in Awake and Sing! sets the tone of lyrical
optimism which critics, both in 1935 and 1974, find so difficult to accept:[2]

> Sure, inventory tomorrow. Coletti to Driscoll to
> Berger--that's how we work. It's a team down
> the warehouse. Driscoll's a show-off, a wiseguy,
> and Joe talks pigeons day and night. But they're
> like me, looking for a chance to get to first base
> too. Joe razzed me about my girl. But he don't
> know why. I'll tell him. Hell, he might tell me
> something I don't know. Get teams together all
> over. Spit on your hands and get to work. And
> with enough teams together maybe we'll get steam
> in the warehouse so our fingers don't freeze off.
> Maybe we'll fix it so life won't be printed on dol-
> lar bills (III).

There are several ways critics have reacted to such

speeches: one is to regard them (as Odets did in retrospect) as reflections of the political pressures within the Group Theater and from outside intellectual circles for playwrights of the period to end plays with a Chorus for Survival which would parallel the International in tone if not in tune.[3] Admittedly, these speeches are excrescences on Odets' plays, since they do not develop logically out of the characterizations and seem tacked on.[4] Perhaps, if Odets had had the "know-how" and commitment which he ascribed to Communist functionaries[5] and which he conspicuously lacked, he might have had Ralph join a Communist cell and invent ways to hasten the death of a doomed capitalist system. But, even in Waiting for Lefty, he does not go that far. Ralph chooses to remain at home and, convinced that he has turned an ideological corner, works within the system for some vague and unspecified social reform. From this perspective one can regard these speeches as reflections of Odets' own uncertainty and political naiveté, the kind that brought him frequent lectures from John Howard Lawson[6] and bad notices from the Left-wing press.[7] Another possible critical reaction is to see them as the mystical yearnings of an idealist to escape the trap of solipsism and achieve transcendence; William Gibson felt that his friend's theme "had always been the liberation of the soul from its social shackles."[8] From this perspective, even Leo's closing speech at the end of Paradise Lost, so bitterly attacked by James T. Farrell,[9] acquires religious and visionary overtones:

> ... Everywhere now men are rising from their sleep. Men, men are understanding the bitter black total of their lives. Their whispers are growing to shouts! They become an ocean of understanding! No man fights alone. Oh, if you could only see with me the greatness of man. I tremble like a bride to see the time when they'll use it. My darling, we must have only one regret--that life is so short! That we must die so soon. (CLARA slowly has turned from JULIE and is listening now to her husband.) Yes, I want to see that new world. I want to kiss all those future men and women. What is this talk of bankrupts, failures, hatred ... they won't know what that means. Oh, yes, I tell you the whole world is for men to possess. Heartbreak and terror are not the heritage of mankind! The world is beautiful. No fruit tree wears a lock and key. Men will sing at their work, men will love. Ohhh,

> darling, the world is in its morning--and <u>no man</u>
> <u>fights alone!</u> ... (III)

Yet somehow the rhetoric does not ring true. It is not
simply that the tone of optimism seems naive, for, as Gerald
Weales points out, it is "certainly no more so than the auto-
matic existential despair that has characterized the last fifteen
years."[10] Rather it fails because it does not proceed from
the play's structure. <u>Paradise Lost,</u> unlike <u>Awake and Sing!,</u>
is patterned on <u>break-ins</u> rather than <u>break-outs,</u> break-ins
such as the visit of the shop delegation, Ben's death, the
appearance of the two homeless men at the end, which invade
the suffocating atmosphere of the Gordon family trap and im-
pinge on Leo's muddled, seeking consciousness. The break-
ins succeed in awakening him from his sleep, but they should
logically bring despair--not hope. There is no reason for
Leo's curtain speech except the willed optimism of the author.

In later plays, the break-out by social commitment
tends to become muted in articulation, or it is placed in the
mouths of subordinate characters. Lorna's appeal in <u>Golden</u>
<u>Boy</u> (III, 2) is simply a yearning for a romantic utopia, and
A. L. Rosenberger in <u>Night Music</u> (III, 2) debases the theme
by turning it into a youth cult and urging the lovers to join a
"Party-to-Marry-My-Girl!" It seems clear that as Odets
matured he saw the difficulties of holding to a collective ideal
in a competitive society and in a culture whose values were
both individualistic and materialistic.[11] He never lost hope
entirely; Noah, in the covenant scene of <u>Peach,</u> says: "Now
it is in man's hands to make or destroy the world" (8), but
Odets had no formula for social cooperation that he knew
would work. His characters hover on the verge of an un-
realized ideal. The only successful break-out by social commitment is that of Frank, Joe's brother, a CIO organizer, in
<u>Golden Boy.</u> But he serves only as a foil and contrast to Joe,
and the thrust of the play belies his self-satisfaction.

Odets' understanding of the middle-class trap was at
its most profound when he was dealing with those who made
no attempt to escape, with the forces that kept the bourgeoisie
content and passive in its family coffin. Though not an astute
political thinker or sociologist, as a dramatic poet, intuitively,
Odets has extraordinary insight into what kept his characters
from achieving the revolutionary goals he espoused. His
knowledge is so precise and uncanny that one suspects that--
down at the roots--he, himself, was affected by the forces
of inertia he wished to destroy. In a real sense, the strength

of his plays lies in his portrait of the submerged and paralyzed American will.

Foremost among the forces that keep the middle class
entrapped are the mass media--movies, radio, the newspaper,
comics, the sports page--all the purveyors of popular culture.
Odets' interest in satirizing the movies is evident in Waiting
for Lefty: Edna tells her amorous husband, "Do it in the
movies, Joe--they pay Clark Gable big money for it" (I);
Fayette, the industrialist, comments on how consumers have
their buying habits shaped by Hollywood: "... just let Mrs.
Consumer know they're used by the Crawfords and Garbos--
more volume of sales than one plant can handle" (II). In
"The Young Hack and His Girl" episode, Sid and Florence
play-act a scene of a wealthy, glamorous lovers' meeting
"... like in the movies" (III). Florence refers to Queen
Marie of Rumania, who had recently made a highly publi-
cized tour of America from which she profited by endorsing
beauty products and writing a woman's column. [12] Sid ends
the scene by miming the "nose camera" bit from Paramount
News--"The Eyes and Ears of the World."

But, unlike Lefty, in the family plays the myths of
America as conveyed by the mass media are not merely
satirized; they serve as both anodynes and stimuli for the
emotional life of the middle class. For the young, like
Ralph in Awake and Sing!, they are standards of measure-
ment for one's self-image. Ralph says, "Who am I--Al
Jolson?" and, "What do I do--go to night clubs with Greta
Garbo?" and, derisively, he snorts, "I'm flying to Hollywood
by plane--that's what I'm doing" (I). Since they are tanta-
lizingly out of reach, the myths underscore the lack of
progress of the young. For the old, however, they are com-
forting--proof that America is indeed the land of opportunity
and that the poverty in the streets is a temporary aberration.
Bessie says: "We saw a very good movie, with Wallace
Beery. He acts like life, very good," and acidly comments,
"Polly Moran too--a woman with a nose from here to Hunts
Point, but a fine player" (II, 2). For Myron the movies provide an escape from harsh reality; he tries to remember
"the great Italian lover in the movies. What was his name?
The Sheik. ... No one remembers?" and, two minutes later
after leaving the room, he returns to announce: "Valentino!
That's the one!" (I) For failures like Myron, and Gus
Michaels in Paradise Lost, the movies are a necessary
dream factory because they make life bearable. When Ben
takes Libby (another ardent movie fan) to see Marlene

Dietrich, Gus remarks, "Marlene--she's the intellect and artistic type," and "Marlene--I got her in the harem of my head" (I).   Then he tells Clara Gordon that he often thinks of committing suicide, but laughingly confesses, "... I turn the radio on instead of the gas" (I).   Jacob in Awake and Sing! diagnoses the appeal of the movies astutely:

> He [Ralph] dreams all night of fortunes.   Why not?
> Don't it say in the movies he should have a per-
> sonal steamship, pyjamas for fifty dollars a pair
> and a toilet like a monument?   But in the morning
> he wakes up and for ten dollars he can't fix the
> teeth.   (II, 1).

Jacob's theory draws laughter from Uncle Morty, the successful businessman of the play.   His mockery illustrates still another function of Hollywood--to turn life into a cartoon and dissipate the social malaise by suggesting that life is fundamentally ridiculous and animalistic.   In his Preface Notes, Odets says that Uncle Morty "sees every Mickey Mouse cartoon that appears," and Morty's worldly wisdom and scorn for Jacob are garnished with cultural tidbits from Popeye the Sailor, the funnies (Ignatz and Boob McNutt) and Charlie Chaplin comedies.   Uncle Morty uses the popular media only to reenforce his crudely stereotyped thinking, but Odets was aware that in a symbolic sense the world of Disney was an ironic paradigm of American values.   In Paradise Lost, there is a striking scene (which I suspect influenced Ralph Ellison in Invisible Man) in which Ben, un- able to find work, returns home with a box containing a Mickey Mouse Drummer Boy, a mechanical toy which he buys for nine cents and sells for fifteen on street corners.   Ben identifies with the toy: "Poor Mickey Mouse!" (II); the all- American hero has been reduced to "a mechanical, capering mouse" (I), as Charlie Castle in a later echo describes him- self in The Big Knife.

Long before The Hidden Persuaders, Marshall Mc- Luhan, and the Yippie media freaks, Odets was aware of the potent forces that could lure the common man into creating a fantasy life more real than reality, and of the none-too- subtle manipulations by means of which the poor could be made to accept their status quo in the capitalistic system. In Clash by Night, Joe Doyle denounces the use of the media as an opiate:

... Earl, Jerry, Mae, millions like them, clinging

to a goofy dream--expecting life to be a picnic.
Who taught them that? Radio, songs, the movies--
you're the greatest people going. Paradise is just
around the corner. Shake that hip, swing that
foot--we're on the Millionaire Express! Don't cultivate your plot of ground--tomorrow you might win
a thousand acre farm! What farm? The dream
farm! (II, 2)

Odets has some of his characters protest directly; in
The Big Knife, Charlie Castle says, "The whole movie thing
is a murder of the people" (III, 2). But more often he shows
us how the media insinuate themselves into the lives of those
enclosed in the family trap, drugging their sensibilities against
pain, offering a tablet of success to lull and tranquilize them.
There is Myron in Awake and Sing! reading "a thing the druggist gave me. 'The Marvel Cosmetic Girl of Hollywood is
going on the air. Give this charming little radio singer a
name and win five thousand dollars. If you will send--'"
(II, 2). And there is Gus in Paradise Lost thinking about
putting in "a complete line of radios," and recalling what "a
certain party in the American Tel and Tel" told him-- "He
says television's comin' in, sure as death" (I). Is it accidental that Myron's leaflet came from a druggist or that
Odets associates the coming of TV with death? The symbolism is on target, though it is not as explicit here as in
the climactic scene of Clash by Night, in which Jerry Wilenski murders Earl Pfeiffer as we listen to the movie dialogue
of "a typical Hollywood 'product'" (II, 3), which Odets tells
us is "so stupid and cruel, so fraudulent in the face of the
present reality."

In his plays Odets constructs a further linkage between
the phony fantasies of Hollywood and the popular press and
the images of power and prestige puffed up by ad men for
American industry. In Golden Boy, Gary Cooper's fourteen
thousand dollar car pictured in the paper inspires Joe Bonaparte to buy the Deusenberg in which he dies. In Paradise
Lost, in the scene in which the newly married Ben and Libby
are interviewed by the press, Odets has the family posing
in front of Gus's shiny, highly decorated motorcycle. "Put
Greta Garbo on the handlebars" (I), suggests a newsman.
In Night Music (II, 4), the backdrop of the New York World's
Fair (commercialism mixed with patriotism) is made to seem
equally fraudulent as it presents to thousands a phantasma-
goria of progress from which the poor are excluded.

Another force which seems temporarily to loosen the

bonds of the family trap, ultimately to knot them even tighter,
is nostalgia for the past: man's natural tendency to look back
on a Golden Age when confronted with an untenable present.
Myron, in Awake and Sing!, survives by ignoring the facts
of the Depression--"Life is an even sweet event to him, but
the 'old days' were sweeter yet" (Preface Notes).   Nearly
everything Myron says or does harks back to the past: his
admiration for Teddy Roosevelt; his treatment of Hennie as
though she were still a little girl--"Where you going, little
Red Riding Hood?" (III); his conviction that "people aren't
the same.   N--O-- The whole world's changing right under
our eyes" (I) He takes solace in his recollections of Nora
Bayes singing "at the old Proctor's on Twenty-third Street, "
and in idly boasting about his two years of law school and
his job as a jewelry salesman on the road before he married.
Even the weather will launch him on a voyage into yesterday:

> There's no more big snows like in the old days....
> I was a little boy when it happened--the Great
> Blizzard.   It snowed three days without a stop that
> time.   Yes, and the horse cars stopped.   A silence
> of death was on the city and little babies got no
> milk ... they say a lot of people died that year
> (II, 2).

Odets' ironic technique in such reminiscent passages is to
juxtapose the shadow of the present on the speaker's haloed
memory, as he places the speech above just before Jacob's
suicide.

There is a similar moment in Paradise Lost when
Gus Michaels, who is a rueful failure like Myron, tries to
recapture his lost youth:

> I can't explain it to you, Mr. G. , how I'm forever
> hungerin' for the past.   It's like a disease in me,
> eatin' away ... some nights I have cried myself
> to sleep--for the old Asbury Park days; the shore
> dinners at old Sheepshead Bay.   In those days
> every house had its little dog--we was no excep-
> tion, as you well remember, with our Spotty, the
> fire dog--it was a common sight to see them out
> walkin' of a summer night, big ones and little
> ones.   How beautiful the summer nights before
> the Big War!   He would sit out there ... and the
> streets fulla laughin' playin' children.   I had Mrs.
> Michaels with me in those days.   Oh, yes, the

> pleasant laughin' talk, when we went around to
> Schoemacher's Ice Cream Parlor. Oh, it was so
> beautiful in those days! (II).

But Gus cannot totally escape into a daydream; in the next
breath he is asking "what'll happen when those barbarian
hordes come sweepin' down on us?" Though Mr. Pike, the
radical raisonneur in this play, states plainly that the system
must be changed, Gus and Leo do not understand, because
they are slaves of custom and habit. Gus calls for "A new
administration, " and Leo can only claim, "God gives us
patience to endure" (II). Previously, in the conclusion to
Act I, in a remarkable scene which blends nostalgia and
ironic fluctuations of hope and despair, Gus, Leo, and Mr.
Pike get drunk, recall their respective fathers, and listen to
a radio announcer repeat the appropriate clichés about God,
flag, and country on Armistice Day. Once again the past
is juxtaposed with the present; Leo remarks, "We cancel
our experience. This is an American habit" (I). Yet Odets
is plainly aware that while we may mis-read the lessons of
history, we cannot resist clinging to our emotional roots.
There is something deeply touching about these three middle-
aged men boozily sentimentalizing over possible alternatives
to the family trap, none of which seems likely to work. In
Act III, when the family is evicted, Leo seems to realize the
fatal consequence of romantic nostalgia: "... So in the end
nothing is real. Nothing is left but our memory of life.
Not as it is ... as it might have been. "

Since the forces of the mass media and the pull of
the past conjoin to seal the family trap, we may wonder what
happens to those who remain and attempt no break-out. For
the most part, we have adumbrated their fates already:
either they become hapless victims of social forces they cannot control or a kind of walking dead, like Myron and Julie.
But the analysis would be incomplete without noting still
another Odetsian motif--that of mendacity or hypocrisy--
which both affects those who remain in the trap and motivates
those who would flee. The Moloch-god of materialism cor-
rodes the family's moral values, and each play usually contains a pivotal scene of deceit which shows the trap closing
on an unanticipated victim. This can best be illustrated by
examining three key moments from the family plays.

In Act II, 2, of Awake and Sing!, Sam Feinschreiber
comes to his in-laws' home disheveled and excited. He has had
a fight with Hennie, and his wife has told him in a burst of

anger that the baby is not his. Humiliated, ashamed at being
"a second fiddle in his own house, " he blurts out the incident
to Jacob and Ralph, then repeats it to Bessie and Myron when
they return home. Sam feels the remark "like a knife in his
heart" and wants to know the truth. Hennie's parents, sens-
ing that he wants consolation more than candor, attribute the
remark to their daughter's "nerves. " They butter up Sam's
ego outrageously:

> BESSIE: We stood right here the first time she
>   said it. "Sam Feinschreiber's a nice boy, "
>   she said it, "a boy he's got good common sense,
>   with a business head. " Right here she said it,
>   in this room. You sent her two boxes of candy
>   together, you remember?
> MYRON: Loft's candy.
> BESSIE: This is when she said it. What do you
>   think?
> MYRON: You were just the only boy she cared for.
> BESSIE: So she married you. Such a world ...
>   plenty of boy friends she had, believe me!
> JACOB: <u>A popular girl</u>.... [my italics]
> MYRON: Y-e-s.
> BESSIE: I'll say it plain out--Moe Axelrod offered
>   her plenty--a servant, a house ... she don't
>   have to pick up a hand.
> MYRON: Oh, Moe? Just wild about her....
> BESSIE: But she didn't care. A girl like Hennie
>   you don't buy. I should never live to see
>   another day if I'm telling a lie.

Sam is pathetically eager to snatch at the bait, soothe his
wounded vanity, and return home to the wife and child he
loves. But the point is not that Bessie and Myron connive to
dissipate the fears of their son-in-law, but that Jacob, the
idealist, <u>joins</u> them in the conspiracy. In a moment of crisis
for the family, for all his lofty moral idealism, Jacob cannot
suppress his feelings of family solidarity. He lies, and a
few moments later--when Myron blurts out the truth--it becomes apparent to Ralph that his grandfather has participated in the trap laid for Sam from the start. Ralph's dis-
gust is unbounded:

> RALPH: I got the whole idea. I get it so quick
>   my head's swimming. Boy, what a laugh! I
>   suppose you know about this, Jake?
> JACOB: Yes.

> RALPH: Why didn't you do something?
> JACOB: I'm an old man.
> RALPH: What's that got to do with the price of
>   bonds? Sits around and lets a thing like that
>   happen! You make me sick too.

This exposure as a moral hypocrite, in combination with the
other motives I have mentioned (page 36), prompts Jacob to
take his own life shortly afterwards. A close reading of the
text will, I believe, confirm that it is the decisive factor
that leads to his death. In this scene, not only is Sam
Feinschreiber a victim of mendacity; Jacob is destroyed by
it.

While The Flowering Peach has been regarded by
some critics as a softening of Odets' critical attitude toward
the family,[13] I find evidence that his basic outlook had not
changed. It is true that the Noah legend as set forth in the
Bible dictated a more conciliatory spirit at the play's conclusion, but the old conflicts still rage before and during the
voyage of the ark. The motif of mendacity is still present,
in comic form, at a crucial moment in Scene 6; after 41 days
of drifting, exploitation already exists on the ark. Shem,
the business-minded son, is bribing Ham with liquor to do
his work for him; Noah finds evidence of lechery and back-
biting; but what sends him into a towering rage is his discovery that Shem has been hoarding "dried manure briquettes,"
fuel which this entrepreneur hopes to sell to his family when
they reach dry land and thus begin a new capitalistic hege-
mony. Previously, Noah had insisted, "On the ark nothing
will be for sale, no investments, hear me? Money is unholy
dirt on the ark--" (4); he had forced Shem to return to the
tax collector the money from his last-minute sale of his
land. Now, while the ark is tipping perilously from the
weight of Shem's fertilizer, Esther makes an artful defense
of her son's action:

> ESTHER: If you made it to sell, Shem, you're a
>   low dog! But if you made it for the family--
> SHEM (picking up the cue): But, Momma, that's
>   what I did--I made it for the family!
> ESTHER (pretending surprise): You hear, Noah?
> NOAH (suspiciously): Esther, you shouldn't take
>   his part, hear me?
> ESTHER: But if it's for the family, why throw it
>   overboard.... ? (NOAH looks at her, aware
>   that she is putting something over on him; he

> turns away with tight lips, hands behind his
> back.   ESTHER, stolidly): Shem made a useful
> thing from nothing, yeh? Why kill the man with
> brains? No. make him use it for the family!
> (Innocently): I said it right, Noah.... ?
> NOAH (mutteringly): Go 'way from me.... (6).

Noah, who had wanted the ark to be "a holy place," is ca-
joled into starting the new world literally with merde. Esther's hypocrisy may be practical--indeed, that trait is the
essence of her character--but her deceit not only dismays
Noah but must surely have an injurious effect on the idealistic son, Japheth, who remains silent.

The motif of mendacity begins with bourgeois rationalizations like Esther's; its more serious implications can be
seen at the end of Act II of Paradise Lost, when another
mother makes a plea for her son.   Leo has been paid a visit
by Mr. May, a business-like arsonist, brought to the Gordons' home by Leo's partner, Sam Katz.   May is proud of
his record of 53 fires set for "respected citizens" who cash
in their insurance policies to save their foundering businesses.
Indignant at the illegality, but more shocked by the man's
inhumanity, the idealistic Leo ejects him from his home.
There follows a terrifying showdown with his partner, in
which Katz is revealed as an impotent, twisted deceiver; not
only has he lied to his friend about the firm's books, but he
has placed the blame for his sterility on his wife, deceiving
the whole world.   After this moment of Sam's exposure,
mendacity claims still another victim.   Clara Gordon finds
the card which Mr. May has left behind and learns of his
profession.

> CLARA: What did you say to him?
> LEO: To who?
> CLARA: To him....
> LEO (in a low voice): I said no.
> CLARA: Leo, we live once....
> LEO: What do you want?
> CLARA: Think of tomorrow.
> LEO: I am....
> CLARA: Leo ...
> LEO: Please ...
> CLARA: If you think ... (LEO jumps up.)
> LEO: Don't say that!
> CLARA: Where will we go?

There is something chilling in this transformation of

the gay Clara who, in Act I, said, "I never worried a day
in my life," into a creature so bedeviled by anxiety for her
dying son and family misfortune that she is tempted to commit a criminal act.   Clara does finally tear up the card, but
Odets has shown that no inhabitant of the family trap is un-
touched by moral hypocrisy.

So the vicious circle completes itself.   Those who remain in the family trap become its victims.   Aged idealists
like Jacob or Noah become corrupted or compromised.   Loving mothers like Bessie, Clara, and Esther become moral
hypocrites.   Sons and daughters may be docile victims, like
Pearl and Julie Gordon, or they may writhe and pull like
Ben, Ralph, Hennie, Japheth, or Joe Bonaparte, in an attempt to break out.   Most of these attempts, as we have
seen, are failures.   But Odets, who is interested primarily
in his characters' humanity and only secondarily in their
ideology, insists that there must be a way out.   Outside the
closely knit family circle looms a world of strangers, of
fierce competition and external pressures, of economic dangers and, in some plays, global cataclysms.   But the idealist
cannot rest content in an island of mendacity, nor can he be
lulled by media myths and nostalgia.   He is driven forth by
his conscience to meet the world's body, seeking a link with
the rest of mankind and a chance for self-fulfillment. [14]   For
if death, running away, and social commitment do not work,
there is another way out of the family trap, and that is to
accept society on its own terms temporarily, to strike out
for independence and power that will put you on top rather
than keep you bottom-dog.   This is a second major territory
Odets explores as he moves from the family trap to the
societal, from the world of blood relations to the bloody
world outside.

2.   The Sell-out

Half-idealism is the peritonitis of
the soul.
                    --Hank, The Big Knife

No one has ever doubted Odets' peculiar qualifications
to deal with the next major theme which preoccupied him:
the individual's barter of moral principle in exchange for
money, power, and status.   His enemies insisted that he

sold himself again and again to Hollywood, and even his
friends found it difficult to defend the paradox of a revolutionary playwright in the Depression era who maintained a
penthouse at One University Place and an apartment at Beek-
man Place, and in later years decorated the walls of his
Beverly Hills mansion with Klees and the French impression-
ists.   The accounts of Clifford Odets, playwright, "king
among the ju-ven-niles," his associations with the great and
famous, his peregrinations to the Mecca of Materialism he
alternately praised and despised, were exploited in the press
at the expense of Odets the artist, the writer of passionate
plays about serious dilemmas in American life.   Indeed, it
is difficult to disentangle the work and the man in Odets'
career, for Odets' major plays on the subject of selling-out,
Golden Boy and The Big Knife, are rooted in his personal
experience.

He had left New York early in 1936, after previously
refusing repeated offers from Hollywood studios, when the
poor critical reception afforded the Group's production of
Paradise Lost threatened to close the play.   From his weekly
Hollywood salary of $2500, he sent back $4000[15] to pay the
actors' salaries; further contributions were donated from his
earnings from the script of The General Died at Dawn and
others.   But money and a near-flop were not the only factors
behind his move to Hollywood.   With such other Leftist playwrights as John Howard Lawson and Albert Maltz, he was
fascinated by the potential of the new medium of film.   An
interview of the period reflects his enthusiasm: "They have
a better conception of story structure here than on the stage...
every playwright should come to Hollywood at least once and
learn this technique of story-telling."   The interview also reflects his naiveté: "... I have found there is no attempt in
Hollywood to stop anyone from doing good writing."   And, in
the same article, he could admire the honesty of an industry
which openly admitted its dependence on the boy-meets-girl
formula and call this "refreshing candor."   As for the pos-
sibility that the movies might change him, he scoffed at it:
"I won't be a party to the fraud the screen has been perpe-
trating on the public for years.   Boy gets girl.   Life is
swell.   I won't do that."[16]

Always brashly confident about his own talent, Odets
was convinced that Hollywood would give him a broader base
from which to promulgate his critical view of American life.
There was something dizzily alluring about a medium that
reached 80 million Americans each week.[17]   Nor was he

alone in this view. According to Eric Bentley, "Before the talkies were a decade old, even the kind of people who had earlier despised the screen began to see in it the successor to the living actor ... the drama was a thing of the past, the future belonged to the motion picture."[18]

Had Odets been only deluding himself, he could be written off as just another slick second-rater easily purchased by Hollywood. But Odets remained a serious writer. He really believed he could write socially significant dramas in movieland, and the process of disillusionment caused him much pain, guilt, and anger. Why, then, didn't he leave? Frequently he did: once to rejoin the Group for an extended period from 1938 to 1940, and again in the post-war years to supervise the three dramas with which he hoped to re-establish himself in New York. But he vacillated between the two capitals, and he was back in Beverly Hills when he died. Hollywood was like a powerful magnet or, more aptly, an incubus which he could not shake off and sometimes seemed to welcome.

The underlying reasons for this vacillation are complex, but I believe the most salient explanation is that Odets, himself, was fascinated by power and the men who wielded it. Like Dreiser, another writer who both sympathized with the poor and admired the rich, he was absorbed by the large-scale manipulations of men like Louis B. Mayer and the Brothers Warner who, by the sheer dynamism of their personalities, carved out personal fiefdoms in a competitive capitalist society. Such men were latter-day Cowperwoods, titans who shaped the tastes and attitudes of millions, while they dealt out princely sums to their favorites and annihilated their enemies. That Odets had an appreciation for raw power was apparent from his earliest work. Young Ralph Berger had listened avidly to the sound of the Boston mail plane cutting its way across the Bronx, a symbol of purposeful movement in a paralyzed world. On a cross-country trip by train back to Hollywood in 1940, Odets was impressed by the sound of a freight train huffing and puffing on the opposite siding in some small town in Arizona. According to his companion, Oscar Levant, he shouted excitedly as he made rhythmic pumping movements with his feet in imitation of the train. "Chug! Chug! Chug! That's power!"[19] The episode seems childlike, yet it is precisely in this lack of sophistication that one detects Odets' vulnerability to Hollywood. He knew the axiom that material success and power corrupt, but his awareness was complicated by his psychological identification

with success, his sympathy with its victims, and his knowledge of the seductive strength of the American Dream. Here,
in Hollywood, he could record it all, like Fitzgerald docu-
menting the rise and fall of Monroe Stahr. Once he had
blithely announced: "Let N. Y. see the rest of the country.
Hollywood too. Play material to keep six dozen writers
going. "[20] But, though he kept a plaster bust of Walt Whitman in his workroom and named his son after the poet, [21]
Odets did not try to encompass all of America's vistas in
his plays. More and more his subject became the sweet
smell of success and what it did to people. Although Hollywood was his microcosm, he intuited that much the same
process occurred in the steel cities, the ranching communities and real estate boom towns across the nation. Perhaps
if he had bestirred himself and traveled more about the
country, he might have been a more diverse and epical writer.
But he was at his best when his imagination was most deeply
engaged; thus, after the family plays, the Broadway-Hollywood
axis became his intensely explored personal landscape.

It would be too simple to suggest that Odets' attraction
to Hollywood grew out of the old Marxist cliché, "bore from
within. " Years later, he told the HUAC Committee just how
laughable were the prospects of writing propaganda in the
collaboratively produced, mass-market-oriented picture industry. [22] Nor is it a sufficient explanation to maintain that
Odets' genuine interest in men of power drew him to Hollywood as a detached and dispassionate observer. For it is
patently true that he wanted to be part of the world of the
Bad and the Beautiful. Harold Clurman, who visited his
friend in Hollywood in 1937, could not understand why Odets
cared so much about winning the approval of the movie moguls
and the entrenched celebrities:

> I did not understand the closeness Odets sought with
> these people he was bent on converting. He wanted
> their admiration, their plaudits, their goodwill. He
> needed their love; or, lacking that, power over
> them. Above all, he did not want them to believe
> that if he thought as he did or wrote as he did, it
> was because he could think or write no other way....
> He wished to be one with them--if in no other way,
> by winning them over, by licking them. It was a
> profoundly human pattern of adjustment by coercion.
> It is often followed by adjustment through self-
> abasement. It is an old drama, of which America
> offers fascinatingly new versions. [23]

Clurman's perceptive comments tell us much about the role Odets eventually came to play in the movie community; it was the classic role of Mr. Inside-Outside. As Mr. Outside, he could be the ghost-like conscience of the commercial world: argue for movies which had social content or were time-tested classics; convince Cary Grant to do the hauntingly memorable and financially unsuccessful None But the Lonely Heart; accept or decline credit on pictures like Humoresque (a spin-off on Golden Boy) and Blockade (Hollywood's truncated tribute to the Spanish Civil War). As Mr. Inside, he could enjoy the perquisites of that same world: attend private parties with friends like Franchot Tone and Eddie Robinson; float in his swimming pool and upon his king-size salary, yet pass them off as "the contradictions of capitalism";[24] accept a call from a major studio to do a craftsman-like suspense melodrama, Deadline at Dawn, or hone the dialogue razor-sharp for The Sweet Smell of Success; even slap together a vehicle for Elvis Presley. His movie work, with the exception of the Grant picture, could not have been emotionally satisfying to him because he must have known he was whoring. Later he would devise elaborate rationalizations: Mozart and Beethoven had done occasional pieces for money; there was nothing wrong with working on trivia for a living, except that puritanic strain in American morality which sat in judgment on professional artists; sheer craft had a value all its own, etc.[25] There was always a plaintive and defensive note to his estimate of the merit of his scriptwriting. In 1963, he told Michael J. Mendelsohn:

> Well, let them [the scripts] stand for what they
> are. They are technically very adept. I have
> learned a great deal from making and shaping these
> scripts.... One need not be ashamed of them. I
> have not expressed anywhere any loss of standards.
> I haven't dehumanized people in them.... It's
> professional work: I'm a professional writer. And
> I am never ashamed of the professional competence
> which is in these scripts. I have never down-
> graded human beings or a certain kind of morality.
> I'm not ashamed of any of them....[26]

Defiance and half-truths. Perhaps Odets had not turned from his basic humanitarianism, but, in art, oversimplification and compromise are immoral, and no one knew better the double standards he used in writing for the camera and writing for the stage. He said as much each time he brought a new play to Broadway.[27] Earlier he had been

positive that affluence and success would not change his thinking or his art; his reasoning was both ironic and prophetic:

> I am fortunate in being associated with a group
> that believes as I do. With them [the Group
> Theater] I get a living. The reason men change
> is either because of success or failure. The first
> isolates them and the other drives them to a more
> secure method of living. There is a substantial
> enough stratum that thinks as I do to encourage
> me and make existence possible. 28

Odets' psychological needs as a writer lie in those
words. Like all men, he feared isolation, but more than
most, he needed people. While the Group surrounded him
with kindred spirits and a tough intellectual atmosphere
against which he could sharpen his ideas, he was at his most
productive. When the Group finally dissolved in 1940, Odets,
after two humiliating stage failures, Night Music and Clash
by Night, headed West. 29 Clurman's earlier remark, "For
Odets at this time Hollywood was Sin, "30 could be revised;
on this occasion it was also Security. But for Odets, existence in Hollywood would have been impossible without the
encouragement of friends who thought and felt as he did.
He sought out this circle in the professionalism of the Screen
Writer's Guild, in artists of cultivation and taste, like Levant and, later, Jean Renoir, who shared his enthusiasm for
classical music and painting. However, Harold Clurman's
crucial role as aesthetic advisor was assumed by the inspired huckster, Jerry Wald. 31 The price he paid was the
ambiguous role of Mr. Inside-Outside and the dilution of his
energies.

There were some compensations, however. In addition
to the needed security (Odets' second wife died in 1950 and
he had two small children to bring up), and the compatible
friends that he found in Hollywood, Odets exercised the
artist's supreme right to sit in judgment on the system and
still be compassionate; he could cultivate a detachment
through his dual role which was denied to others. A striking incident will serve to illustrate what I mean. It was
common knowledge that the characterization of Marcus Hoff,
the megalomaniacal boss in The Big Knife, was based on
Harry Cohn, the tyrannical head of Columbia Pictures. When
Cohn died in 1958, he had been called "a sadistic son of a
bitch" by scores of actors and directors, and much worse in

more elegant language.   Yet the man who wrote the funeral
eulogy for Cohn (with Danny Kaye) was the same Clifford
Odets who had pilloried him mercilessly in his play.   It was a
moving and unblinkingly honest tribute to a tough, ruthless and
dedicated studio czar.   When John Ford heard it at the
funeral, he asked, "Who is that intelligent young rabbi?"[32]

      That Odets' personal encounter with Hollywood, with
success, and with men of power, was filled with ambiguities
and contradictions should now be evident.   Whether his personal drama was an inglorious sell-out or a lifelong struggle
that he never resolved I shall leave to his biographers and
to those people who insist on making judgments before all
the facts and memoirs and letters have been gathered and
evaluated.

      Two facts are indisputable, however.   Odets learned
much from the seasoned professionals who labored in the
Hollywood vineyards, and his admiration for sheer craftsmanship in cinema-making did not ruin him as a serious
dramatist.   If anything, the lessons he learned enhanced his
versatility and furthered his willingness to experiment, e. g. ,
Night Music and, later, The Country Girl--a play that is
partially about the crafts of acting and directing.   The second
fact is that Odets kept inviolate his love for his original commitment.   Whatever his vacillations in attitude toward the
film industry, he always thought of himself as a playwright.
In several articles and interviews he talked of the creative
writer's need to write "out of his own state of being" and to
make "a personal statement, " and he recognized, after a few
painful experiences, that the high-finance, cooperatively-pro-
duced, box-office and star-dependent Hollywood system did
not permit such artistic independence. [33]   He knew that the
theater in New York--though it might sometimes mimic
Hollywood's big business tactics--was the place "where personal affiliation with one's writing (the first premise of
truth) does not constitute lese majesty. "[34]   So whenever he
wanted to express "a state of being" instead of a "construct, "
he headed for Broadway.

      Yet to know a thing is not enough for a playwright;
he must work out its objective correlatives in his art.   The
crucial question is whether Odets' ambivalent attitude toward
power and success led to confusion and contradiction in his
serious dramas or to artistically productive tension.   In the
family plays, his simultaneous feelings of love and hate had
produced dramas of richness and complexity, flawed mainly

by their forced conclusions. But double vision in art can be
both a blessing and a curse. What was Odets' conception of
the sell-out? Was it consistent? Was it valid? Did he
embody this theme in artistically achieved wholes? At this
point I shall turn to an examination of the theme as it evolved
in his plays, conscious of Odets' deep emotional entanglement
in it but also aware of the artist's transforming imagination.

Remarkably early in his career, Odets became concerned with the man who sells himself for a price. Recurring throughout his political plays are vivid cameos and vignettes of turncoats and traitors, who are consciously dis-
loyal to a political cause. In Waiting for Lefty, the Labor
Spy Episode is a pointed reminder that greed and defection
can poison the solidarity of the working class. Tom Clayton,
"a thin, modest individual," is introduced by Fatt, the corrupt union boss, as a man with practical strike experience
from Philadelphia. His purpose is to put a damper on the
proposed taxi strike. "If I thought it would help us hacks
get better living conditions, I'd let you walk all over me,
cut me up to little pieces. I'm one of you myself. But what
I wanna say is that Harry Fatt's right ... the time ain't
ripe." A persistent voice heckles him from the audience,
calls him a liar and a rat, and identifies him as belonging
to a professional strike-breaking organization. When Clayton denies it, the man strides onstage and applies the clinch-
er: "Boys, I slept with him in the same bed sixteen years,
HE'S MY OWN LOUSY BROTHER!"

In Till the Day I Die, the entire plot spins around a
supposed traitor, Ernst Tausig, who is isolated from his
Communist brethren when the SS arrests him and then, by
allowing him to move freely, though shadowed by gunmen,
the SS suggests to the underground that he is a stool pigeon.
Ernst, alienated from friends and the girl carrying his child,
becomes a living ghost who begs to be put out of his misery.
Almost as though he is foreshadowing the theme he was later
to explore in greater depth, Odets allows his imagination to
weave and circle around the consequences of real and ima-
gined defection. In this artificial and often meretricious
play wherein the villains are caricatured brutes and the
heroes idealized pacifists, a vision wholly conjured up by
Odets from newspaper materials and his stereotyped view of
Nazi mentality, there is one fairly complex or at least interesting character. Significantly, he is a sell-out figure:
Major Duhring, "a tired civilized man," who interviews
Ernst privately and informs him that he is in Nazi uniform

because of "a realistic necessity"--he had married into one
of the finest old German families but is, in reality, of Jewish
stock. Courteously ironic, he hints that his work hinders
rather than helps the National Socialist State and mocks his
insipid wife's radio speech which she plans to deliver for the
Minister of Propaganda. When they are alone he tries to
help Ernst by realistically describing his fate and urging him
to kill himself. There follows a melodramatic encounter with
his arch-enemy, the homosexual Captain Schlegal, whom he
impulsively kills. Among his final words to Ernst are: "Say,
I am not despised. Please say it.... You see, the contradictions of my own nature have backed up on me" (4).

With these black-and-white vignettes, Odets was beginning to grapple with his theme. An even greater stride
was taken when he wrote a short piece entitled "I Can't
Sleep," which was first performed on May 19, 1935, for the
benefit of the Marine Workers Industrial Union at Mecca
Temple, New York. Essentially a bravura soliloquy by a
worker who encounters a hungry beggar, "an American
spectre," on a street corner, the work was performed by
Morris Carnovsky and Art Smith of the Group during the
dreary days of 1935.

Sam Blitzstein, a worker in the garment industry in
New York City, refuses a handout to the silent figure since
he does not believe in charity, especially at a time when
"Poverty is whistling from every corner of the country."
But he immediately changes his mind and pours out his
troubled heart to the beggar, whom he now implores for forgiveness. He has committed the crime of remaining aloof
and apolitical while ignoring the suffering of his brothers.
But his immigrant, working-class conscience nags at him.
At home, reacting to his selfishness, his wife and children
have withdrawn from him. Debarred from those he loves,
he develops a paranoic suspicion that his youngest child is
not his own. Tormented by conflicting emotions of love and
hatred, he lies awake at night:

> Oh, I don't sleep. At night my heart cries blood.
> A fish swims all night in the black ocean--and
> this is how I am all night with one eye open. A
> mixed up man like me crawls away to die alone.
> No woman should hold his head. In the whole city
> no one speaks to me. A very peculiar proposition.
> Maybe I would like to say to a man, "Brother."
> But what happens? They bring in a verdict--

crazy! It's a civilized world today in America?
Columbus should live so long. [35]

Here, in miniature, Odets had worked out the pattern
for what happens to the sell-out figure. Having struggled to
secure a niche in the amoral business-competitive society,
he becomes an acceptable commodity; but guilt feelings nag
at him. He alienates his true friends and loved ones and
succumbs to intolerable loneliness. He tries to find solace
in material rewards and phony status, but an inner core of
incorruptability becomes his cross. He may lash out in
paranoic reprisal at his loved ones, but the real target of
his hatred is himself. Suicide, in some cases, is both his
release and transcendence.

This pattern is developed in complex detail in Golden
Boy and The Big Knife, yet it is implicit in early Odets
works other than those already mentioned. As his art matured, Odets came to recognize that the sell-out has two
phases: a person can be a conscious traitor to a political
cause (as in these early vignettes); but the most tragic sell-
out, and the most endemic to American life, is to be forced
by economic circumstance to desert one's highest principles
and negate one's deepest potentialities. The first phase
rapidly became a cliché of leftist writing in the 1930's, with
the Party as the Supreme Judge, branding the defector as a
miscreant whenever he deviated from the political dogmas
which were, in themselves, straightjackets to individual
growth. Some critics still insist on reading Odets' plays
(and judging Odets the man) as though he were concerned
with this first kind of sell-out primarily; ironically, he had
bolted the Party precisely because he did not want to be
boxed in. Odets' most astute critics--Harold Clurman, William Gibson, Michael Mendelsohn--have always recognized
that his major concern was to depict the broader issue, and
to liberate the individual soul from those forces in American
society which shackle and prevent it from achieving its highest fulfillment.

Implicit in Awake and Sing! there are already prototypes of this kind of sell-out figure. Jacob, the failed idealist, confesses to Ralph that he has been a talker rather than
a doer all his life: "But you should act. Not like me. A
man who had golden opportunities but drank instead a glass
tea" (I, 2). Opposed to Jacob is Moe Axelrod, the cynical
legless veteran, who has joined the bootleggers and numbers
boys and whose motto is: "It's all a racket--from horse

racing down. Marriage, politics, big business--everybody
plays cops and robbers" (II, 1). Poised between them is
young Ralph, who must choose between the easy money represented by Moe, and the hard road of revolutionizing
society represented by Jacob.

Yet in Awake and Sing! the forces which comprise
the sell-out theme, idealism vs. materialistic corruption,
are set in juxtaposition; there is no head-on collision, nor
do we see them actively struggling for domination in the
mind of the youthful protagonist. In Paradise Lost Odets
etched his first memorable and pathetic sell-out figure,
young Ben Gordon, but even here the theme is a sub-strand
in the larger tragedy of the dissolution of the family. By
the time he wrote Golden Boy, Odets' attitudes toward the
theme had coalesced, and in The Big Knife he deepened and
embellished his insights, so that we can discover a consistency as discernible as the development of a morality play
(Odets' Everyman).

First and foremost the sell-out figure sins by "living
against his own nature" (The Big Knife, II). Each of the
characters has a desire compatible with his "nature": in
Ben's case, it is his ambition to be a champion Olympic
runner; for Joe Bonaparte, it is his love of music and the
violin; and for Charlie Castle, his ardor for acting in serious
Broadway theater (presumably, if we are to judge by hints
in the text, the kind of anti-establishment, left-wing drama
characteristic of the Group Theater). Odets establishes the
authenticity of his characters' natures by giving them lyrical,
affirmative speeches that convey youth's fervor and truth:

> ... I used to like to be out in front. When I fell
> in that rhythm and knew my reserve--the steady
> driving forward--I sang inside when I ran. Yeah,
> sang like an airplane, powerful motors humming in
> oil. I wanted to run till my heart exploded ...
> --Ben, Paradise Lost, II

> With music I'm never alone when I'm alone--Play-
> ing music ... that's like saying, "I am man. I
> belong here. How do you do, world--good evening!"
> When I play music nothing is closed to me. I'm
> not afraid of people and what they say. There's
> no war in music. It's not like the streets.
> --Joe, Golden Boy, I, 4

The cynical and older Charlie Castle must see his youthful
nature reflected through the eyes of his wife, Marion:

> ... You used to take sides. Golly, the zest with
> which you fought. You used to grab your theater
> parts and eat 'em like a tiger.
>> --Marion, The Big Knife, I

It does not matter to Odets that these fields--athletics,
music, acting--are in themselves highly competitive. They
are associated with the protagonists' youthful innocence, and
each in its own way is an art form. The trouble is that art,
to say nothing of liberal politics, is incompatible with the
climate of a materialistic, capitalist society. As Mr. Carp
says to Mr. Bonaparte:

> ... could a boy make a living playing this instru-
> ment in our competitive civilization today?...
> Could the Muses put bread and butter on the table?
> (Golden Boy, I, 2)

These are indeed pertinent remarks and the answer is obvious
in a world where, as Roxy Gottlieb tells Mr. Bonaparte:
"... Five hundred fiddlers stand on Broadway and 48th Street,
on the corner, every day, rain or shine, hot or cold" (I, 3).

To each of the sell-out figures this lesson of frustration and uselessness is forcefully driven home. For Ben
Gordon, who learns from the doctor that he has a heart condition and cannot run again, there is no alternative. In the
depths of the Great Depression and with no training or apti-
tude, he indulges in false hopes that his personal magnetism
will find him some means of support on Wall Street, and
finally makes a rash marriage to the shallow, pleasure-loving
Libby Michaels. Joe Bonaparte's disillusionment is more
complicated. He has discovered that music cannot gain him
the respect and admiration he seeks from the world:

> People have hurt my feelings for years. I never
> forget. You can't get even with people by playing
> the fiddle. If music shot bullets I'd like it better--
> artists and people like that are freaks today. The
> world moves fast and they sit around like forgotten
> dopes (I, 4).

Part of Joe's disaffection from his true self stems from his
inferiority complex about his eyes: the "cockeyed" kid in

Act I, who persuades Tom Moody into taking him on as a fighter, is compensating for the taunts of hostile schoolmates who regarded him as "a shrimp with glasses." The motif runs all through the play. Joe tells Lorna Moon in Act II: "I develop the ability to knock down anyone my weight. But what point have I made? Don't you think I know that? I went off to the wars 'cause someone called me a name--because I wanted to be two other guys. Now it's happening ... I'm not sure I like it." And, at the end, at the moment of his greatest triumph in the ring, Joe is still exulting: "... that veritable cockeye wonder, Bonaparte.... Well, how do you like me, boys? Am I good or am I good?" (III, 2).

Harold Clurman felt it was a mistake for Odets to place such emphasis on the hero's eyes, "a subjective flaw due to a reliance on a personal interpretation where a social one is required."[36] But surely if we are to read Golden Boy as a moral allegory--and how else can we take this fable of the fiddle and the fist?--Odets was symbolically on target by making young Joe both an artistic and physical freak. Odets, unlike Tennessee Williams, rarely makes his characters into psychological case histories, and despite Joe's Napoleonic complex, his major motivation for selling out is clear. In the beginning he may have wanted to prove his manhood; mostly, however, he wanted to earn money, as he tells his father in Act I, 2. What Joe wants is what the society esteems: success, fame, and the status that comes with owning a $14,000 Deusenberg. As his brother-in-law Siggie puts it: "... Joe went in the boxing game 'cause he's ashamed to be poor. That's his way to enter a little enterprise. All other remarks are so much alfalfa!" (I, 5).

The vivid American images of overnight success, millionaires created by their prowess in sports or by their photogenic profiles are far more alluring to Joe than the gold medal he won for his musicianship and a scholarship from the Frickson Institute. Joe wants a taste of the "fat cat" life which America has always promised its immigrants like Mr. Carp: "Fortunes! I used to hear it in my youth--the streets of America is paved with gold" (I, 2). Only the aggressive side of Joe's nature can win him this trophy; as his brother Frank says, "It looks like the gold bug has visited our house" (I, 2).

Charlie Castle's deviation from his true nature is a little more difficult to trace. In part this is because we meet him already corrupted, a famous movie star worth "millions a year ... in ice-cold profits" to Hoff-Federated, a man who "is apt to mask his best qualities behind a cynical, guying manner and certain jazzy small-talk" (Preface Notes, Act I). Mainly, we learn about his early years by inference, that he was brought up by an uncle in Philly who "had a nose for the rebels--London, Upton Sinclair--all the way back to Ibsen and Hugo.... Sounds grandiose, but Hugo said to me: 'Be a good boy, Charlie. Love people, do good, help the lost and fallen, make the world happy, if you can!'" (I). The people around Charlie give us tantalizing glimpses of the man behind the mask: Polly Benedict, the gossip columnist, elicits from him the remark that when he first came to Hollywood he believed in FDR (I); his business agent scolds him for giving $200 to a hungry writer; Nat Danzinger, his agent, says to him, "You're a special, idealist type" (I), and the venomous Smiley Coy characterizes him as "the warrior minstrel of the forlorn hope" (II). Marion, his wife, recalls "the critic who called you the Van Gogh of the American Theater" (II).

Yet all this, though it establishes Charlie's inner sensitivity, drive, and liberal bent, does not explain why he abandoned Broadway acting, his calling, and came to Hollywood. The fact is that we must infer his motives from what we know about Odets' motives. It is no coincidence that in this play, written in 1948, we are told Charlie Castle has lived in Hollywood 12 years. This would place the year of his emigration in 1936, the same year Odets made his first trip. If my analogy is correct, Odets is certainly at fault in failing to flesh out his character's motivations with the truths derived from his own experience. Odets placed too much reliance on John Garfield, who played Charlie on the stage and was Odets' favorite alter-ego, to carry the burden of Odets' confession, suggesting by his mere presence in the play all that Odets himself felt about the attraction of Hollywood.

The denaturing process for the sell-out figure is only what Dreiser called "a single step in a long tragedy." Once a man has mortgaged his true talent and become tainted by "success"--American style--he can never regain his full humanity. Realizing that he is a mere commodity, he lashes out at his friends and enemies, moved by guilt feelings and self-hatred.

Ben Gordon, who has been forced to become a peddler of mechanical toys which no one will buy, is drawn into the racketeering of his boyhood chum, Kewpie. In his bitterness he gratuitously wounds the pitiable, barren Mrs. Katz.

> BEN (to MRS. KATZ, (passing through)): Mrs. Katz, can I sell you a gross of these drummer boys? A helluva lot of toys for a kid to play with, if you had the kid.
> MRS. KATZ: If I had a boy I would buy gold toys. (Exits.)
> LEO: Why do you hurt her feelings?
> BEN: Leo, did you ever see the stuff these guys write on toilet walls? They write because they don't have! Like Kewpie--socking away because that's all he's got (II).

Later it develops that Kewpie, long a rival for Libby's affections, has been cheating on his friend and leaving money with his wife, so that Ben is utterly dependent on the man who has cuckolded him. The irony is that Ben, the man who won all the medals and whom Kewpie has both hero-worshiped and hated, no longer cares.

> KEWPIE: Libby don't care for you three cents. You're sand in her shoes. I buy her clothes, keep your house running. The new fancy carriage for the kid? My dough! The money in your pocket? Mine! I'm in you like a tape worm.
> BEN: You pushed me out of bed....
> KEWPIE: You're out--I'm in!
> BEN: Better than me? You want to be better than me? You picked a lousy model to beat! What an honor to be a better guy than Ben Gordon! (II)

At last, Ben perceives his degradation, the triviality of Kewpie's twisted love-hatred, and the meaninglessness of love itself. Kewpie, Libby, and Ben are all victims of the same inexorable economic forces. Before leaving to do his last "job" for Kewpie, he spits violently in the face of the life-size statue of himself in athletic garb.

To Joe Bonaparte it quickly becomes obvious that he is a mere fighting machine to his handlers, to be kept well oiled and handled gently because of his monetary value. He sees through Moody's attempt to use Lorna as a decoy, and rebels against his manager's attempts to run his life:

LORNA: Moody's against that car of yours.
JOE: I'm against Moody, so we're even.
LORNA: Why don't you like him?
JOE: He's a manager! He treats me like a pos-
    session! I'm just a little silver mine for him--
    he bangs me around with a shovel! (II, 2)

Moody, who senses Joe's interest in Lorna, later con-
firms his callous attitude: "It's a business--Joe does his
work, I do mine. Like this telephone--I pay the bill and I
use it!" (II, 3). The more Joe encounters such attitudes,
the more he is transformed from musician into fighter, to
the degree that by his first important fight his gentle father
can say:

MR. BONAPARTE: ... he gotta wild wolf inside--
    eat him up!
LORNA: You could build a city with his ambition
    to be somebody.
MR. BONAPARTE (sadly, shaking his head): No ...
    burn down! (II, 4)

In The Big Knife, Charlie Castle's situation is hardly
more satisfactory than Joe Bonaparte's. Twelve years of
stardom in mediocre gangster pictures--MARION: "... in
your last ten pictures you were electrocuted four times!"
(I)--have made him virtually the studio's prisoner. His estranged wife calls him "Hoff's Mr. Castle," and he recognizes that once he signs his new 14-year contract guarantee-
ing him three and one-half million a year, "Hoff's got me
by the tail and he won't let go...." (I). It is not that Charlie bleeds internally at the thought of making money: "I'm
in the movie business, darling. I can't afford these acute
attacks of integrity" (I); and "I never heard you kick about
barbecuing four-inch steaks!" (II), he tells his somewhat-too-
smug liberal wife. He has even lost faith in the legitimate
stage: "The theatre's a stunted bleeding stump" (I). It is
simply that the actor who began as Charlie Cass has become
"a mechanical, capering mouse." As his talent degenerated,
a coarsening process of character also set in, and his wife
can no longer live with "the half a man that is me" (I), as
Charlie describes himself in a moment of truth. Charlie,
too, has recognized the irony that the more he has become
a star, the more he is increasingly used as a commodity by
his studio. His agent tries to remonstrate with him:

NAT: ... Darling, you expect too much from

yourself. A movie isn't a movie to you--it's a
gospel. But you're mistaken, dear sir and
friend. In all humility--
CHARLIE: Don't get me wrong, Nat. I live out
here like a rajah and I love it! But what about
the work? The place is hell on married life!
I can't make peace with this place--I don't wanna
live under the same blanket with Marcus Hoff
and his feudal friends. The color of their money
is getting pale white, with blood-shot eyes, and
I don't want it! (I)

We may perhaps infer something of the author himself in this
passage, for Odets recognized that despite the sell-out's
qualms, he was often a willing victim. Caught between the
lure of status and power and a lingering idealism, he becomes an anomaly. Charlie Castle admits that "... Charlie
Cass is still around in dribs and drabs--don't you think he'd
like to do a fine play every other year?" (I). But his wife
points out that this sort of temporizing is futile:

Aren't you the one who says he wants to live a
certain way and do a certain kind of work?...
And then pushes a pie in the face of everything he
says? Men like Hoff and Coy have their own in-
tegrity--they're what they are! The beetle and
the fervid Christian can't be equally corrupted!
But the critic who called you the Van Gogh of the
American theatre saw, as I did, that you had a
Christian fervor! (Beginning to cry) And now
you're nothing, common trash--coarsened down to
something I don't even recognize! (II)

Once the sell-out has made his deal with Moloch, however much he may writhe and twist, he cannot break away.
His wants multiply: Ben must support Libby; Joe falls in
love with Lorna Moon and tries to steal her away from Tom
Moody; Charlie Castle's marriage goes on the rocks and he
must bolster his sagging ego with what he calls "those occasional girls." Moreover, in Odets' view greed inevitably
leads to illicit as well as self-indulgent behavior. Thus,
each of the sell-out figures commits a crime and each is
involved with power-brokers who do not shrink from violence
and murder. Ben, as I have already indicated, accepts an
unspecified "job" from Kewpie and dies in a shoot-out with
the cops. Joe Bonaparte, in a more subtle way, becomes a
"killer" in the ring and links his destiny with the gangster,

Eddie Fuseli. Charlie Castle has participated in a hit-and-run accident which his studio has covered up, and then is asked by Smiley Coy to be a silent accomplice to the murder of the only witness.

There are two concepts or motifs in which Odets' sell-out pattern seems to transcend melodrama and the familiar moral that the drive for wealth does not necessarily bring happiness. First, the men who manipulate the sell-out figures are themselves victims, end-products of the system. Odets' villains are not mere stereotypes but are accorded a measure of sympathy and understanding. Thus, Kewpie in Paradise Lost seeks more than Ben's girl and good name; he sees in Ben an idealism he admires but which he cannot pragmatically accept. When Ben spits at his own statue, Kewpie "carefully wipes off the face with a silk handkerchief" (II) and, earlier, after a scuffle over Libby's affections, Kewpie cares more about the loss of Ben's friendship and respect than the girl's. A curious conversation occurs:

> KEWPIE: Did I hurt you, Ben?
> BEN: I didn't feel it.
> KEWPIE (ashamed): You know how I am--in there
> boppin' away before I know it. I don't work
> with my head, Ben.
> BEN: Sure ...
> KEWPIE: Smack me in the mouth, Ben. Hit me ...
> BEN: Don't be a kid!
> LIBBY: What's this, a love duet? (II)

Kewpie, who recognizes that he is "a pro-anti,"[37] admires in Ben everything he lacks; but he also knows that to survive in a racketeering society one must be smart and follow the rackets. Even so, the bronze statue of Ben is his one bright emblem in a sordid world. He redeems Ben's medals, and later, when Ben has been gunned down, Kewpie, guilt-stricken, visits the sorely pressed Gordon family with a gift of conscience-money. When the family turns on Kewpie, Odets gives him an impassioned speech in reply:

> (furiously, in defense of his entire life): You gim-
> me worms, the whole bunch! A pack of tramps
> making believe they own the world because they
> read a book! I don't read, see! But I saw the
> handwriting on the wall. I don't stop to say it
> ain't my cake. I cut a piece without asking! I
> done something to help myself. You don't! Well,

>take a lesson from little Kewpie--if you don't like
the Constitution, make it over!... Don't think I'll
ever forget my friend Ben. I carry him around
like a medal. He wanted to show he was better
than me--that's why he killed himself. He was
better. (IV)

Though the others despise and reject Kewpie, the foolish and
saintly Leo Gordon describes him as "a lonely boy crying in
the wilderness" (IV).

Odets carried the motif of the victimizer-as-victim
even further in Golden Boy. From his first appearance,
Eddie Fuseli, "a renowned gambler and gunman" (II, 1), with
his mirthless laugh, his threats, and his catlike movements,
is evil incarnate. As Lorna Moon puts it: "What exhaust
pipe did he crawl out of?" (II, 1). Yet Fuseli's motives in
his entire relationship with Joe are complicated. Despite
his homosexuality and foreign origin, he explains to Joe, he
has his pride and dignity:

>... I'm Eyetalian too--Eyetalian born, but an Amer-
ican citizen. I like to buy a piece of you. I don't
care for no profit. I could turn it back to you--
you could take my share. But I like a good fighter;
I like a good boy who could win the crown. It's
the in-ter-est of my life. It would be a proud
thing for me when Bonaparte could win the crown
like I think he can (II, 1).

Later we perceive that this speech was not without
guile, for before Joe meets the Chocolate Drop in the climactic fight, Eddie tells him that he has eighteen thousand
bet on him and that he "better be on his toes ... tomorrow,"
to which Joe replies, "Your loyalty makes me shiver" (III,
1). Eddie Fuseli, like Kewpie, is a "pro-anti" type, and
his admiration for Joe is tempered by his tendency to treat
all humans on a cash basis. As he says to Joe: "You wanna
walk in a parade? Everybody's lonely. Get the money and
you're not so lonely" (III, 1). Yet there is pathos in the
spectacle of the "queer" criminal, almost embarrassed by
his affection, hovering over his fighter, buying him expensive
silk shirts and tickets to the Scandals, trying to manage his
personal life like a fussy parent. Eddie, too, is given his
moment of impassioned dignity. It comes when he releases
his wrath against Lorna Moon, whose misguided loyalty to
Tom Moody has caused her to hurt and unsettle Joe on the

night of the crucial fight. He turns on her when the roar of
the crowd informs him that his boy is taking a beating:

> Get outa my sight! You turned down the sweetest
> boy who ever walked in shoes! You turned him
> down, the golden boy, that king among the ju-ven-
> niles! He gave you his hand--you spit in his face!
> You led him on like Gertie's whoore! You sold
> him down the river! (III, 2)

Yet in the final scene Eddie, along with the other ex-
ploiters, reverts to type and is again haggling over Joe as
commodity, the dollar's ultimate triumph.

Because The Big Knife deals with a presumably more
cultured and complex milieu, we might expect a more complex treatment of character and motive. Unfortunately, such
is not the case. Marcus Hoff and his aide-de-camp, Smiley
Coy, are a pair of Machiavellian villains without a redeeming trait. Marcus is a bloated monster of egotism--an etched-
in-acid type. He can be, in turn, unctuous, self-dramatizing
(he cries real tears at the memory of his first wife's per-
fidy), but he is quintessentially money-hungry, guileful--"I
want you to sign these papers with one of the pens that ended
the last war. It was used by a great American, General
MacArthur" (I)--and ruthless. He will do anything to keep
Charlie Castle on the lot and preserve his value as an investment to the stockholders. Only in Act III, 2, is Hoff
granted a shred of dignity. When Charlie accuses him to
his face of ordering the murder of Dixie Evans and taunts
him about his "phony cathedral eloquence," it momentarily
seems that Charlie's ego-baiting has angered Hoff enough to
tear up his contract. But even after he has slapped Hoff's
face, Charlie quickly realizes that Hoff will cool off and continue to "protect his property."

Odets seems carried away in his vitriolic characterization of Hoff; the part is wonderfully actable, but it remains somewhat stereotyped--"What are you without Hoff-
Federated behind you? I built that studio with my brains
and hands--I ripped it out of the world!" (III, 2). Unlike
Kewpie and Eddie Fuseli, Hoff has no psychological identification with his victim, nor is there any suggestion that he,
too, marches on the treadmill of success. Marcus Hoff is
Uncle Morty of Awake and Sing!, magnified, more suave
perhaps, but essentially one-dimensional. Strange that the
man who wrote a dignified eulogy for Harry Cohn in 1958

should have failed to visualize the factors that transplant an Uncle Morty to Hollywood and transform him into a predatory Marcus Hoff. The reason for this failure probably lies in the bitterness which Odets felt toward Hollywood in 1950, a bitterness which pervades the play and weakens its overall effectiveness. [38]

The other major insight Odets brought to the morality fable of the sell-out was that sinning against one's nature was a purgatory from which suicide could be an almost-welcome release. Just before his last "job," Ben Gordon has a Joycean epiphany, a vivid image of a childhood incident which illuminates his psychological condition:

> BEN (looking at his friend a long time before he speaks): We're still under the ice, you and me--we never escaped! Christ, Kewpie! Are we the same kids who used to go up to Whitey Aimer's roof and watch the pigeons fly? You and me and Danny? There's one old pal we know what happened to, where he is. The three of us under the ice with our skates on and not being able to get him out. Then sticking him dead in the box. Dressed in a blue serge suit and stiff white collar ... Christ, Kewpie, tell me---who died there--me or you or him or what?
> KEWPIE: What the hell you talking about!
> BEN: Is Danny wearing wings in paradise? Or is he a cheap cluck like you and me, trying to make a living, trying to be a man and look the world in the face in some other hell? (II)

The point of Ben's vision--so rich in metaphoric content-- is that the loss of innocence and the perversion of character are indeed a form of death. Failure has not destroyed Ben; the surrender of his dreams and aspirations has--"Columbus was wrong--we're being pushed over the edge" (II)--and robbed him of the will to go on living. This is confirmed in Act III when Kewpie visits the family and gives his version of how Ben Gordon died:

> He stood there like a rock--.... He stood there soaking up cops' bullets like a sponge--A guy with fifty medals for running. Ben Gordon wanted to die.

Similarly, Joe Bonaparte becomes a symbol of Death-

in-Life, although he is not initially aware of the consequences
of his ride on the Millionaire Express. By the end of Act II
he has abandoned friends and family and is figuratively trying
to punch his way through life. He tells Tokio, his trainer:

> ... Now I'm alone. They're all against me--Moody,
> the girl ... you're my family now, Tokio--you and
> Eddie! I'll show them all--nobody stands in my
> way! My father's had his hand on me for years.
> No more. No more for her either--she had her
> chance! When a bullet sings through the air it has
> no past--only a future--like me! Nobody, nothing
> stands in my way!

Joe has turned himself into a killer; when he breaks his fist
in the Lombardo fight, permanently flattening the knuckles
on the hand that might have played the violin, he "begins to
laugh loudly, victoriously, exultantly--with a deep thrill of
satisfaction" (Stage Directions, II, 4). Joe does not seem to
realize that he has destroyed his better self, despite Lorna
Moon's indictment:

> ... When did you look in the mirror last? Getting
> to be a killer! You're getting to be like Fuseli!
> You're not the boy I cared about, not you. You
> murdered that boy with the generous face--God
> knows where you hid the body! I don't know you.
> (III, 1)

Full knowledge only comes to Joe as he concentrates
"the fury of a lifetime" in a final punch that floors the
Chocolate Drop permanently. When the fighter's distraught
manager accuses him of murdering his boy, Joe, legally
"innocent," knows that in fact he is morally responsible for
a double murder. The full force of conscience overwhelms
him, beyond any attempt to rationalize his complicity:

> But I did it! That's the thing--I did it! What will
> my father say when he hears I murdered a man?
> Lorna, I see what I did. I murdered myself, too!
> I've been running around in circles. Now I'm
> smashed! That's the truth. Yes, I was a real
> sparrow, and I wanted to be a fake eagle! But
> now I'm hung up by my finger tips--I'm no good--
> my feet are off the earth! (III, 2)

Lorna, who loves him, tries to instill some hope that he can

recover some goodness and return to music, but Joe knows
that his hands are ruined and that he is "Half a man, nothing,
useless... " (III, 2). Their mutual decision to ride off in
Joe's Deusenberg can be seen as a suicide pact, though Odets
does not make this explicit. Nevertheless, though this climax
is superficially similar to Moe and Hennie's break-out attempt
in Awake and Sing!, one can find no Edenic imagery in Joe's
final appeal. Rather, the language connotes destruction.
There can be no mistaking the self-immolation implicit in
Joe's words:

> Ride! That's it, we ride--clear my head. We'll
> drive through the night. When you mow down the
> night with headlights, nobody gets you! You're on
> top of the world then--nobody laughs! That's it--
> speed! We're off the earth--unconnected! We
> don't have to think! That's what speed's for, an
> easy way to live! Lorna darling, we'll burn up
> the night! (III, 2)

When Frank Bonaparte, Joe's brother, receives the news that
Joe and Lorna have both been killed in a crash near Babylon,
Long Island, there can be no surprise for the audience--only
a sense of inevitability.

Finally, in The Big Knife, though Charlie Castle early
admits to his wife that his integrity is impaired by his life
in Hollywood, he continues to struggle and rationalize during
the first two acts. Only when he learns of the threat to
Dixie Evans' life and measures the depth of the moral sewer
into which he has sunk does Charlie recognize that, in Odets'
sense, he is a living dead man. The recognition is voiced
in an emotionally charged exchange between Charlie and Hank
Teagle, his author-friend, who wants to marry Marion but
leaves for New York when he learns that the couple has
reconciled. Hank plans to write a novel "about moral values
and success, " whose hero is a popular movie star like Charlie. Though he respects Marion's wishes, he warns his
friend that he has not given up and taunts Charlie about his
indecisiveness:

> ... You've sold out! You'll be here for another
> fourteen years! Stop torturing yourself, Charlie--
> don't resist! Your wild, native idealism is a fatal
> flaw in the context of your life out here. Half-
> idealism is the peritonitis of the soul--America is
> full of it! Give up and really march to Hoff's
> bugle call! Forget what you used to be! (III, 1)

Charlie bitterly counterattacks Teagle at these accusations,
but his bluster quickly collapses. Because he loves and
respects Hank, he admits to the honesty of the portrait:

> ... You're right, Hank.   Your hero's half a man,
> neither here nor there, dead from the gizzard up.
> Stick him with a pin and see, psst! No feelings!
> When I came home from Germany ... I saw most
> of the war dead were here, not in Africa and Italy.
> And Roosevelt was dead ... and the war was only
> last week's snowball fight ... and we plunged our-
> selves, all of us, into the noble work of making
> the buck reproduce itself! (III, 1)

From this scene of psychological recognition, Charlie
belatedly attempts to save Dixie Evans and win some freedom from Hoff. "If you wrestle, Charlie, you may win a
blessing..." (III, 1), Hank had said.   But it is too late for
Charlie to extricate himself from this filth, and he fears
dragging others down with him.   That is why he refuses Nat
Danziger's offer of help and personal intervention with Dixie:

> You're sweet, darling, but it's too late, from my
> point of view.   I can't go on, covering one crime
> with another.   That's Macbeth....   But Macbeth
> is an allegory, too: one by one, he kills his better
> selves (III, 2).

Whatever was once the source of Charlie's strength and purpose, it has long been lost, and, in the end, he is too weak
to admit the crime his studio has been covering up.   But,
though he is weak, he possesses enough self-knowledge to
see that he cannot compromise indefinitely.   He tells Marion:

> ... My life is sworn away and now they wanna
> murder for me and I see what I am!...   You see,
> you have Castle.   He murdered Cass....   I was
> there....   I saw him do it!   Look at me!   Can
> you face it?   Look at this dripping fat of the land?
> Could you ever know that all my life I yearned for
> a world and people to call out the best in me?
> How can life be so empty?   But it can't be!   It
> can't!   It's proven--statistics and graphs prove
> it--we are the world's happiest, earth's best ...
> (Stopping) I'll go up and bathe and change my
> clothes....   (III, 2)

However one interprets Charlie's bathtub suicide--Hank calls

it "a final act of faith"--there is no question that, like Kewpie and Joe Bonaparte, spiritually he was dead before his
heart stopped beating.   Though suicide--whether by police-
man's bullets, auto wreck or slashing one's wrists--may
seem cowardly to certain sensibilities, Odets implies that it
brings a measure of peace and release from the intolerable
pain of the sell-out.   Hank Teagle says of Charlie: "He ...
killed himself ... because that was the only way he could
live" (III, 2).   For the sell-out, suicide is partially an act
of atonement but, more importantly, a form of transcendence.

     I have traced at some length the pattern of the sell-
out figure as Odets envisioned it in order to demonstrate the
consistency of his treatment of this theme, and the touch of
originality he added to what was, after all, a well-worn concept of Left-wing theater.   Two questions remain: How profound was Odets' understanding of the sell-out?   Was he able
to embody his theme in artistic plays that fully conveyed his
moral fable concretely and dramatically to an audience?

     The answers are related because over the years Odets
modified his concept only slightly, but the modification was
aesthetically damaging to The Big Knife.   One factor that
did not change was Odets' stubborn belief that materialism
was rotten and that it could and did corrupt the finest instincts of American youth.   In each of the plays the blame
for the hero's corruption is placed squarely on a competitive
society where "in a jungle you have to look out for the wild
life" (Paradise Lost, I).   Kewpie may blame himself for
Ben's death and displace some of his guilt on Ben's family and
their fool's paradise.   Frank, Joe's brother, may accuse
Fuseli and Moody of being killers.   Nat Danziger may rail
against Hoff-Federated.   Ultimately, however, the real killer
is Industrial Society itself, which murders the dreams of
its young people with its soul-destroying materialism.

     Nevertheless, Odets did afford a measure of choice to
the sell-out and a suggestion that psychological as well as
social factors contributed to his fate.   Where the psychological and social do indeed combine, there his plays assume tension and credibility.

     In Paradise Lost, Ben Gordon has almost no freedom
of choice.   An arbitrary event, a heart condition, forces
him out of athletics and subsequently the Depression over-
powers him.   Ben's marriage to the silly Libby Michaels
seems psychologically unmotivated; one might question what

both he and Kewpie see in this selfish bitch who is so lacking in the generous impulses of her father.   Consequently,
Ben, while an interesting and pathetic figure, is not fully
fleshed out.   He, like so many other characters in this rich
but uneven play, is a walking symbol.   Odets, in the doctrinaire mood of 1935, bent his talent to the Marxist thesis
that the middle class was dying, rather than to the development of each character's motivation.   Still, the sub-theme
of Ben's sell-out is one of the more interesting dramatic
motifs in this depressing, poetic, haunting, and overwrought
play.

Golden Boy is something different.   It was and has
remained Odets' most popular play, if one can judge from
its numerous revivals and the spin-offs (The Set-Up, Body
and Soul, etc.)   turned out in Hollywood.   In it, Joe Bonaparte is given some degree of both choice and depth.   Not
only is his complex about his eyes important in his motivation, but Odets had the happy inspiration of juxtaposing in
one person the twin drives toward artistic beauty and aggressive brutality that are the components of the sell-out's
dichotomy.   (Those literal-minded critics who complain that
realistically the combination of musical and pugilistic skills
in one individual is unlikely--that Joe Bonaparte is a side-
show oddity--would demand a medical report on Janus; they
represent the ultimate in critical Gradgrindism.)[39]   By juxtaposing the values of Joe's music-loving father, his homely
and simple philosophy against the hard, competitive world
of the boxing ring, Odets externalizes the psychomachia inside Joe Bonaparte's head and keeps the dramatic action
taut from start to finish.

But even more important to the play's success is the
fact that materialistic corrosion affects subordinate as well
as central characters.   Money and "the sweet smell" permeate the atmosphere.   Siggie, Joe's brother-in-law, nags
Mr. Bonaparte to buy him a new cab and, later, hopes to
get the money from Joe.   Tom Moody is struggling to find
a good "boy" so he can pay his divorced wife's alimony and
eventually make a settlement with her and marry Lorna
Moon.   Lorna, herself, was nine weeks behind in rent when
Moody rescued her from a tacky hotel on 39th Street.   Roxy
Gottlieb, the perennial promoter, aspires to the luxury of
"an eight-cylinder lunch" (I, 3).   Even so minor a figure
as Pepper Young, the punch-drunk fighter who precedes Joe
on the card, proudly exclaims: "I don't fight for under one
thousand bucks" (II, 4).   Money and its pulsations dominate

the play, and the destructiveness of selling out is not treated
didactically but mythically. Odets, as did Henry Adams in
"The Dynamo and the Virgin," found appropriate metaphors
that illuminate the ethos of American materialism--both its
subtle attractions and terrible dangers.

In spite of its well-made story-line and cinematic
structure, Golden Boy is a major American play because it
contains poetic truth. Odets knew little about the fight business, but his metaphors are convincing. Ironically, when
he wrote The Big Knife, he knew too much about Hollywood
and was less convincing. The flaws in the later play are
apparent. If Charlie Castle had any freedom of choice when
he left Broadway for motion pictures, we are not told about
it. His psychological thrust toward power and success is
implied but never fully explored. Critics have pointed out
that he feels too little guilt about his role in the hit-and-run
cover-up. Why, they ask, if he hated his decadent life, did
he not leave it instead of whining about it?[40]

Some of these criticisms are justified, yet the play
is not without dramatic interest. Odets erred by shrouding
Charlie's early years in mystery, by expecting his audience
to accept Charlie's youthful idealism as a donnée. When we
meet him in Act I, he is already a sell-out and a weak man
masquerading as a demi-god. Despite these flaws, Odets
was aiming at a variation of the sell-out figure, presenting
him as a victim of doubt and hesitation. The Big Knife is
Odets' Hamlet, as certain references make plain. Gone is
the atmosphere of ferocious competition of Golden Boy; instead, there is depicted a world of flattery and deceit in
which Charlie Castle is slowly suffocating. In the rottenness
of post-war America--where McCarthyism, race prejudice,
affluence and militarism rub shoulders--there is no longer
a clear-cut issue for the sell-out figure. Charlie asks Hank,
whom he calls Horatio, "... do you say in your book it
isn't even easy to go to hell today? That there's nothing
left to sin against?" (III, 1). The sick characters who parade
through Charlie Castle's playroom are puzzling to the former Depression rebel. In a world where everything is for
sale, where, as Hank Teagle puts it, the eagle as the American symbol has given way to "the cocker spaniel, paws up,
saying, 'Like me, like me, I'm a good dog, like me!'" (III,
1), it seems pointless to fight for outworn principles.

Accordingly, Odets tried to translate the sell-out
fable into a tragedy of moral weakness with Shakespearean

overtones; i. e. , Smiley Coy tells Charlie, ". . . you marry
the scheme and the scheme's children" (III, 1), and there
are references to Horatio and Macbeth.   But Charlie Castle,
though he has bursts of verbal eloquence (end of Act II) and
inveighs against the rottenness of sunny California, is not
Hamlet, just as Marcus Hoff is not Claudius.   He lacks not
only Hamlet's philosophical mind, humor, and bravery, but
also the psychological complexity that make the Dane so fascinating a figure.   Only in Act III, when Charlie finally decides to kill the King-murderer--himself--does he assume
dignity and stature.   After his farewell conversation with
Hank Teagle, both men embrace; and Hank foreshadows Charlie's final act of courage: "You still know that the failure
is the best of American life" (III, 1).   When Charlie is dead,
Hank, in a moving tribute to his friend, refuses to allow
the studio to cover up the suicide; he tells the truth that
Charlie could not bring himself to tell.

   If Odets had really come to grips with the central
character, he might have written his most profound study of
the sell-out in The Big Knife.   As the play stands, it is difficult to know whether Charlie's weakness is to be pitied or
abhorred. [41]   Obviously, Odets intended the former, but to
accomplish this he needed to explore Charlie's inner life,
his dreams, ambitions, drives.   He may have intended this,
for the play's original title was Winter Journey, suggestive
of a psychological voyage that might more fully explain the
route his hero takes.   But he changed the title to The Big
Knife, probably a reference to the killing scalpel of success
which destroys Charlie Castle. [42]   The onus in the play is
directed at the Hollywood social structure as represented by
the powerbrokers, Hoff and Coy, and when, at the play's
conclusion, Charlie slashes his veins in the bathtub, metaphorically the Big Knife has finished its work.   Odets stubbornly (or carelessly) refused to permit psychological factors
to outweigh the social criticism inherent in his theme and,
indeed, he may have believed that changing the world was
more important than analyzing the psyche.   Hence The Big
Knife as a title indicates his abiding social concerns.

   If this is so, we may legitimately ask why Odets does
not suggest some solution to the sell-out's dilemma, to present an alternative to the pattern he traced so consistently
and with such anger.   The answer is that he did.   In each
of the plays under discussion there is a minor character who
hints at the role the protagonist should have taken: in
Paradise Lost, it is Mr. Pike, the furnace man, who em-

bodies the alternative of class revolution; in Golden Boy, it
is Frank, Joe's brother, the union organizer, who travels
around the country "at harmony with millions of others!"
(III, 3), fighting for what he believes in; in The Big Knife,
it is Dr. Frary, Charlie's next-door neighbor who, retired
after a lifetime of service to others, peacefully cultivates
his garden in the jungle world of Beverly Hills. Not every-
one has to sell out, and strong men can remain true to their
natures. These were the exceptional men Odets respected;
The Big Knife is dedicated "to M. V. Leof, M. D. in his
seventy-eighth year with love. " Yet the overall thrust of
Odets' plays suggests that, even more than in the family trap,
for most men there is no breaking out of the societal trap except through death.

One may argue that Odets completely ignores the spiritual dimension in these plays, that religion cannot be omitted
from the parable of the self and society. (Odets' religious
views are ambiguous; they emerge only in The Flowering
Peach.) Also, we may inquire why he did not recognize--as
did a later generation--that turning inward, that exploring of
the Imperial Self, was a form of defense against the materialistic, dehumanizing world. There are no existential rebels
in his plays, no Yossarians, no Herzogs. Yet one cannot
say that this later generation has discovered better solutions
than did Odets to the problems that produce the sell-out.
Yossarian flees, but things may not be any better for him in
Sweden; and Herzog may arrive at a temporary tranquility,
but he still inhabits the same world where the Gersbachs
manipulate and corrupt others, seemingly at will.

Perhaps it is naive to expect even socially dedicated
playwrights to present more than hints of solutions to social
problems. Odets' main concern was dramatizing the problem
itself. In the final analysis, his projection of the sell-out
was an honest exploration of the theme in compassionate
terms. He, himself, had lived inside the citadels of power,
and his original contribution was to show that half-idealism
was not strong enough to resist the seductive lure of Success.
He knew, too, that the attractions of status and material
wealth were too much for most Americans to withstand.
From his personal experience he understood better than most
the emotional cost and tragic waste of selling out.

3. The Crisis of Love

> All the jazz bands and crooners in
> America singin' one sad song--"Give
> Me Love, Baby. " Well, I never seen
> that solve no problems--
>   --Gus, Paradise Lost

Long before he became a Marxist, Odets was a lover--
a poet of romantic love, with a deep understanding of youth's
yearnings and fears, marital love's emotional entanglements
and fulfillments, and the saving quality of a transcendent
emotion. In fact, it may be argued that the social criticism
in Odets' dramas was sometimes secondary or co-equal in
significance to his exploration of love's effect on human relationships. To understand this, one has only to look at
Awake and Sing!, where Jacob's love for Ralph, Ralph's for
Blanche, Moe's for Hennie, as well as other emotional attach-
ments dominate the action. Passions spin the plot for Odets,
and few American dramatists have excelled him in his exploration of the turbulence of the human heart.

It is true that Odets' early plays and some later ones
deal with the effect of economics and chaotic social conditions on the hopes and aspirations of young lovers. Scarred
as he was by the Great Depression, it was inevitable that
Odets should be preoccupied with the practical difficulties
and pitfalls of marriage in a time of deprivation and despair.
Lack of work and opportunity made it seem positively dangerous to marry in 1935. [43] In the Joe-Edna sequence in Waiting for Lefty, Edna excoriates her underpaid husband, who
drives a hack and is too passive to strike for higher wages;
she calls him a "four-star bust!" and tells him their marriage is "stalled like a flivver in the snow, " even threatens
to leave him. In reality, she is pleading for her two blonde
children who need food and clothes and their shoes soled
before they go to school. Her anger is really inverted love
for Joe and her family; as she admits in a moment of candor,
"I'm turning into a sour old nag. " The other reflection of
the effect of economics on love in Lefty is in "The Young
Hack and His Girl" sequence; interestingly, these two vignettes between lovers are the best in the play. [44] Florrie
and Sid engage in a poignant leave-taking when the opposition of Florrie's brother, Irv, makes it apparent that "This
ain't no time to get married. " The two lovers review their
stringent finances and family obligations, decide "If we can't

climb higher than this together--we better stay apart," and close the chapter in their lives. The lyricism of their love declarations starkly counterpoints brother Irv's statement: "Nowadays is no time to be soft. You gotta be hard as a rock or go under."

In Till the Day I Die, Tilly and Ernst also decide to follow the hard course and, in the face of growing Nazi hostility, postpone marriage and the children they desire. Both look to some glowing revolutionary future of international brotherhood "when the day comes that we don't have to live like rats in sewers--" (1). Unfortunately, despite their dedication to self-control, a baby is born to Tilly and Ernst which complicates and intensifies the play's emotional dénouement.

Instances of what I shall call the "love-economic" motif occur prominently in Paradise Lost. Not only does Odets stress the foolhardiness of Ben's marriage to Libby Michaels when he has no job or prospects, but a sub-strand of the plot deals with the metamorphosis of Pearl, the Gordons' only daughter, from a talented and hopeful girl into a spinsterish pianist who plays requiems for romance in an upstairs bedroom. Pearl has been engaged to Felix, a violinist, for two years, but he visits her in the opening act, dispirited by his inability to find a permanent berth with an orchestra, and unwilling to struggle along on odd jobs and Pearl's piano lesson fees. He tells her:

> Listen--I'm a worm in the ground and you're a worm in the ground. Pearlie, I used to think I was a wonderful guy--a musician with a big head of hair. Have a good time--love everybody. Play in the orchestra--play quartets--culture, but without the bucks--who'll get culture?... (bitterly): The best things in life are free. What lies we believe! (I)

Though he loves her more than his fiddle, he has determined to leave New York and tells his sweetheart to find a better man, "the kind who supports the orchestra." Embittered, Pearl's sense of loss is expressed through her intermittent offstage playing as she joins her family in its slow process of fossilization and disintegration.

Echoes of the "love-economic" motif pervade Odets' work: minor characters like Anna and Siggie in Golden Boy

cannot raise a family because they are in a financial bind;
Ben and Belle Stark's marriage goes sour in Rocket to the
Moon partially because, as he puts it, "We're always wor-
ried ... we're two machines counting up the petty cash" (III);
Fay's and Steve's romance in Night Music is almost frozen
by what Steve calls "an economic blizzard"; similarly, Joe
W. Doyle and Peggy Coffey, the young lovers in Clash by
Night, are deterred from marrying because the former can
only find work as a part-time truck driver.

All this is not surprising since Odets, even in 1940,
when the economy rallied because of the war boom, was not
duped by superficial changes in conditions. There were still
poverty and inequality. And the price to be paid for artificial recovery was too high; as Steve Takis says in Night
Music: "Sure, boom-boom an' you're dead" (II, 4). What
is surprising is that the "love-economic" motif still operates
in The Big Knife and Country Girl, which were produced
during the prosperous early Fifties. The motif becomes al-
tered and ironically reversed, as we shall see, but it is
present. Small wonder that a playwright conditioned by such
events as Odets had witnessed would have a subliminal fear
of untimely marriage. Amusingly, Japheth, facing an apocalyptic disaster in The Flowering Peach, tells Noah: "How
can I take a wife in times like these?" (3).

But Odets was too much of an artist to view human
relationships simplistically, and his plays have value quite
aside from their socio-economic message. The complexity
of their characterizations would make them penetrating domestic dramas even without their criticism of capitalistic
society. Robert J. Griffin, in an excellent article, calls
the plays "Love Songs," and remarks: "When Odets set
himself the task of staging the realities of middle class life ...
he managed to show selected segments of that life with a wise
wholeness of vision. I mean, though he may have a humane
social gospel to announce, his 'message' does not mislead
him into oversimplifying the experience he is dealing with:
the issues he may treat simplistically but not the facts."[45]
Although this comment is made apropos of Awake and Sing!,
it can be justly applied to almost all of Odets' plays--and
especially to the triangle dramas: Rocket to the Moon, Clash
by Night, and The Country Girl. In these plays, Odets explores marital discord and the attraction of philandering to
those caught in what I may refer to (if the reader is not
tired of this metaphor) as "The Marriage Trap." Ben and
Belle Stark, estranged by Ben's growing attraction to Cleo
Singer, the naive, sensual assistant in his dental office;

Mae and Jerry Wilenski, living the lumpenproletariat life on
Staten Island where Earl Pfeiffer, a swaggering friend of
her husband from "the pro-jec," moves in on them; Frank
and Georgie Elgin, struggling to hang on to Frank's hand-to-
mouth alcoholic theatrical career--all are complicated and
credible people, not social types. Odets' lovers are, indeed,
in a state of crisis, but the crises are only partly economic
and derive from the mysteries and conflicts of human character.

      Not all of the characterizations are equally rich and
penetrating, nor are Rocket to the Moon and Clash by Night
completely successful plays; the deficiencies in them may
derive precisely from Odets' compulsion to preach a social
gospel, when his major interest lay in exploring the intri-
cacies of clashing personalities. But there are ample compensations in both plays. What remains with the audience is
the indecisiveness of Ben, the agony of Belle, the anguish of
Jerry Wilenski in the sweltering summers of their mutual
discontent. And in The Country Girl, the most soundly
crafted of Odets' plays, we remember the loyalty of Georgie,
struggling with her loathing for what the intolerable burden
of coping with an alcoholic husband has done to her. These
are the moments that count. The compassionate playwright
of lovers in crisis permits one to ignore the insistent propagandist who, on occasions, dashes in from the wings.

      Even so, one must recognize that Odets saw individual
relationships as a microcosm of the condition of society and
mankind. Odets not only took the title of Clash by Night
from Matthew Arnold's "Dover Beach," but, in the published
version, he placed in the frontispiece the section of the poem
which begins: "Ah, love, let us be true/ To one another!"
Arnold, representing an earlier generation which was facing
the emptiness of a mechanistic, Godless universe--which
had, in fact, given its modern sense to a favorite twentieth
century word: alienation--was a meaningful figure to Odets.
Arnold's only positive recommendation in a chaotic, destructive world was: "Ah, love, let us be true." There were
times when Odets' views on love matched Arnold's extreme
pessimism; in Awake and Sing! Jake tells Ralph: "... in a
society like this today people don't love. Hate!" (II, 2).
But Odets was too much the incorrigible romantic to accept
so bleak a prospect. He could not retreat to the nihilism
of Nathanael West, nor even assume the detachment of Dos
Passos. He was too committed to life, and while he did
not see love as a panacea, he regarded it as the only viable

response to his generation's loneliness and angst. Tokio's advice to Joe Bonaparte in Golden Boy is "Find something to love, or someone":

> Joe, you're loaded with love. Find something to give it to. Your heart ain't in fighting ... your hate is. But a man with hate and nothing else ... he's half a man ... is no man. (III, 1)

A similar human need thrusts Cleo Singer and Ben Stark together in Rocket to the Moon; both have witnessed the agonized outbursts of Ben's colleague, Phil Cooper, the Job of the Depression, and are shaken by his human misery. Cleo cries out:

> CLEO: ... Don't want to be lonely, never left alone! Why should I cry? I have a throat to sing with, a heart to love with! Why don't you love me, Dr. Stark? I was ten, then fifteen-- I'm almost twenty now. Everything is in a hurry and you ought to love me.
> STARK: Cleo, please....
> CLEO: You're good, you're kind, you're like a father. Do you love your wife? I'm intuitive-- I know you don't!
> STARK (making a last effort to stop her): Cleo!
> CLEO: We're both alone, so alone. You might be like Cooper in a year or two. Maybe I lie. You know why. Because I'm alone--nobody loves me. But I won't have it that way. I'll change life. (II, 1)

Odets' lovers are usually in a state of turmoil, and love is always the prerequisite to change. Without it, people are homeless drifters even though they may be temporarily anchored in one place. A good example is the divorced Earl Pfeiffer who, despite his bimbos, binges, and outward bravado, is really reaching out to Mae to assert his desperate needs:

> MAE (Intently): Why can't you sleep?
> EARL (Passionately): 'Cause I'm always outside looking in! Because I wanna get in somewhere! Someone has to need me, love me ... I'm not a barge goin' down the river! How do people go on this way? Tell me that--how do they do it? The blues for home, for home sweet home,

> but where is home? (<u>Almost frantically</u>) Help
> me, Mae, help me!
> MAE: How can I help you...?
> EARL: Love me, need me! Common sense don't
> do it! Common sense is dirt!... Mae, I'm
> dying of lonesomeness!... (<u>Clash by Night</u>, I,
> 3)

Thus, love to Odets is either a necessary illusion or
a saving grace. Though this view implies ambivalence, it
serves to indicate Odets' knowledge of the dangers and pretenses that threaten sincerity and authenticity in love. Joe
Doyle tells Peggy Coffey in <u>Clash by Night</u>: "Marriage is
not a convent. It's not a harbor--it's the open world, Peg.
It's being out at sea in a boat" (I, 4). Risk-taking is an
unavoidable element that lovers must share; not only economics but inimical hidden factors in the psyches of the lovers
can wreck them. But the risk is worth taking when the alternatives are monotony and sterility.

<u>Rocket to the Moon</u> dramatizes these various attitudes
toward love more searchingly than any other Odets drama. [46]
Around the fringes of the central triangle, two peripheral
characters voice contrasting views of love. There is rich
old Mr. Prince, Belle's father, who describes himself as
"the American King Lear." A magnificent dandy of a man
who bubbles aphorisms, he befriends his son-in-law but is
anathema to his daughter because of his alleged cruelty
toward his now dead wife. Fiercely, Mr. Prince defends
himself to Ben, claiming that his timid wife stifled his ambitions to be a great actor:

> ... I shouldn't be ambitious. Go work for some-
> body else for twenty dollars a week--a man with
> my brains! Play safe! A housewife's conception
> of life! In the bargain, she had more respect-
> ability under the blankets than you have on Fifth
> Avenue! A man of my strength, my fire! Drip,
> Drip, the matrimonial waters go, and a man wears
> away.... (I)

And yet this cynical and polished old man-of-the-
world uses all the guile and eloquence at his command to
convince Cleo Singer to forget her affair with Ben, and pro-
poses a marriage of convenience with more than a hint that
his sexual ardor has not waned. When Dr. Stark (who reads
Shakespeare) calls him "a damned smiling villain," he is
met with no servile apologies:

PRINCE: ... Remember, Dr. Benny, I want what
I want! There are seven fundamental words in
life, and one of these is love, and I didn't have
it! And another one is love, and I don't have
it! And the third of these is love, and I shall
have it! (III)

There is something dauntless and courageous in Prince's
willingness to buy and bully his way out of his "long winter
night," and though he loses twice, he represents the courage
to risk all for love, which is one side of the Odetsian dialectic in this play.

The other side is represented by Frenchy, a bachelor
chiropodist from Utica, New York, who shares Ben's office,
"a self-educated, amateur student of human nature in all its
aspects" (I). Frenchy, aware of Cleo's potent sexuality and
Stark's growing attraction to her, opposes the affair and
ridicules her because he fears she is just an ephemeral ano-
dyne for his friend's basic unhappiness. Frenchy believes
that work and creative accomplishment are primary male
needs, and he suspects that Cleo will hurt rather than help
Ben. When Ben asks him why he has never married or
fallen in love, he delivers a most eloquent and almost convincing rationale:

FRENCHY: Love? Depends on what you mean by
love. Love, for most people, is a curious sen-
sation below the equator. Love--as they call
it--is easy--even the rabbits do it! The girl
I want ... she'd have to be made in heaven.
That's why I wait--
STARK: You're that good, you think?
FRENCHY: That bad, Doc! She'll have to be the
good one. This is why: Love is a beginning,
a jumping-off place. It's like what heat is at
the forge--makes the metal easy to handle and
shape. But love and the grace to use it!--To
develop, expand it, variate it!--Oh, dearie me,
that's the problem, as the poet said!
STARK: Yes, I see your point....
FRENCHY: Who can do that today? Who's got
time and place for "love and the grace to use
it"? Is it something apart, love? A good
book you go to in a spare hour? An entertain-
ment? Christ, no! It's a synthesis of good
and bad, economics, work, play, all contacts ...

it's not a Sunday suit for special occasions.
That's why Broadway songs are phony, Doc!--
Love is no solution of life!   Au contraire, as
the Frenchman says--the opposite.   You have
to bring a whole balanced normal life to love if
you want it to go!   (III)

Once again we are listening to an exponent of the
"love-economic" motif, except that Frenchy has the imagination to envision love's potential, and even can concede that
an exceptional creature might exist who could share his vision
of "the free exercise of love. "   But only for a moment.   Detached and practical, he is by nature an observer and a fence-
sitter; we intuit that he is one of Odets' messengers from the
wings, and hence slightly contemptible, for all his pragmatic
wisdom.

The most important figure in the play is Cleo Singer,
around whom the men cluster and the dialectic centers.
Though there have been critics who wonder what the fuss is
all about, [47] I find her one of Odets' most charming characters, and her characterization the key to an understanding of
Odets' commitment to love.   Cleo is naive and sensual--"I
never adjust my shoulder straps or girdle in public, as
some women do.   God knows, it's so warm I'm practically
naked underneath" (II, 1).   She is uneducated, given to
bromides, and yet capable of a genuine lyricism on occa-
sion--"Summer is beautiful, I think,   All the people have
such an unbuttoned mood, don't they?" (II, 1).   Cleo is also
a congenital liar, a prefiguration of those O'Neill characters
who subsist on pipe dreams in Harry Hope's saloon.   At
various times, she tells the men in her life that she doesn't
need her job, that she has been a dancer with several shows,
that her perfume costs forty dollars an ounce, that she has
often visited California, that her parents wanted to send her
to a fashionable girl's college, that her mother was an opera
singer, that her brother is at West Point.   When Ben Stark
gently but insistently exposes her lies, she tearfully tells
him: "You never show anyone they're wrong by showing
them you're right" (II, 1).   She admits that she lies, but
says she does it to escape an insufferable home life--her
father dead, and eight assorted relatives in one apartment.
Unlike O'Neill's characters, Cleo's fantasies are willed and
a reflection of her romantic aspirations--alternatives to her
sisters, who are "washed out, bleached ... everybody forgets how to dream.... " (II, 1).   Cleo is a fighter who up-
braids Dr. Stark for his loss of enterprise and spirit; she
blames Belle Stark for stifling his courage.

STARK: Courage for what?

CLEO: To go out to things, to new experiences.... Don't you think life is to live all you can and experience everything? Isn't that the only way you can develop to be a real human being? Shouldn't a wife help a man do that? (II, 1)

These insistent questions bring us back to risk-taking and individual fulfillment as essential elements in marriage and among lovers. Odets believed this, and he makes Cleo Singer his instrument to demonstrate the point dramatically. At the play's climax, Mr. Prince forces Ben Stark's hand, exposes his dependence on Belle--"He won't leave her. That needs courage, strength, and he's not strong" (III)--and Cleo is convinced by Ben's lame excuses that he will never divorce his wife. She rejects Mr. Prince and Willy Wax, a Hollywood smoothie-director who has been besieging her, and says that she will continue to search for genuine love and a sense of her own identity.

PRINCE: ... You'll never get what you're looking for! You want a life like Heifetz's music--up from the roots, perfect, clean, every note in place. But that, my girl, is music!

CLEO: I'm looking for love....

PRINCE: From a book of stories!

CLEO: Don't say that. I know what's real. (Of STARK): Is his love real?

PRINCE: But mine!...

CLEO: It's real for you. If I can't find love here, I'll find it there.

PRINCE (insistently): Where?

CLEO: Somewhere.... How can I tell you what I mean?...

PRINCE: You'll go down the road alone--like Charlie Chaplin?

CLEO (to both men): Yes, if there's roads, I'll take them. I'll go up all those roads till I find what I want. I want a love that uses me, that needs me. Don't you think there's a world of joyful men and women? Must all men live afraid to laugh and sing? Can't we sing at work and love our work? It's getting late to play at life; I want to live it. Something has to feel real for me, more than both of you. You see? I don't ask for much....

PRINCE: She's an artist.

The cynical Mr. Prince is quite correct; Cleo is projecting
an artist's vision--the singing note of a joyous world trans-
formed--characteristic of Odets in his moments of lyrical
affirmation. We can see how the political overtones of the
closing speeches of Awake and Sing! and Paradise Lost have
given way to a poet's yearning for a lover's Utopia. It may
seem naive (especially on the lips of the childlike Cleo), but
Odets was expressing the unvoiced and inchoate longings of
millions who listened to the jazz bands and crooners singing,
"Give Me Love, Baby. "

But we should not attribute the character's naiveté to
the author. Odets was perfectly aware of how difficult would
be the dream's attainment. In Golden Boy, Lorna has a
pathetic eleventh-hour hope that somehow she and Joe can
salvage their broken lives:

> ... Two together! We have each other! Somewhere
> there must be happy boys and girls who can teach
> us the way of life! We'll find some city where
> poverty's no shame--where music is no crime!--
> where there's no war in the streets--where a man
> is glad to be himself, to live and make his woman
> herself!

Unfortunately, Lorna's Utopia does not exist; instead, their
quest ends in disaster in the portentous locale of Babylon,
Long Island.

In Clash by Night, Mae Wilenski hears a juke box
playing an oldie, "Avalon, " but she has mixed feelings about
its Edenic spell. She tells Earl, who is listening appreci-
atively:

> ... It gives me the jim-jams ... always gets me.
> I used to sell sheet music in the dime store. A
> place called Avalon ... no worries there, sort of
> flowers in the winter. I don't know how all that
> stuff gets in a song, but it does (I, 2).

Mae's Utopia is buried in her girlhood dreams, but her
present is a desperate bid to escape "the marriage trap, "
which ends with the death of her loved one and the crackup
of her cuckolded husband. So Odets is anything but naive
about the millenium.

Even Night Music, the most light-hearted and facile

play Odets ever wrote, in which the two lovers join hands
at the end and agree to take a chance against the economic
odds, is overshadowed by scenes of melancholy.   The theme
of homelessness[48] is so emphasized throughout that the courage and determination of "Suitcase Steve" and Fay to make a
home at the play's end seems to be a quixotic gesture.   It
is noteworthy that these lovers would have no chance at all
without the presence of a deus ex machina.   He is Detective
Abraham Lincoln Rosenberger, who, though dying of cancer,
brings them together, watches over them, wards off their
enemies--especially Fay's relatives--provides them with
physical and emotional sustenance, and finally exhorts them
to form a "Party-to-Marry-My-Girl."   But without Rosenberger's intervention--without the almost religious awe with
which police and criminals and assorted denizens of Manhattan regard this aging law officer--there would be no miracle.   He is a comic Christ figure, and he represents Odets'
conviction that redemption through love is a quasi-religious
concept which a secular age must not ignore.   Odets explores this redemption motif more fully in several plays,
most notably in The Country Girl and The Flowering Peach;
it is an important concept to which I shall return.

Before doing so, I must emphasize how poignantly
Odets dramatized love relationships gone awry, and how the
motif of love's limitations adds realistic depth to what others
have wrongly designated a shallow optimism. [49]   Despite the
yearning lyricism in his plays, Odets knew he was dealing
with a world in which love destroyed as often as it saved,
and he faced squarely the failure of love for psychological--
not social--reasons.   In his view, the primary reason for
love's failure is that it cannot survive where it becomes
mixed with pity.

In Awake and Sing!, Hennie and Sam Feinschreiber's
relationship is wrong from the beginning, since she regards
him as a "poor foreigner," and resents being bullied into a
hypocritical marriage.   But Sam--whose last name means
"fine writer" in Yiddish--is a lonely man who wants to find
a home, and "he approaches his wife as if he were always
offering her a delicate flower" (Preface Notes).   He knows
that he is a comic figure to the second generation and the
more Americanized Bergers, and his poet's soul intuits Hennie's hateful looks at night.   "I make a nice living from the
store.   But it's no use--she looks for a star in the sky"
(II, 2), he complains.   Beguiled only temporarily by his in-
laws, he feels sympathy for Hennie's growing restlessness--

"I know ... to my worst enemy I don't wish such a life--"
(III)--just as she feels pity for his loneliness. At the very
moment when she senses the end of their relationship, she
tells him she loves him and "kisses him with real feeling"
(III).   Sam's humiliation when Hennie leaves him for Moe
Axelrod is predictable; no synthesis of affection and pity could
have resolved the problems in their ersatz union.

In Golden Boy, Lorna Moon, in becoming the mistress
of Tom Moody, the fight manager, has confused love with
physical passion and gratitude. Impatiently waiting for Moody's
divorce so they can marry, she explains to Joe Bonaparte,
his rival, the basis of her tie to Moody:

> ... He loved me in a world of enemies, of stags
> and bulls! ... and I loved him for that.   He
> picked me up in Friskin's hotel on 39th Street.   I
> was nine weeks behind in rent.   I hadn't hit the
> gutter yet, but I was near.   He washed my face
> and combed my hair.   He stiffened the space be-
> tween my shoulder blades.   Misery reached out to
> misery--(II, 2)

Still, Joe's youthful ardor and intensity are too much for
Lorna to withstand; their attraction had been growing from
their first meeting.   After yielding to Joe, she determines
to tell Moody the truth about her love for him.   But Moody
surprises her with the jubilant news that his divorce is
coming through.   When she guiltily hints that there is another
man, Moody turns pale and reveals the depth of his need for
her.   Heartsick, motivated by loyalty and pity, Lorna adroitly
passes her confession off as a joke and determines to sustain Moody, as he is the weaker of the two lovers.   But love
based on pity, despite Lorna's rationalizations, cannot last,
and in the climax Lorna is back in Joe's corner, aware of
their bond, telling him, "It isn't too late to tell the world
good evening again" (III, 2).   Unfortunately for both of them,
their recognition of true values comes too late.

In Clash by Night, Mae is unable to sustain her marriage to the generous but "child-hearted" Jerry Wilenski,
who "doesn't know there's a battle of the bread and butter.
He expects his wife to fight those battles!" (I, 2).   She had
married him on the rebound from an affair with a Pennsylvania politician, and now she finds her "shoulders aren't
strong enough for crosses" (I, 2), which Jerry and her child
have become to her.   She agrees to run off with Earl Pfeiffer,

whose divorced wife is <u>his</u> cross, but is reluctant to hurt
Jerry, saying: "Do you expect me to throw him away like
a little stone?" (II, 1). Earl is not without compassion, but
he urges Mae not to let softness stand in the way of their
flight: "Mae, don't make me sorry for him. If I feel sorry
for him I won't feel sorry for us--then we'll both be sorry
love was ever invented" (II, 1). Ironically, this action
parallels <u>Awake and Sing!</u> (with the exception that Mae and
Earl plan to take her child with them); it is another break-
out attempt, but with tragic consequences. Thematically,
what is most interesting is that though both Hennie and Mae
pity their respective spouses and respect their finer qualities,
that very pity is a motivating force for their flight with
stronger, more confident men.

Another obvious reason for love's failure is disloyalty
and betrayal on the part of one's spouse. What is fresh and
dramatically compelling is Odets' insight into the capacity of
the spurned lover to rationalize rejection and offer forgiveness, provided that he or she can salvage a shred of dignity.
Belle Stark, in <u>Rocket to the Moon,</u> treats her husband as
a lovable child, undercuts his dreams of opening a new dental office with practical objections, nags him with her itch
to travel--"Why can't we do what Jack and Milly Heitner
do?" (I)--and tries to possess him completely. Some explanation for her bitchy behavior lies in her childlessness--
she had a stillborn birth, cannot conceive again, and Ben
does not want to adopt a child--and she musters her single
generous impulse when Cooper bemoans the plight of his
children, offering him a month's extension in the rent. But,
generally, Belle is an insecure and neurotic woman, quite
capable of driving even her understanding and tolerant husband into his assistant's arms. When her suspicions of
Cleo are confirmed, the blood figuratively drains from this
pushy and pitiful woman, and she refuses to regard Ben's
attachment as anything more than a casual sexual interlude.

> But you don't love her! You had an affair, all
> right, but you don't love her! (STARK sits, head
> in hands. BELLE continues with fearful agitation.)
> The girl was here all day. You were close to-
> gether and you fell into that thing. I can forget
> it, I can forget it, Ben. I'm your wife. It doesn't
> involve our whole relationship. We can have many
> happy years together. I'll do anything you want.
> We're young--we have our life together in common,
> our ten years. We can talk it out--we're civilized

> beings--I'll never mention it.   We'll both forget it!
> We need each other, Ben....   (III)

Much the same reaction is elicited from the childlike
Jerry Wilenski when, on discovering his wife's infidelity,
stunned and unable to comprehend life without Mae, he returns after his abortive flight from the house with an offer
of forgiveness.

> JERRY: ... Mae, a certain thing happened.   I
>   guess you didn't realize what it meant to me ...
> MAE: I guess I didn't, Jerry ...
> JERRY: But now you do ...
> MAE: I now do ...
> JERRY: Well ... if it didn't mean anything to you,
>   if it was somethin' that just happened ... I can
>   understand it.   Maybe I'm short on brains, how
>   I kept puttin' you together ... it didn't occur to
>   me.   It goes to show ... sometimes you forget
>   you're alive ... (Then with fresh attack) Now
>   there's the past--that's what I wanna say.
>   There's a past an' there's the future.   The
>   past don't interest me if we could have a future.
>   The best of the people lose their heads some-
>   time, as I see it ...   (II, 1)

Odets' realistic grasp of character and theme is evident: long-standing marital relationships cannot be sundered
by what is viewed as casual sex, except when the cheated
partner feels robbed of dignity and self-respect.   Belle slaps
Ben's face when he admits that he has doubts about where
his responsibilities lie, and Jerry, totally distraught when
Mae tells him not to have false hopes and that "It's over between us," flings a hammer at Earl's head.   Love's labor
is lost when one of the partners refuses to be forgiven, and
hate fills the vacuum temporarily.

Of all the lovers in crisis, there are only a few who
maintain an uneasy accommodation based on proximity and
despair.   We rarely find in Odets' dramas prototypes of the
self-lacerating and mutually recriminating George and Martha
of Albee's Who's Afraid of Virginia Woolf?, or any of Williams' or Hellman's marriages of inconvenience.   Love
usually succeeds or fails in Odets; rarely is there a delicate
balance.   Charlie and Marion Castle in The Big Knife may
be at odds over Charlie's loss of idealism, but the issue
between them is clear-cut, and is resolved by his suicide.

Affection for one another undergirds all the Castles' quarrels.
The same can be said of Georgie Elgin who, at the beginning
of Act I of The Country Girl, is planning to abandon her self-
indulgent, dependent husband after years of struggles. But
the appearance of Bernie Dodd, the director, and a possible
new opportunity for Frank are enough to make her unpack
her suitcase and try again. Perhaps Georgie and Frank's
relationship has reached the love-hate stage when we meet
them, but Georgie still clings to her memory of her "naive
belief in Frank's worldliness and competence ... " (II, 2) when
she first married him. She tells Dodd: "Yes, I saw he
drank. But that was only a pathetic hint of frailty in a wonderful, glowing man. It was touching and sweet--it made me
love him more" (II, 2). Throughout the vicissitudes of
Frank's comeback attempt, one feels that sustaining affection--
attentuated but still there--in Georgie.

Ben and Belle Stark in Rocket to the Moon resolve
their difficulties at the end of the play; presumably, his affair with Cleo has given this reflective dentist a new, clear
insight into himself and his wife: "... for the first time in
years I looked out on the world and saw things as they really
are ... " (III), he tells Mr. Prince. Free from guilt and
no longer insensitive to his wife and his own needs, he and
Belle will build their lives anew. Personally, along with
Mr. Prince, who cynically undercuts Ben's optimism, I have
always found this conclusion a bit slick and incredible. But
Odets' belief in the transforming power of love was strong,
and he evidently concluded that this pair would successfully
repair their damaged marriage.

If I have been implying that Odets' lovers are healthier
than some of the sick specimens found in the plays of his
successors, this is not to say that he was unaware of psycho-
sexual reasons for the failure of love. One need hardly look
further than Paradise Lost for a depressing example of a
twisted marital relationship, one in which a sexually impotent male builds a fantasy world with the tacit agreement
of his wife. Sam Katz bullies Bertha unmercifully and
blames her in front of others for their childlessness. According to Pearl, "Mr. Katz hits her some times." This
and his verbal abuse--"In the circus they got a bearded
lady.... And in my house I got a baldy woman (II)--explain
why, as Sam selfishly complains, "All night she cries!" (I).
But when Sam is exposed as a thief and a liar at work, concurrently, his sexual pretenses crumble. When Clara Gordon
slaps him, Bertha, the quiet one, defends him: "Don't hit

him, a sick man. God put a mark on his face! ... We
have upstairs a closet full of pills, medicine, electric machines. For seven years Sam Katz didn't sleep with a girl"
(II). Bertha intercedes for him with the Gordons and reveals
a martyr's ability to absorb punishment and still minister to
this sterile man's deep hurt. It is one of the most harrow-
ing scenes in the play. From a man who bragged that he
was "like an ox," Sam is reduced to a whimpering, helpless
child who calls Bertha "Momma, Momma" as she escorts
him to their upstairs room.

The Oedipal relationship between them is clear, just
as Kewpie's latent homosexual feelings for Ben are unmis-
takable in the same play. Odets knew his Freud and did not
neglect to dramatize the family romance, suppression of the
libido, the dominant-passive roles, or any other of the now-
familiar psychological concepts in his study of lovers in crisis. It is important that we examine some of these patterns,
but I shall not do so in detail since W. David Sievers, in
his valuable Freud on Broadway, has a useful chapter on
Odets' plays in their psychological context, and a detailed
article on the same subject is imminent from Dr. Margaret
Brenman-Gibson, a psychiatrist who is writing Odets' biography. However, it is illuminating to read Odets' reply to
a questionnaire Sievers sent him, which makes clear his
position in regard to the creative artist's relation to psychi-
atric theory:

> My method of writing is to bring to characters and
> situations whatever fullness of psychological aware-
> ness and experience I have on my own. Let the
> psychologist beware, not the artist, is my belief!
> I suspect writers who consciously bring psychologi-
> cal principles to their work....
>
> If a writer is really creative, let him write as
> fully as possible what he is and what he knows.
> After that let the psychologists, the religionists,
> Communists (or what you will) bring their analysis
> to bear. But the other way around is sterilizing
> and deodorizing, and is a position that I for one
> would fight as vigorously as possible.

Although he claimed he never deliberately sought devices to
dramatize the workings of the unconscious, Odets had read
many books by post-Freudians, such as Fromm and Sullivan,
and praised aspects of Freud's theories.

> The best of Freud is already so deeply in creative
> writing that it is bootless to stop for examination
> of where one always knew or where Freud opened
> up knowledge of self or others.   Freud seems to
> me great in the discovery of the "Unconscious"
> motivation, the analytic situation and its resultant
> therapy and the big matter of "transference. "   As
> for the rest, I don't give a hang, except for Freud's
> greatness of spirit, his human nobility as it were.

Sievers calls the last paragraph "perhaps the most eloquently
expressed appreciation of Freud yet written by an American
playwright, "[50] but he is forced into the Procrustean bed so
enticing to psychological critics and, ignoring the warning
implicit in Odets' words, sums up his analysis of the plays
with the following statement:

> The psychological themes which appear recurrently
> in Odets are passive-dependency in men coupled
> with a hint of latent homosexuality and the wish to
> return to the security of childhood; the matriarchal
> family pattern; childhood inferiority feelings con-
> verted into adult aggression and hostility; the
> search for psychological integrity and the struggle
> with guilt over "selling out"; and, finally, the de-
> vious conversions of suppressed sexual energy into
> sadism, Fascism, alcoholism and voyeurism.   To
> ascribe psychoanalytic influence to the plays of
> Odets, however, is not to detract in any way from
> his own powers of creative observation and his in-
> tuitive feeling for people. [51]

Despite Sievers' disclaimer, it is somehow unsatisfy-
ing to me--as I believe it would have been to Odets--to
think of the body of his plays in this way.   It is true that
there is a passive-dependency pattern in Odets' males and a
matriarchal family pattern, but what is important is the use
Odets made of this knowledge and of "experience I have on my
own. "   What really matter are the differences, not the similarities, in Odets' treatment of the husband-wife relationship.
We can see similarities between Edna and Joe in Lefty and
Bessie and Myron in Awake and Sing!, and we can cite the
"child-man" Jerry or the dependent Ben Stark and Frank
Elgin if we wish to emphasize that Odets often shows weakness inherent in the husband's role.   Then we could point
out that the "sell-out" figures, Charlie Castle and Joe Bonaparte, are no longer dependent on their wives and girl friends,

who either urge them to return to the passive state (Lorna: "You've murdered that boy with the generous face" Golden Boy, II, 1), or resent their derelictions from hearth and home (Marion: "... away from this atmosphere of flattery and deceit we might make our marriage work" The Big Knife, I). This insight could lead us to infer that their guilts over selling out are allied to their assuming overly aggressive male roles.

It is an interesting theory, but somehow it seems irrelevant to the experiential texture of Odets' dramas. The truth is that Odets saw nothing necessarily abnormal or unhealthy in the passive husband-strong wife relationship. The most enduring and endearing lovers in Odets are Leo and Clara Gordon of Paradise Lost, and Noah and Esther in The Flowering Peach. These relationships are balanced; by that I mean that Leo and Noah may be impractical and idealistic, but they stand firm on their principles; Clara and Esther are eminently practical, often critical of their husbands' ideas, but they dote upon them. Their attitudes are epitomized by Clara's offhand comment: "I found out many years ago that I married a fool but I love him" (I). And in The Flowering Peach we could point to instance after instance of Noah's and Esther's constant bickering. Yet, as Odets remarks in his stage directions for Scene 1, Esther "is very fond of him ... She lifts one hand in a mock slapping gesture. He backs away from her with a typical snarl, all part of an almost ritualized by-play between them."

It is by such insights and his awareness of the importance of psychological adjustments that Odets was able to create a gallery of lovers who were more than simple types. It seems to me significant (as it does to Mr. Sievers) that so many of Odets' males suffer childhood inferiority feelings which they convert into adult aggression and hostility, e. g., Moe Axelrod, Kewpie, Earl, Steve, and Ham (Noah's second son). And if we wish to regard the "sell-out" figures, Joe Bonaparte and Charlie Castle, as projections of Odets himself, it is very tempting to see this psychological syndrome as the prime source of the restless energy and vitality that Odets instilled in his characters. Perhaps on some deeper level Odets drew on this source, but he was also able to transform the type endlessly: Moody is aggressive, but he has a weak underbelly, "a certain vulnerable quality" (Golden Boy, Stage Directions, I, 1); Fuseli is aggressive, but he is a homosexual--it is hard to imagine he ever had a childhood; Mr. Prince is a pushy, proud man--so proud one guesses he was the cockiest kid on his block.

Odets leaves out important information that would
flesh out the psychological backgrounds of these last three
characters, but I suspect the omission is deliberate. [52]   His
words to Sievers imply that he had a writer's suspicion of
psychological cant and a fear of turning dramatic characters
into case histories.   A good example is his refusal to state
exactly why Frank Elgin in The Country Girl became an alcoholic.   We get hints that his child's death started him down-
hill, as well as some bad financial judgments.   But, as
Georgie says, "There's no one reason a man becomes a
drinker" (II, 1).   Contrast this with the movie version of the
play in which Bing Crosby is supplied by the writers with a
standard traumatic incident portrayed in flashback: at the
peak of his fame, he pauses outside a recording studio to
pose for some photographers, releases his little boy's hand
to do so, and the child promptly dashes into the street and
is killed.   Result?   Crosby is provided with a convenient
motivation for excessive drinking, a guilt from which he
must be purged.

Now there is nothing wrong with such an approach to
character (it worked rather well in the film), except that it
reduces the mystery of human personality to a hidden find-
me-and-I'm-cured trick.   Think of the profusion of such
scenes in modern drama: Biff in Miller's Death of a Salesman, Blanche in Streetcar, and other of Williams' characters,
George in Who's Afraid, and other of Albee's.   The childhood
trauma was almost obligatory in Fifties and Sixties drama.
Odets stubbornly refused to treat his characters like patients
in an analyst's waiting room--that tendency was passed on to
the others by O'Neill.   Undoubtedly, Odets' conviction that
the large social picture was of paramount importance influenced his reticence in this area, but it may be that his psychological understatement was in his case wiser and more
artistically honest.   He himself never consulted a psychoanalyst, and he considered that a playwright should be a
heart-shocker, not a head-shrinker.

Therefore, I feel Odets' plays resist doctrinaire psychological criticism, even though I believe that when used
sparingly it can yield some fundamental truths about them.
For example, I would hypothesize that the aforementioned
hostility and aggression of his characters are accompanied
by strong guilt feelings in the males.   Steve Takis' behavior
toward Fay in Night Music is almost puritanical; he is
shocked when foul language is used in Fay's presence, hor-
rified when a hotel manager suggests he share her room,

apologizes for saying to her he has "a bitch of a cold. "
Moe, in Awake and Sing!, rags Ralph about not sleeping with
his girl friend Blanche, but only a few minutes later Bessie
denies Ralph's request that Blanche be permitted to move in
with them, saying: "Maybe you'll sleep in the same bed
without marriage" (II, 2). Here and elsewhere, the procreative males are enveloped in an atmosphere of suffocating
middle-class morality fostered by the females. Yet part of
Odets is committed to this morality; certainly, Cleo is not
intended to be laughable when she takes umbrage at Mr.
Prince's suggestion that she barter her sexual favors:

> CLEO: Nobody supports me!
> PRINCE: A beautiful girl like you? Nobody sup-
> ports you?
> CLEO: No!
> PRINCE: My remark makes you angry?
> CLEO: Yes! I come from a very good home--
> (Rocket to the Moon, I)

A middle-class view of respectability suffuses Lorna's
relationship with Tom Moody in Golden Boy. Lorna does not
like the feeling of being "a tramp from Newark, " and Joe
reads her accurately when he calls her "a lost baby" and
"a miserable creature who never knew what to pick" (I, 3).
Lorna desperately wants marriage, just as the whores in
Night Music want it, and, paradoxically, Odets sympathizes
with them. That is to say Odets was partially committed to
a middle-class view of morals which--sometimes consciously,
often unconsciously--he rejected, and the resulting stresses
and strains make for that underlying psychological tension
that is characteristic of Odets' plays.

Unlike Shaw, Odets is not concerned with ridiculing
the absurdities of bourgeois morality; he presents the experiential facts and does not strive consciously to be radical.
But because he thinks and feels poetically about the facts as
he knows them, we can discover in the spectrum of his plays
certain psychological insights into the role of women in our
society which foreshadow the issues of the modern women's
liberation movement. Male chauvinists abound in Odets'
dramas, but then so do independent, searching women. He
seems to have regarded the cultural role of women as inextricably bound up with the home and the roles of helpmate
and mother, but his view of the female is characterized by
her freedom--indeed, her necessity--to grow within accepted
middle-class standards. I shall not cite chapter and verse

to support my statement, lest I stray from my central purpose in this section.   I believe I have shown that, sensitive
as he was to love's triumphs and tragedies, Odets had a
penetrating understanding of the psycho-sexual dynamics which
undergird human relationships, and that he used this understanding to dramatize the failures of love as well as its
successes.   I also believe that his attitudes were, on the
whole, consistent and added richness and complexity to his
characterizations and thematic content.

    We return now to what I have called the redemptive
motif in Odets' plays.   In his last two dramas, The Country
Girl and The Flowering Peach, the intensity of Odets' treatment of this motif, coupled with a tighter control of form,
solved the problem of lovers in crisis as well as it ever
could be solved for him.   These plays, so different in subject and in tone, share a common belief in the redeeming
power of love to overcome human difficulties, together with
a new, quiet affirmation of human values that is different
from the strident assertion and sometimes meretricious conclusions of the earlier dramas.   It is not that the ideas are
new; as early as Awake and Sing!, Jacob's love and self-
sacrifice for Ralph are seen as redemptive, and there are
other instances in Night Music and Golden Boy.   It is rather
that Odets is building in controlled fashion on what he knows
and, for the first time, he allows the poet equal voice with
the ideologue.   The results are two plays that rival in excellence those of his brilliant beginning.

    The Country Girl is a modern miracle play that mas-
querades as an actors' vehicle.   Viewed on one level, it is
about a show business cliché--the once-great star struggling
to make a comeback, assisted by his loyal, much-put-upon
wife, at cross purposes with his ambitious young director,
who does not really understand him, but falls in love with
her.   Capsuled in these terms, it smacks of the backstage
pathos of Pagliacci and seems just the sort of plot which a
reviewer for The New Yorker would satirize. [53]   But repeated successful revivals of this play have revealed its
remarkable craftsmanship and durability.   It is a work that
concerns itself with the interplay of charged emotions during
a period of intense pressure--the initial rehearsals, then
the try-out in Boston and eventual opening on Broadway of
a new drama.   One has the general impression of a world
stripped bare of everything but sheer emotional force, symbolically expressed by the utilization of the naked stage for
several crucial scenes.   Odets drives toward psychological

truth in the gradual unfolding of his characterizations; successively, he reveals Elgin's cunning lies and rationalizations, Georgie's self-loathing because of her enforced wife-mother role and her repressed womanhood, Bernie Dodd's misogyny which marks his loneliness. In addition, he creates tension by building a rivalry between Georgie and Bernie based on misunderstanding. In the beginning, Bernie, who had hero-worshiped Frank in his youth, tells him: "I'll commit myself to you--we'll work and worry together--it's a marriage" (I, 2). This inverted marriage and the struggle over who can best save Frank is but one of the play's abundant ironies. Although I will later analyze Odets' craft, I must mention here the perfect structuring of the last two scenes which unravel Frank's lies, Bernie's love, Georgie's choice, and Frank's recovery of his lost potency. [54]

Odets knew he had achieved a success in this play; indeed, he directed it himself to insure that no outsider marred his conception of it. Yet his satisfaction was also contaminated by some guilt. For example, he told Elliot Norton before the Broadway opening that in omitting social significance from the play, he may have taken "a step backward as a playwright." He felt compelled to state that he believed in a Federal Theater and was deeply concerned about the social problems of actors, and to utter lame platitudes like "limitation is the beginning of wisdom." [55] Even after the play was a commercial success, he never lost his feeling that he had betrayed his reputation as embattled social critic. The review by his old mentor, Harold Clurman, must have been particularly wounding: "The Country Girl is lightweight Odets.... To my mind the play is thin in characterization, meager in authentic feeling, shallow in invention." [56] Even in the last years of his life he clung to this crotchety attitude; he told Arthur Wagner: "It [The Country Girl] doesn't mean anything to me; it's just a theater piece." [57] And in his interview with Michael J. Mendelsohn, he talked of "a play like The Country Girl which is relatively, in the body of my work, a superficial play. I knew just exactly how that play should become successful." [58]

The taint of the "sell-out" hung over the play, and not even Brooks Atkinson's encomiums--"The Country Girl is the best play he has written for years, perhaps the best play of his career"[59]--could rid Odets of this misguided notion. But the truth is that Odets had indeed written a play with social meaning, not overtly didactic but with cues that are perceived by the audience. Never once are we allowed to forget that the production of a play is a hazardous financial enterprise, and there is the constant presence of Phil Cook, the producer, blood-brother to Marcus Hoff and Uncle Morty, to remind us of this fact. He ridicules Bernie's choice of Frank for the leading role, constantly worries over his investment, chafes at expenditures and, after Elgin's triumph, fawningly apologizes to Frank in order to secure a favorable run-of-the-play contract with the star. Once again the artist is being maltreated and manipulated by a capitalist exploiter, albeit in this play he is hardly ruthless and assumes a subordinate role; even the stage manager rebukes him when he berates Frank after his bender (II, 2). Malcolm Goldstein, who gives a simplistic and hostile summary of this play, has noted: "The money motive, once more, looms as a destructive force."[60]

But Odets extends himself in conjoining the psychological conflicts with the social undercurrents implicit in the play. There is a suggestion that outside the profit-and-fame world of the theater a different life-style might have awaited the Elgins. The title of the play conveys the classic opposition between pastoral simplicity and purity (symbolized by Georgie) and urban complexity and corruption. Although Odets never makes explicit the reasons for Frank's alcoholism, any American audience knows the pressures which fame and success exert on our celebrities. The very word "celebrity" connotes a need to party and play in the public eye; only the most iron-clad ego can avoid the feeling that one may be slipping, the fear failure will strike, the vulnerability to gossip. Odets understood this, as he demonstrated in his screenplay for The Sweet Smell of Success, wherein a gossip columnist and his press-agent toady are rendered as villains. He had undergone the process himself. Therefore, we intuit--without any specific references needed--that the causes of Frank Elgin's deep-seated fears and tremendous ego needs are social as well as psychological.

Furthermore, Odets was quite wrong in seeing the play as uncharacteristic, written to regain his status on Broadway, since the problem the play poses and the tentative solution it provides are consonant with his other major works. A combination of social and psychological forces have forced Frank Elgin into an alcoholic trap--he is a sell-out to the bottle. Like the other sell-outs, he must struggle to escape, and the allegory that Odets dramatizes is the story of love transcendent. Bernie Dodd determines in Act I that he wants to unleash "all that power and majesty" that Unger, the play-

wright, also sees in Frank, and witness the same theatrical
resurrection that had recently occurred when Laurette Taylor
starred in The Glass Menagerie. Before he can do this, he
must learn the true nature of the woman he mistakenly
taunts--"Lady, you ride the man like a broom! You're a
bitch!" (I, 5)--just as she must penetrate the deceptively
frank self-portrait he presents to her:

> ... I'm ambitious--I wanna get my picture on a
> green postage stamp, too. There's a difference
> between us, of course. Way up on the twenty-
> fourth floor is where I live. And sometimes, late
> at night, I look out way over the sleeping city and
> think how I'd like to change the history of the
> world. I know I won't--the idea is talented but
> phony. I admit I'm a gifted mountebank. (I, 5)

Beneath the self-derogatory tone, Bernie Dodd is a man of
feeling, an idealist with a touch of the fanatic in him. Unger
reads him accurately: "Despite the talent, he's a dumb innocent kid in more ways than one. He's in love with art,
for instance, and would make it a felony that you are not"
(II, 1).

In her uneasy alliance with Dodd, Georgie Elgin
comes to see that he really is a loving man and a redemptive
force. Her derisive nickname for him--Bernardo the Great--
comes to have tender meaning by the play's conclusion;
"Haven't you been a magician to Frank? To both of us, in
fact?" (II, 3), she asks him. Yet without the strength and
candor of Georgie, the miracle could not have occurred. It
takes the combined qualities of Bernie, the artistic visionary,
and Georgie--"Steadfast. And loyal ... reliable" (II, 3)--
possessor of the old-fashioned virtues which Bernie and Odets
himself admired, to place Frank back at center stage before
warmly applauding first-nighters. Love can perform miracles,
but Odets implies that man must not rest complacent. At
the play's conclusion, Georgie feels that both their lives are
at a pivotal point, that there are grounds for hope, but she
warns: "I married you for happiness, Frank. And, if nec-
cessary, I'll leave you for the same reasons." And Frank,
pulling himself together for a fresh onslaught at the world,
says: "I think I have a chance." But the fact is that no
beatific vision has transformed the world for Frank and
Georgie. They must still cope with the crises of love, and
subsist in an uncertain world. Or, as Rosamond Gilder
once aptly put it in reviewing Rocket to the Moon: "The
mood is apocalyptic but there is no revelation."[61]

By the time he wrote The Flowering Peach Odets had
collected all the themes that represented a lifetime's con-
cerns--the family trap, the sell-out, and the crisis of love--
and found a fable which could present his mature reflections
on aspects of all of them.   With his usual bravado and élan,
he went to Genesis to write "a work of secular piety"[62] about
the Noah legend, which would be broad instead of narrow--
encompassing all of his ambiguities--as well as introducing
a motif of spirituality hitherto absent from his work.   As he
told Herbert Mitgang in a pre-opening interview, "The Country Girl was like a pen-and-ink drawing.   The Flowering
Peach is, to me, more like a heavily detailed oil painting.
Here there is something extra, the people in the play are
extensions, the whole thing is richer. "[63]   What matter if
the canvas becomes overcrowded at times, if (as some
critics complain)[64] the brush strokes which should have filled
in details of important characters are lacking?   The whole
is like some collaborative masterpiece by Breughel and
Gauguin, alive with color and action and light and darkness.
Here I will not deal with the analogue between the Bergers
squabbling in their Bronx apartment and Noah's family trapped by the waters of God's wrath (see p. 102), or dwell on
the implications of Noah's decision to settle down after long
travail with Shem, his materialistic son (a sell-out! implied
some critics). [65]   Instead, I will concentrate on the motif of
love's redemptive power, which overshadows the other themes
and keeps the Ark afloat--that love which Walt Whitman said
was "the keelson of the Creation. "

There are many lovers in this play: male and female,
father and son, mother and children, and of course the animals, two by two.   Foremost among them are the parents,
whose relationship is consistently moving.   Their affection
is conveyed partially by bantering dialogue:

> ESTHER: Noah, tell the truth--when they gave
> out the brains, you weren't hiding behind the
> house? You had enough to drink....
> NOAH (loftily): You should be satisfied I drink,
> otherwise I'd leave you.   (1)

But it is also a matter of grunts, raised eyebrows, worried
frowns and tender, fleeting looks.   When Noah miraculously
changes from a septuagenarian to a virile man of forty, the
wife whose bed he shared for sixty years puts on an old
fruit-and-flower-bedecked hat and says to Noah: "I'm pretty?
You'll take me for a walk?" (5).   And, later, when Esther

becomes ill near the end of their voyage, Noah's furtive
visits to her, his brooding silence and admission to Japheth
that he cannot conceive of her dying or of facing the future
without her, are all evidence that such potentially sentimental situations can move us if presented with dignity and
restraint.

There has been criticism that, once the voyage gets
underway, "there is too much argufying about marriage and
divorce," and that Odets includes the subplot about the crossed
love affairs among the children "driven by some irrelevant
compulsion."[66] I disagree. Not only must the forty-day voyage be filled with some dramatic tension, but Noah's recognition of love's demands and their resolution is essential to
the symbolic journey Odets was depicting. First, Odets shows
the "love-economic" motif ironically reversed by the greedy
son Shem and his selfish wife Leah, who try to make world
catastrophe profitable; in contrast, we see how the idealistic
Japheth cannot conceive of taking a wife because of the terrible picture before his eyes of "bushels of babies who will die
in the flood" (3). Then Odets makes us aware of the in-
compatibility of Ham, the lazy, cynical son, who is a gamester
and womanizer, and Rachel, his delicate, hopeful and somehow
uncertain wife. Japheth, the sensitive idealist and artist (he
carves wooden spoons), returns from his trip to town with an
attractive orphan in tow, Goldie, who has rescued him from
a hostile crowd. Ham immediately courts her and she, while
resisting him, admires his wit. With a mother's instinct,
Esther sees at once that there is a mutual attraction: "A
person like her, she fits to Ham," she tells Rachel solemnly,
"the way you fit to Japhie" (4).

Thus the scene is set for lovers in crisis, and a
comic analogue to Awake and Sing! is played out, with Ham
substituting for Moe Axelrod, Goldie for Hennie, Japheth for
Ralph, and Rachel for Blanche (who never appears on stage).
Esther assumes Bessie's dominant role and pushes for the
practical divorce which will bring the true lovers together
against the moral horror and repugnance of Noah, the Jacob
prototype in this play. There are differences, of course.
Esther can accept a poor orphan because the entire world is
going under the waves which will drown middle-class distinc-
tions, and Noah is a stubborn believer in Jehovah, not Karl
Marx. As archetypal forces in both plays, Marx and Jehovah,
are not very different after all.

The humbling of Noah's pride and stiff-necked tradi-

tionalism takes place at two key moments in the play: when
Japheth convinces his father that his man-made rudder is
necessary to steer the Ark and keep it from foundering (7);
and when Esther dies, sitting in the sun, wearing her absurd
hat, just before the dove brings a small green leaf to the
eager travelers (8). Her last request to Noah had been:
"Marry the children before I go ... their happiness ... is
my last promised land...." (8) The bereaved patriarch per-
forms the shipboard rites and, in the final scene, with the
Ark aground against a lucent sky, beside a flowering tree,
we discover that the lovers are fitly paired and that each
wife is swollen with child. Noah's injunction to go forth and
replenish the earth has already been obeyed. Love can redeem, but the essence of the play's meaning lies in the
changed relationship between Japheth and Noah.

From the beginning, Noah's love for his youngest son
is special: "... because Noah makes unconscious identification with Japheth ... the boy has always panged the old man's
heart: they are two outcasts in the more competent and
fluent world" (Stage Directions, 2). Therefore, Japheth's
questioning of God's judgment, and insistence that the Ark be
steered by a rudder, had seemed to Noah not only blasphe-
mous and rebellious but also a kind of personal desertion.
At odds with his father even before they embark, Japheth
finds some solace in his growing attraction to Rachel. She
tries to convince him "to bend a little" to his father's will,
but he can only think of "men crazy not to be alone or apart"
whose world is about "to be brushed away by a peevish boy!"
Then, Rachel says: "Japheth, I beg you to think! There is
idealism now in just survival!" (5).

Much has been made of this line by critics[67] who take
it as proof that Odets had rationalized away his former social
commitment and was now ready to "settle for half," as Arthur
Miller put it in A View from the Bridge. It is true that the
threatening flood invites comparison with the atomic bomb
threat, which permeated the cold-war Fifties, and Rachel's
words may reflect Odets' sense of the changed social and
political environment in a world that could easily terminate
itself. But critics forget the dramatic context of these
words: once again we have the practical female urging restraint upon an idealistic male, as so many Odetsian wives
and sweethearts had done before her. My study of this pattern has shown that the men rarely listen, and, sure enough,
Japheth refuses to board the Ark when the rains begin; thus,
Noah must strike him unconscious so that they can literally

drag him on board.   In the light of these events it is surely
wrong to take Rachel's words as evidence of a significant
change in Odets' idealistic posture.

Japheth carries the guerdon of social protest against
injustice and a sturdy independence with him on the voyage
to a new beginning on Mount Ararat.   It is he who insists to
the moralistic and more naive Noah that "if He doesn't like
it that human beings act like human beings, He's out of
luck!" (6); even God must accept man's humanity.   Japheth
will marry his brother's wife and not be bound by convention,
and he will not rely on Divine Providence but his own two
hands in steering the Ark through turbulent waters.   Withal,
he loves and respects his father and begs him to accept him
as he is.   When Esther dies, it is in Japheth's arms that
Noah seeks comfort, and after the landing both father and
son have undergone a sea change.   Noah has learned humility
and Japheth has gained maturity.   And what of God?   Japheth
says: "Maybe God changes when men change" (9).   Noah
blesses his favorite son and receives the sign of the covenant.
But in Odets' version of the fable, Noah, though grateful,
knows God is not handing him the rainbow as an emblem of
security: "Now it's in man's hands to make or destroy the
world!" (9).

It should be evident from my discussion that Odets'
work shows respect for the religious spirit but remains secular and, on one occasion, irreverent in tone.   During
colloquies with God, Noah and the audience hear a humming
noise: "the Presence of God ... is expressed by a certain
musical rustle or widening shimmer, as if a gigantic tuning
fork had been struck" (Stage Directions, 1).   The effect
may be awesome in the theater when combined with occasional thunder rolls, but Odets cannot resist informing us
that these can be "made by one good union stagehand in the
theater rolling a lead ball across the back of the stage"
(Stage Directions, 1).   One might gather that only an agnos-
tic could have made so offhand an observation.   Yet there
is deep appreciation for the transcendent power of love in
this play, for the miraculous cycle of fertility and renewal.
As for metaphysics and the source and purpose of mankind,
Noah concludes by saying, "I'll tell you a mystery...." (9).

In The Flowering Peach, Odets made good use of the
myth of Genesis as a confirmation of his artist's vision.   In
the words of Denis de Rougement: "Art is an exercise of
the whole being of man, not to compete with God, but to

coincide better with the order of Creation, to love it better, and to reestablish ourselves in it. "[68] Here, as in the other plays, life for Odets is the mystery, happiness the goal, but only man's striving can make the mystery meaningful. That was about as far as he was willing to go--and in the last quarter of the twentieth century, most of us have not gone much further.

NOTES

[1]"For Ralph, moreover, to applaud his sister's abandonment of her child and flight with Moe as an awakening does not speak well for his own awakening. " John Gassner, "The Long Journey of a Talent, " Theatre Arts, 33 (July 1949), 28. "The incongruity of the situation is enhanced by Ralph's approval of Hennie's elopement, an act which in purport is precisely the opposite of his own plan to fight it out at home. " Malcolm Goldstein, The Political Stage (New York, 1974), p. 96. For an argument that Ralph is merely calling for action for its own sake, not because he believes the break-out will succeed, see Shuman, p. 64.

[2]See summary of Michael Blankfort's review from New Masses, 5 Mar. 1935, in Morgan Y. Himelstein's Drama Was a Weapon (New York, 1963), p. 167, and Goldstein, pp. 96-97.

[3]Quoted above, p. 21. Wagner, p. 73. See also HUAC, pp. 3475-6.

[4]Moe's comment on Ralph's speech, "Graduation Day!, " seems particularly inept, since it comes from a cynical racketeer. The only explanation for it is that Moe admires Ralph's fighting spirit and tone; but it sounds almost as though Odets was patting himself on the back for a rousing curtain speech.

[5]HUAC, p. 3468.

[6]Lawson, Theory and Technique of Playwriting and Screenwriting (1936; rpt. New York, 1960), pp. 249-54, passim.

[7]Himelstein, pp. 166-69.

[8]William Gibson, Introduction to Golden Boy (musical version, New York, 1966), p. 9.

[9]James T. Farrell, rev. of <u>Paradise Lost</u>, <u>Partisan Review and Anvil</u>, 3 (Feb. 1936), 28-29.

[10]Weales, "The Group Theatre and Its Plays," in <u>American Theatre</u>, Stratford-Upon-Avon Studies 10 (New York, 1967), p. 72.

[11]Weales, p. 69.

[12]Robert Warnock, ed., <u>Representative American Plays</u> (Oakland, N.J., 1952), p. 564.

[13]See Michael J. Mendelsohn, "American Family," p. 242; and Shuman, <u>Clifford Odets</u>, p. 136.

[14]Shuman, "Thematic Consistency in Odets' Early Plays," <u>Revue des Langues Vivantes</u>, 35 (1969), 418-19.

[15]Odets told McCarten in 1938 that he sent back $4000 to aid the ailing play (McCarten, p. 26). However, when Wagner interviewed him in 1961, Odets claimed that he sent back half of his $2500 per week salary to the Group for an unspecified period (Wagner, pp. 72-73).

[16]"Mr. Odets Is Acclimated," <u>New York Times</u>, 3 May 1936, Sec. 10, p. 4.

[17]Odets, "Democratic Vistas in Drama," <u>New York Times</u>, 1 Feb. 1942, Sec. 9, p. 3.

[18]Eric Bentley, <u>The Playwright as Thinker</u> (New York, 1955), p. 30.

[19]Levant, p. 190.

[20]Mersand, p. 63.

[21]Odets, "Vistas."

[22]HUAC, p. 3509.

[23]Clurman, p. 169. Later in his book, when describing the breakup of the Group, Clurman expresses the same idea more angrily:

> Odets wanted to run with the hares and hunt with the hounds; he wanted to be the great revolutionary

playwright of our day and the white-haired boy of
Broadway. He wanted the devotion of the man in the
cellar and the congratulations of the boys at "21. "
He wanted the praise of the philosophers and the
votes of Variety's box-score. (p. 249)

[24]"Mr. Odets Is Acclimated. "

[25]"The Sum and Substance: A Dialogue on Contemporary Values, " telecast (Burbank, Calif. , 1963). Interview
of Clifford Odets by Dr. Herman Harvey. See Appendix,
pp. 206-213.

[26]"Center Stage" June 1963, p. 29.

[27]See Odets, "Vistas, " pp. 1-2; Peck, p. 1; Odets,
"On Coming Home, " New York Times, 25 July 1948, Sec.
2, p. 1; Herbert Mitgang, "Odets Goes to Genesis, " New
York Times, 26 Dec. 1954, Sec. 2, pp. 1, 3.

[28]"Mr. Odets Is Acclimated. "

[29]Odets never completely deserted Broadway during
the war years. He adapted The Russian People from a play
by Konstantin Simonov for the Theater Guild in 1942; see
Weales, Clifford Odets, pp. 151-54, and Lawrence Langner,
The Magic Curtain (New York, 1951), pp. 338-40. Later,
in the early 1940s, he made an abortive attempt to adapt
Franz Werfel's Jacobowsky and the Colonel, but the Guild
and its director, Elia Kazan, were dissatisfied, and the work
was handed over to S. N. Behrman; see Behrman, People in
a Diary (Boston, 1972), pp. 171-72.

[30]Clurman, p. 159.

[31]It was well known in Hollywood that Jerry Wald was
the model for Budd Schulberg's protagonist in What Makes
Sammy Run?

[32]Bob Thomas, King Cohn (New York, 1967), pp. xv-
xvii. Thomas cites, on p. 322, an interesting remark which
Wald once made to Budd Schulberg: "For years I have been
fighting the Sammy Glick image; people thought that I was
Sammy. Let me tell you something: Sammy Glick was a
Boy Scout leader compared to Harry Cohn. "

[33]See "The Sum and Substance," pp. 210-211, and Mendelsohn, "Center Stage," May 1963, p. 19, and June 1963, p. 28.

[34]Odets, "On Coming Home," p. 1.

[35]"I Can't Sleep," in The Anxious Years, ed. Louis Filler (New York, 1964), p. 216.

[36]Clurman, "Introduction to Golden Boy," in Six Plays of Clifford Odets (New York, 1939), p. 433.

[37]Although Kewpie recognizes, through the use of the term "pro-anti," his schizoid personality, he is also behaving as if he were a jilted lover. Malcolm Goldstein also has noted this point: "Odets subtly suggests that this minor monster feels a homosexual attraction for Ben and that he asserts his manliness by sleeping with Ben's wife." Political Stage, p. 307. See also my discussion of Odets' attitudes toward psycho-sexual relations, pp. 91-97.

[38]See Peck, passim. It should also be noted that the "Hollywood Ten" were cited for contempt on Nov. 24, 1947, and that by 1949 HUAC had succeeded in intimidating all of the major studios into instituting a blacklist. See Stefan Kanfer, A Journal of the Plague Years (New York, 1973), pp. 74-97. Odets, who would make his appearance before the Committee in 1952, makes allusions in The Big Knife to the atmosphere of oppression and intimidation in Hollywood.

[39]Examples are Goldstein, Political Stage, p. 328, and Eleanor Flexner, American Playwrights, 1918-1938 (New York, 1938), p. 319.

[40]See T. C. Worsley, rev. of The Big Knife, New Statesman, 47 (9 Jan. 1954), 40; John Mason Brown, rev. of The Big Knife, "Biting the Hand," Saturday Review, 32 (19 Mar. 1949), 34-35; and Joseph Wood Krutch, rev. of The Big Knife, Nation, 168 (19 Mar. 1949), 340-41.

[41]See Kappo Phelan, rev. of The Big Knife, Commonweal, 49 (25 Mar. 1949), 390-91, and Anthony Hartley, rev. of The Big Knife, Spectator, 192 (29 May 1942), 507.

[42]It is equally possible to link the title with the mode of Charlie's suicide; also, by extension, to the motifs of Charlie's emasculation and self-betrayal. However, in Peck, Odets stated: "The big knife is that force in modern life which is against people and their aspirations, which seeks to cut people off in their best flower."

[43]There are some revealing statistics on declining marriage rates in Frederick Lewis Allen, Since Yesterday, 1929-1939 (New York, 1940), pp. 132-33; see also Caroline Bird, The Invisible Scar (New York, 1966), p. 283.

[44]I agree with Sievers, p. 261: "Of all the episodes only two seem today to have flesh and blood characters, the scene with Joe and his wife, Edna ... and the scene between the young hack and his girl. The other episodes are written with the mawkish zeal of a young propagandist." W. David Sievers, Freud on Broadway (New York, 1955), p. 261.

[45]Robert J. Griffin, "On the Love Songs of Clifford Odets," in The Thirties, ed. Warren French (DeLand, Fla., 1967), p. 198.

[46]George Jean Nathan delivered a withering and contemptuous attack on this play. Encyclopedia of the Theatre (New York, 1940), pp. 288-90. For contrast, Joseph Wood Krutch found the play "impressive" and noted that "the intensity which makes the play at moments almost unbearable is responsible also for the fact that it is more than a tale of frustration and rises above mere realism toward the tragic level." American Drama, p. 276.

[47]Among the critics who disparage Cleo Singer, Murray (who admires her) lists Clurman, Gassner, and Edmond M. Gagey. Clifford Odets, p. 87. Also, Weales feels that her awakening at the conclusion is not credible. Clifford Odets, p. 135.

[48]For a discussion of the theme of homelessness, see Clurman's Introduction to Night Music (New York, 1940), pp. viii-xi, and Winifred L. Dusenbury, The Theme of Loneliness in Modern American Drama (Gainesville, 1960), pp. 38-45.

[49]In his interview with Mendelsohn, Odets was asked: "Do you accept the label 'optimist' that has very often been pinned on you?" Odets replied: "'Optimist'? I would say that I have a belief in man and his possibilities as the measure of things, but I would not say that I was an optimistic writer. I would say that I have shown as much of the seamy side of life as any other playwright of the twentieth century, if not more." "Center Stage," May 1963, p. 17.

[50]Sievers, p. 262.

[51]Sievers, pp. 274-75.

[52]Moody, Fuseli, and Mr. Prince are important but not central characters. I have criticized Odets for omitting the psychological background of Charlie Castle in The Big Knife, but Charlie is the central character and his motivation is essential to our understanding of him.

[53]See Wolcott Gibbs, "A Review of The Country Girl," New Yorker, 26 (18 Nov. 1950), 77-79.

[54]Odets was particularly proud of the last scene, which he called "the best technical job I ever did." See Armand Aulicino, "How The Country Girl Came About," Theatre Arts, 36 (May 1954), 57.

[55]Elliot Norton, "Clifford Odets Sans Message," New York Times, 5 Nov. 1950, Sec. 2, p. 3.

[56]Clurman, "The First Fifteen Years," New Republic, 123 (11 Dec. 1950), 30.

[57]Wagner, p. 74.

[58]Mendelsohn, "Center Stage," May 1963, p. 18.

[59]Atkinson, "A Review of The Country Girl," New York Times, 11 Nov. 1950, p. 10.

[60]Goldstein, "Clifford Odets and the Found Generation," in American Drama and its Critics, ed. Alan S. Downer (Chicago, 1965), p. 144.

[61]Gilder, rev. of Rocket to the Moon, Theatre Arts, 23 (Jan. 1939), 13.

[62]Richard Hayes, "The Flowering Peach," Commonweal, 61 (11 Feb. 1955), 502.

[63]Mitgang, p. 3.

[64]See William Becker, "Reflections on Three New Plays," Hudson Review, 8 (Summer 1955), 263-68, and Eric Bentley, "Poetry of the Theater," in What Is Theater? (New York, 1968), pp. 207-11.

[65]"... at the conclusion of the play, Noah pathetically

chooses to spend his feeble old age at the home of his mono-
polistic, well-to-do son because he will be more comfortable
there.   It seemed as if Odets ... had given up hopes for a
better world and is ready to accept humanity on its own
second-best terms. " John Gassner, Theatre at the Crossroads (New York, 1960), p. 155.   See also Rabkin, p. 210.

[66]Bentley, "Poetry of the Theater, " p. 208.

[67]See Weales, Clifford Odets, pp. 177-78, and Barry
Hyams, "Twenty Years on a Tightrope, " Theatre Arts, 39
(Apr. 1955), 86.

[68]Denis de Rougemont, "Religion and the Mission of
the Artist, " in Spiritual Problems in Contemporary Literature,
ed. Stanley Romaine Hopper (1952; rpt. Gloucester, Mass.,
1969), p. 186.

CHAPTER III

THE PLAYWRIGHT AS POET

1. Structure and Symbol

> Don't ask him to change his style. A
> style is best when it's individual, when
> it comes out of the inner personality
> and the lay of the muscles and the set
> of the bones.
> --Tokio, Golden Boy

When the young Kenneth Burke went to see a performance of Paradise Lost shortly before it ended its brief
run in February, 1936, he found to his surprise that he
liked the play enormously. He had been led by the play's
brutal reviews to expect a work with a "scandalous number
of exits and entrances," grotesque characters, and an arbitrary ending--in short, the work of a tyro. Instead, he was
deeply impressed. "And as I had witnessed, not pedestrian
realism, but the idealizations of an expert stylist, I carried
away something of the exhilaration that good art gives us
when, by the ingratiations of style, it enables us to contem-
plate even abhorrent things with calmness."

Later, when Burke had an opportunity to examine the
printed text of the play, his admiration for "the subtlety,
complexity and depths of the internal adjustments" increased;
he thought he perceived beneath the conscious allegory of
Odets what he called a ritualistic process embodying references to ice, fire and decay which imparted a structural unity
to the work. Extrapolating from Gus' remark at the close
of Act I about Pearl's piano-playing ("And when the last day
comes--by ice or fire--she'll be up there playin' away") and
Mr. Pike's enigmatic but crucial symbolic statement in Act
II ("I'm sayin' the smell of decay may sometimes be a sweet
smell"), he postulated that "the play deals with three modes

112

of 'redemption'--redemption by ice, fire, or decay--and
finally chooses the third. " Ben's speech in Act II about
being under the ice with Kewpie and their dead friend, Danny, is taken as a refutation of the "life-in-death" of ice;
Leo's rejection of Mr. May, the arsonist, is a denial of puri-
fication and rebirth by fire; and, in Act III, amid the process
of decay, Leo's closing speech is a "prophecy of rebirth ...
from the rotten grain. ... " To Kenneth Burke, "Acts II and
III show us the author's attempts to shape a magic incantation
whereby the spell is broken. "[1]

Burke's brilliant analysis of Paradise Lost was first
published in The New Republic and later included in his The
Philosophy of Literary Form. There, to illustrate his critical concept of symbolic action, he again turned to Odets,
this time to Golden Boy. Burke found Odets' play "an especially convenient work to use as illustration of 'cluster' or
'equations' ... since it is formed about two opposed principles
symbolized as an opposition between 'violin' and 'prizefight.'"
According to Burke, "prizefight equals competition, cult of
money, leaving home, getting the girl, while violin equals
cooperative social unity, disdain of money, staying home,
not needing the girl. " He goes on to suggest other "leads"
one might garner from Odets by "statistical" or "symbolic"
analysis, noting that to trace the playwright's "psychic economy" further, "we might ... borrow help from his other
plays, " and concludes with some fascinating but cryptic hints
about what might be gleaned from the study of Odets' use of
music and references to musical instruments. [2]

Such attention and intensive analysis from a highly influential critic would have seemed strange to the Broadway
reviewers who sat in judgment on Odets' plays, for they had
been accustomed to scold him for his lack of form and subtlety. As it was said of Stendhal, it seemed to some of
them that he went about writing as casually as a man would
puff on a cigar. Brooks Atkinson had written in his first
review of Awake and Sing! that "his drama in the first two
acts is wanting in the ordinary fluidity of a play, "[3] and later
found Paradise Lost replete with "frowzy characterization,
random form and ... inchoate material. "[4] Joseph Wood
Krutch, after his savage review of Paradise Lost entitled
"The Apocalypse of St. Clifford" in The Nation, found in
retrospect that "it carries exaggeration almost to the point
of burlesque and seemed to suggest that its author had completely lost his grip on reality. "[5] Not only were many
critics irritated by Odets' crowded stage and rhetorical con-

clusions in the family plays, but they somehow expected Ibsenite realism. Thus they were puzzled to discover what John Gassner accurately described in New Theatre: "His is the method of realistic symbolism rather than realistic representation."[6] There were also those critics from the Left, such as John Howard Lawson and Michael Blankfort, who masked their ideological disagreements with Odets by criticizing, for instance, his lack of "progression" and properly motivated recognition scenes.[7] Much later, The Big Knife was to be as effectively butchered as Paradise Lost by critics who wanted to lecture the erring playwright and use his play as object lesson (see Kappo Phelan's review in Commonweal).[8]

But I do not wish to linger over the critical controversies raised by Odets' plays (they have been ably documented elsewhere),[9] but rather to suggest that while some of the slurs were justified, and almost all the reviewers affirmed Odets' talent, very few perceived him as a stylist in Burke's sense. As a fledgling playwright, Odets worked too fast, and as a mature one, he made mistakes; but his critics were short-sighted in not recognizing that he had brought something radically different to the American stage. His plays are all organic shapes and grow out of what he called "the material," and his best plays have an underlying unity of symbol, metaphor, and language that works toward a satisfying cohesion.

Odets told Mendelsohn: "I don't think I've written two plays alike. This makes trouble for me, because the materials of the play or its shape always seem to baffle not the audience, but the critics."[10] One could not expect that a playwright employing such an organic methodology would place prime importance on Aristotelian considerations of plot, complications and dénouement. And it is a fact that prescribed structural elements, such as those applied to the Scribean "well-made play," were of secondary interest to Odets. That is not to say that Odets lacked skill in this aspect of his craft. He was always a strong storyteller, and in his apprentice years as an amateur actor and later with the Group, he learned much about how to write a workmanlike, realistic play. In fact, a whole chapter of this work might be devoted to Odets' adeptness in dispensing with lengthy exposition, his use of dramatic irony in planning strategic entrances and exits, his sure sense of when to bring a curtain down, etc. However, I am convinced that such a study would teach us only a little about what makes him a dramatic poet.

In his 1961 interview with Arthur Wagner, Odets said: "The form [of a play] is always dictated by the material; there can be nothing ready-made about it.... Form is viability."[11] Ultimately, structure for Odets was a matter of choosing the best available scaffolding for the imaginative or poetic vision that he wished to impart. That is why it is difficult to generalize about the dramatic architecture of his plays, and why critics have tended to contradict each other in analyzing it. Despite his disclaimer to Mendelsohn that "my forms are not Ibsen's,"[12] it seems clear that he was most successful in his early plays with a conventional Ibsenite "realistic" three-act structure, to which he added the focus on an ensemble cast rather than on a few individuals (influenced, as he correctly surmised, by his interaction with the Group Theater players). He also added the indirect and contrapuntal dialogue of a drama by O'Casey or Chekhov. Edward Murray seems closest to the truth when he states, "... the basic structure of an Odets play is Ibsenite; that is, one can perceive in it a single rising line of action which can be analyzed in terms of a point of attack, a turning point, and a resolution composed of a crisis, climax and conclusion."[13]

But Odets was also a restless experimenter with variations on this basic form. Gerald Weales has shown that Waiting for Lefty was not only inspired by the American minstrel show (as Odets claimed), but by the ground-breaking agitprop dramas of the early Thirties.[14] Odets soon discarded the emphasis on the ensemble cast (most evident in Awake and Sing! and Paradise Lost) and concentrated on a single hero (Golden Boy, The Big Knife) or a triangle (Rocket to the Moon, Clash by Night, The Country Girl), only to return to the ensemble grouping in The Flowering Peach. John Howard Lawson, in the course of his pedantic critique of Odets' craftsmanship early in Odets' career, remarked: "Odets remains more of a scenewright than a playwright"[15] because individual scenes in Odets seemed to him more powerful than his plays as integrated wholes. But after Odets returned from his Hollywood sojourn with Golden Boy, which is written in 12 scenes, the epithet took on a different meaning; George Jean Nathan, who would have headed a list of Odets' detractors, wrote in 1940 about the cinematic influence on Odets' structure: "... in almost all his plays, he reduces the epic of life to a 'quickie,' and the deliberations of mankind to a series of 'rushes.' He can write scenes, beautiful scenes, but the noisy express train that is his drama steams past them so furiously that one recalls

only a quick and insufficient glimpse of them. "16   Even in
1973 we find Malcolm Goldstein observing: "Out of his experience and education as a screen writer he acquired some
details of construction useful in the making of Golden Boy:
the vision [sic] of the play into numerous short scenes--
twelve in all--to provide a logical basis for a shift in tone,
and the 'fadeout' to replace the 'curtain' or 'blackout' as a
device for ending them. "17   Yet before Odets went to Hollywood he constructed Till the Day I Die in seven short scenes
and several slow "fadeouts" as well as "blackouts. " In addition, he employed the imaginative bridging device of "the
shrill sounds of a half dozen whistles" (Stage Direction, 1),
which is carried out between all the scenes and provides an
aural symbol for the Fascist terror which engulfs the characters.   Thus, it appears that it is both dangerous and difficult
to generalize about Odets' forms--except to say that he was
always willing to vary them in his quest for the organic.

Among the few generalizations we can make about
Odets' structure is that, with one exception (Paradise Lost),
his plays use relatively short time sequences.   The on-stage
action of Lefty occupies less than an hour; Till the Day I
Die is 6 to 8 months; Awake and Sing! covers exactly one
year and a week; Rocket to the Moon is 3 months; Golden
Boy's rise and fall occur in 16 months; Night Music, the
most compressed, is 3 days and nights; Clash by Night
takes 8 or 9 weeks; The Big Knife's action covers about 1-
1/2 weeks; The Country Girl's less than 2 months; and in
The Flowering Peach, if we follow Genesis carefully, we
find that Odets had confined the action to a year and 10 days.
The temporal mode of a typical Odets drama, then, is swift
and highly compressed.   There are no lengthy expository
scenes; seven of his eleven plays begin with a quarrel plung-
ing the audience into the heart of a conflict.   The action of
the plays proceeds with urgency, and has the speed and dramatic punch that Tokio so admired: "Where do you see
speed like that?   That's style, real style--you can't tag
him" (Golden Boy, II, 1).

When Odets wanted to adopt a different temporal
mode and increase the time span, he utilized another technique entirely. Paradise Lost covers the longest period of
any of Odets' dramas--2-3/4 years, or about 33 months.
In his canon, this play comes the closest to one of O'Neill's
mammoth dramas, in which characters are presented as
youths in the first act, mature between Acts I and II, and
age and die in Act III.   It is the only play in which Odets

deliberately adopted an historical perspective. To dramatize
the slow death of the Gordon clan, he employed a variety of
devices: a slow curtain, the insistent counterpoint of Pearl's
piano playing, the piling up of numerous exits and entrances
within the house, and, most important, sustained circularity
in dialogue. The audience's sense of clock time is lengthened
as characters appear and reappear, as they wander aimlessly
about the claustrophobic Gordon parlor and dining room. A
stage direction reads: "He [Julie] starts out one exit, but
changes his mind and goes the other way. It doesn't quite
matter where he goes is the intention here" (II). This pattern of aimless circularity is reenforced by dialogue which
suggests that time also is circular, suspended, meaningless.

> LEO: Sometimes life is unreal to me. I'm not a
> practical person. What is to be done?
> GUS (portentously): That is the question--"What
> is to be done?"
> LEO: My brain has been sleeping, My mind is
> made up: our workers must have better condi-
> tions! Tomorrow I mean to start fresh. In
> life we must face certain facts.
> GUS: Yes. Only last night I was thinkin' about
> selling my stamp collection. I figger she's
> easily worth a few thousand---- But I guess I
> could never do it ... Maybe some day though--
> and go far away to the South Sea Isles and eat
> coconuts. (I)

Odets never equaled the craftsmanship of O'Neill in
structuring a perfectly unified play like Long Day's Journey
into Night, wherein time, place, and theme fuse almost
magically. He used a dubious contrivance in Rocket to the
Moon, where Phil Cooper's trips to the water cooler to escape the heat serve to graft a subplot onto the play. And
even in the generally well-constructed The Flowering Peach,
one senses the absence of a pivotal scene which might have
more clearly explored the crucial issues between Noah and
Japheth.

But though Odets may have occasional structural
flaws in his plays, he has a sure theatrical instinct and an
unerring sense of timing. His plays may seem deceptively
casual about the unities of time and place, but he never
forgets the unity of action. Though several plays retain a
single setting, the majority do not. He sacrifices unity of
place twice in Clash by Night, but each time he does so for

perfectly valid dramatic reasons--once to contrast the opening mood of sodden torpor at the Wilenski home with a scene
of liveliness and vivacity at the dance pavilion; and again, in
the final scene, to create a symbolic climax in the projection
booth, a climax with impact and relevance. He ends Night
Music, after touring New York City, not at the Lieutenant's
desk where he began, but at the airport, which is a more
striking symbolic jumping-off place for the lovers.

Since all of his plays were experimental, he was bound
to have occasional failures. I would place in this category
Till the Day I Die, Night Music, and Clash by Night, though
I would add that none of them is without occasional interest,
either thematic or stylistic. Generally these are the plays
in which Odets was least himself. The early anti-Nazi play
was conjured up from a clipping that appeared in the New
Masses. Night Music, despite Clurman's defensive denials, 18
borrows from Saroyan's The Time of Your Life in its presentation of oddball, walk-on characters, and its loose construction. Clash by Night seems to have derived from Stein-
beck's Of Mice and Men, not only in Jerry Wilenski's sharing
of some traits with the peanut-brained strong man, Lennie,
but in the giveaway appearance of a drunk in I, 2, who keeps
muttering George and Lennie's catch-phrase, "Fat-o-the-land. "

But eight of Odets' eleven plays are densely textured,
interestingly shaped, and rich in language. Following the
hints in Burke, I propose now to examine closely the symbolic and imagistic clusters in Odets' plays as a whole, recognizing that the substratum of a writer's art functions at the
unconscious level and that the different forms of his plays are
all dictated by outward circumstances, changes in the historical and personal environment, and reaction to criticism.
Odets may have thought he was creating discrete and individual
works, but when he "rolled his eye around an inner landscape,"19
he saw many of the same metaphoric visions. By examining
the recurrent elements in his plays, I shall try to identify the
strengths which caused James Agee to say: "... he is obviously one of the very few genuine dramatic poets alive, "20
and Morris Freedman, more recently, "The genius of Odets
is in his capacity for poetry; his plays come alive and compel us whatever the confusion of their making. Odets is to
be compared with writers of the order of Shakespeare whose
art surpassed their mere understanding. "21

That Odets was a conscious allegorist has long been
established. Harold Clurman's three introductions in Six

Plays and his introduction to Night Music are helpful in showing how Odets wedded theme and metaphor; other critics,
such as Winifred L. Dusenbury and Edward Murray, have increased our understanding of the symbolic structure of individual plays.   Their works suggest that Odets' best plays
are structured around symbolic polarities: passivity vs. ag-
gressiveness, sleep vs. wakefulness, sterility vs. fertility--
ultimately, life vs. death.   But the symbolic referents which
reverberate from play to play have not been given the attention they deserve.

I intend, then, to examine six important symbolic
clusters in Odets' plays: the polarities of water and sleep
images versus procreative and redemptive images; animal
images; images of boats, cars, ships and planes; and then
to briefly examine his symbolic use of music and musical
instruments and certain selected scenic properties.

We begin with an image which haunted Odets' mental
landscape from his earliest play to his last, a metaphor
which may have its origins in that mysterious "neurotic illness" he spoke of to Mendelsohn, [22] or it may derive from
his traumatic experiences of the Thirties.   I refer to Odets'
"imagination of disaster," his apocalyptic sense that, in
Yeats' familiar lines, "Things fall apart.   The center cannot
hold/Mere anarchy is loosed upon the world/The ceremony of
innocence is drowned...." It is, indeed, a drowning world
that we witness in these plays, one in which characters have
a sense of "going under." "I only know we're at the bottom
of the ocean," Edna tells Joe in Lefty (1), and Lorna, desperate to change her lot in Golden Boy, tells Joe Bonaparte:
"They'll all want you, all the girls!   But I don't care!   I've
been undersea a long time!" (II, 2).   Hennie, in Awake and
Sing!, adds a biblical dimension to the image by sarcastically
warning Moe Axelrod: "Come around when it's a flood again
and they put you in the ark with the animals" (II, 1).   In
Paradise Lost, Ben's memories of nearly drowning under
the ice (already quoted) are central to the play's symbolic
structure; more peripheral is Odets' offhand mention that
the pushy wardheeler, Phil Foley, is chairman of the Nemo
Democratic Club, an allusion to Verne's Captain Nemo, a
man who had learned to survive on the ocean's floor.   At
the end of Act II, Mr. Pike ironically sees only one alternative to this oppressive world: "... All picked out for
me: the bottom of the ocean.   Very quiet there, the light
is soft, food is free...." And by Act III, Gus Michaels,

for no apparent logical reason but for a very valid symbolic one, recalls a friend who died in the Titanic disaster.

Rocket to the Moon contains Ben's angry third act speech to Belle: "I'm not going to stay under water like an iceberg the rest of my life" (III, 2); it is a sterile, monotonous existence that he is protesting, the kind that keeps Stark's marriage partially afloat but leaves him basically unsatisfied. More frequently, it was the economic threat that summoned up the image; in Night Music, we find Steve Takis telling Fay, "It's a job--a little island to put your feet on" (III, 2).

By the time he wrote Clash by Night, a work which shows Odets' pessimism at its most intense, the drowning world image had become a conscious symbol which pervades this gloomy Staten Island melodrama. There are first of all the persistent tolling of the bell buoy and the ominous newspaper reports. Jerry's father reads the headline: "Three ships disappear near the tip of Africa ... " (I, 1), and Potter, the proprietor of the dance pavilion, comments: "Yesterday a little girl drowned right off here, too" (I, 2). Jerry Wilenski cannot get the images out of his mind: "Only July an' they're drownin' like flies" (I, 3), he says, as he surveys another photo of a drowned girl with her father looking down. Later, when he is about to lose his own daughter, Gloria, to Earl and Mae, the image returns to him in his drunkenness (II, 2). Mae, too, in her account to Earl of her courtroom battles with the relatives of the Pennsylvania politician she loved, says, "I like to drowned in outraged Irish!" (I, 2), and, at the beginning of Act II, remarks, "A silly line keeps running through my mind--'Three ships disappear near the tip of Africa.'" Earl Pfeiffer thinks of himself, at 38, as a man "floating ... " and, drinking heavily, he tells a waiter, "I'm my own party, son ... a party of thirty-eight sinkin' in a boat" (I, 2).

Thus, by linking the principal characters and the setting of Clash by Night to this central symbol, Odets achieves a poetic and haunting effect. One suspects he had read Eliot's "The Dry Salvages," where the tolling bell buoy sounds a mournful note in a tidal swell that covers the wrecks of sunken ships and drowned fishermen. For Odets, the symbol becomes an objective correlative for the human situation of agonized and unhappy lovers--unhappy because they are separated by loneliness and guilt--as well as a world threatened by Fascism and imminent war.

There is less drowning-world imagery in The Big
Knife than in Odets' other plays, but I think it hardly accidental that Charlie Castle is a bathtub suicide. In the climactic scene, Coy notes water dripping through the ceiling,
and after the door upstairs is forced, Marion returns and
"Her light dress is badly stained with blood and water"
(Stage Direction, III, 2). When "her grief bursts," she expresses it "in one iterated, pleadingly anguished word:
Help! ... Help! ... Help!! ... Help!!! ..." Whatever aid
she is imploring will never arrive in time to help rescue
her and her drowned husband.

In The Country Girl, obviously Frank Elgin is a drowning man; as Phil Cook expresses it, "He's been laying in
pickle for a good ten years!" (I, 1). But Georgie, Frank's
wife, shares with him the sense of their subterranean existence and metaphorically sums up the distance they must
travel: "We're both of us miles behind. Don't try to catch
up all at once. We both know what's happened in the past.
We'll have to live one day at a time, without resentments
and evasions. We're at the bottom--" (I, 4).

In his last play, Odets' account of the flood that God
sent to destroy the earth is the culmination of all the symbolic flood and drowning imagery that had conveyed his per-
ception of a world "going under." Odets does not suggest
specifically what the sins or iniquities were that caused God
to visit this terrible doom on His creations, but there is a
sense in which the early symbol of a world drowning because
of economic injustice is contained as the nucleus within the
larger implications of this global disaster. Shem, the greedy
and materialistic son, stands for the earlier instances of in-
equities, which were, for Odets, iniquities. Noah's vision
is unequivocal: "A rain. He'll bring a flood--a flood of
waters--so much rain the whole damn place will be drowned
off!" (1). And when his vision is confirmed in Scene 5 and
the rain begins to fall in sheets and torrents, turning the
roads into small rivers and sending darkness over the land,
Odets has his nightmarish vision fulfilled: "... the world
seems to shake with thunder.... NOAH lets himself be led
like a child [to the Ark]. More lashing electricity in the
air. THE OLD MEN [denied access to the Ark by God's
commandments] are stone fixtures in the dripping landscape.
An appalling atmosphere" (Stage Directions, 5).

Other symbol clusters of negation that permeate Odets'

plays are those referring to sleep and death. In his plays
sleep does not merely represent death and decay in the
familiar poetic convention; it also symbolizes a state of being
in which characters are unconscious of the social realities of
the world around them.   In addition, sleep often suggests the
monotony of daily existence.   These recurrent metaphors
create a somnambulistic world in which characters are unaware of or unable to cope with impending disaster.

Jacob, in Awake and Sing!, first poses the warning
quite literally when he argues politics with his jeering family:

> Did you found a piece of earth where you could
> live like a human being and die with the sun on
> your face?   Tell me, yes, tell me.   I would like
> to know myself.   But on these questions, on this
> theme--the struggle for existence--you can't make
> an answer.   The answer I see in your face ... the
> answer is your mouth can't talk.   In this dark cor-
> ner you sit and you die....   (II, 1)[23]

In II, 2, just before Jacob commits suicide, Ralph fingers
his shattered Caruso records and says that Bessie did not
have to do it.   Moe snaps: "Tough tit!   Now I can sleep in
the morning," and the word "sleep," in context, takes on
symbolic meaning.   Myron launches into his memories of the
Great Blizzard of his boyhood, while Moe plays cards and
hums a tune he learned in World War I:

> "Lights are blinking while you're drinking,
> That's the place where the good fellows go.
> Good-by to all your sorrows,
> You never hear them talk about the war,
> In the land of Yama Yama
> Funicalee, funicala, funicalo...."

The effect here is one accomplished by mood--not words:
though the word "sleep" is mentioned only once, Odets conveys a sense of characters taking refuge in nostalgia or a
feigned indifference, quite oblivious to Jacob's approaching
suicide or to its meaning.

The sleep symbol is so much a part of the central
theme of Paradise Lost that it is difficult to trace all of its
ramifications.   First, the entire Gordon clan is unconscious
of the fact that people are starving to death in "the richest
city in the world."   When Mr. Pike shows Clara Gordon a

sketch of a dead man he made at the garbage dump, she exclaims: "It sounds like something that happens only in a foreign country!" (I). Ben's pipe dream of "a swell berth waiting for me in Wall Street" (I) is certainly naive, and Libby Michaels shares his naiveté since she tells Kewpie: "I married a man with a big future" (I). Aggressively, Kewpie grabs her, exclaiming: "A sleeping clam at the bottom of the ocean, but I'll wake you up" (I). (Note how deftly the sleep symbol corresponds with the drowned world image.) Leo Gordon is one of the mental ostriches in the play, and after the shop delegation discloses the bad conditions at the factory, his shock elicits a remark from Rogo: "Oh, you sleep, Boss" (I).

By the end of Act I, death images have also infiltrated the play: we have heard Gus Michaels' account of the death of Mrs. Michaels in an open-air car; Sam Katz has threatened, "Some day they'll find me hanging from a chandelier"; and Leo, Gus, and Mr. Pike have tipsily remembered their dead fathers. When in Act II financial calamity overwhelms the Gordons because of Katz's embezzlement of funds, the audience is prepared to accept Sam's agonized cry: "I died so far back...." In Act III, in response to Clara's puzzled question, "Why did we wait so long?" we are given the answer in a virtual monologue by Paul, the homeless man Leo calls in from the street:

> Why, you're sleeping! All over the country people sleeping. Don't argue! Like Napoleon, I been on that battle field. All over millions dreaming of democracy and liberty which don't exist. That's how it comes out on my knitting machine.... I look at you and see myself seven years back. I been there. This kind of dream paralyzes the will--confuses the mind. Courage goes. Daring goes ... and in the nights there is sighing.... You had a sorta little paradise here. Now you lost the paradise. That should teach you something. But no! You ain't awake yet....

The play ends with Leo's peroration, which includes the line, "Everywhere now men are rising from their sleep," but there is irony (which I do not believe Odets intended) in that the youngest son, Julie, is dying of sleeping sickness before our eyes.

Julie Gordon is certainly the most notable sleeper in

the play, but he seems a weak conception precisely because
he is a walking symbol. In Act I, he appears in bathrobe
and slippers, studying the stock quotations in the newspapers
and remarking, "The stock market was a lifeless affair
today." Obviously, he is meant to embody the sickness and
decay of a capitalist system blindly stumbling to its doom.
In Act II, dressed in evening clothes, he resembles an undertaker, and in Act III he sits in a wheel chair, hardly audible,
as Clara reports: "'United aircraft'--it's an active stock, he
says." In a discussion following a television production of
Paradise Lost, Harold Clurman referred to the symbolic
function of Julie Gordon as "natural and unforced." I cannot
agree; he has no function in the play other than to "stand for"
something and he clutters up what is, in many respects, a
remarkable work.

Other of Odets' plays use the sleep symbol less centrally. In Golden Boy, Joe tells his manager's girl: "Lorna
darling, you won't let me wake you up! I feel it all the
time--you're half dead, and you don't know it!" (II, 2). She
replies defensively: "All I want is peace and quiet, not love.
I'm a tired old lady, Joe, and I don't mind being what you
call 'half dead.'" But she is only shamming and fighting her
fears because, like Ben Stark in Rocket to the Moon, she
cannot truly be alive in a mechanical relationship. Mr.
Prince had warned Ben Stark of his daughter's destructive
grip: "She's got you where she wants you.... Like an iceberg, three-quarters under water," and had urged him, "make
a motto for yourself: 'Out of the coffin by Labor Day!'" (I).
Ben, already attracted to Cleo, muses: "A man falls asleep
in marriage. And after a time he wants to keep on sleeping,
undisturbed. I'm surprised how little I've thought about it.
Gee!--What I don't know would fill a book" (I). But it is
doubtful, to me at least, that after Ben has had his amorous
adventure he has awakened to full consciousness, since his
last words in the play are again: "Sonofagun! ... What I
don't know would fill a book!" (III).

In Night Music, Fay is in flight from the monotonous
life of her parents in Philadelphia, and Steve Takis cannot
help blurting out to her father: "... she objects to the dead
life there, Mr. Tucker. She says you're all half alive....
I wouldn't tell a lie--you look like an undertaker to me!"
(II, 2). It is not monotony but the far deeper misery of
alienation that prompts Earl Pfeiffer in Clash by Night to
tell Mae, "with a certain gloomy excitement: You were born
an' now you'd like to get unborn! That's why I drink this
varnish, lady--to get unborn!" (I, 3).

The protagonists of the later plays, in some of their attitudes, are no less lethargic; in Thoreau's sense, none of them is truly "awake." Marion, in The Big Knife, tries to arouse her somnolent husband: "Charlie, you're half asleep right now! I haven't seen you sparkle since the day Billy was born! ... Now you act with droopy eyes--they have to call you away from a card game" (I). Yet Charlie is aware that his talent, as well as the wife and friend who epitomize his lost idealism, are all leaving him, and he tells Marion:

> It's all a bleak and bitter dream, a real dish of
> doves. The only friends I can keep are the classy
> pimps, like Coy. There's only two ways to forget
> everything--get drunk or stick a pencil in your eye
> (II).

Those doves in Charlie's colorful metaphor actually appear in Act II as mourning doves who try to awaken him. He imitates their sound and, after Hank leaves for New York, recalls them again as he turns to face Coy's and Hoff's murderous designs on Dixie Evans. The doves prefigure his death, for their source is biblical--the same beautiful prayer that Fay reads for Steve Takis in Night Music:

> My heart is sore pained within me; and the ter-
> rors of death are fallen upon me. Fearfulness
> and trembling are come upon me, and horror hath
> overwhelmed me. And I said, Oh that I had wings
> like a dove! for then would I fly away, and be at
> rest.... (II, 5).

It would be surprising if there was no sleep reference in The Country Girl; we find one when Bernie Dodd visits the shabby furnished room west of Eighth Avenue where Frank and Georgie Elgin live, and where Georgie burns in-cense "to cut the restaurant odors from down below." Georgie capsulizes the drowsy atmosphere, emblematic of their lives: "You could fall asleep here and not wake up till they called you for the Judgment Day" (I, 2).

And when God visits a judgment on mankind in The Flowering Peach, He first imparts it to the slumbering Noah who, in turn, "Dazed, half in sleep" (Stage Direction, 1), recounts the horror of his vision to Esther. Noah had gone out many times before to "preach repentance to the world!" (6) and hurt his head against the stone wall of evil; then, his worries and troubles and bills began to accumulate--"I

began to drink! I started to go down!" (6). Now he has
been called upon again, but he shrinks from the message he
must deliver: "You're talking a total destruction of the
whole world an' this is something terrible ... ! Am I awake
or am I asleep? I'm awake, but I wish I was dead" (1).

To balance the negative forces of a drowning world
inhabited by sleeping men and women, many of whom long
for "easeful death," Odets' psychic landscape contains two
counter-forces, powerful in their life-affirming qualities.
The first of these is a symbol cluster that stands for fertility and the life cycle of birth, growth, and fruition. Its
images are redolent of lush tropical vegetation, of procreation and sexual desire and, sometimes, are accompanied by
a note of sadness at the transiency of man's earth-bound
appetites and lusts. Odets has varied perspectives in which
he views these fertility images: sometimes he uses them
for ironic or humorous effect; often they swell with the
vitality of life itself and merge with a yearning for transcendence.

In his earliest success, Lefty, Agate's triumphant
speech at the play's climax contains some of Odets' best-
known lines: "WE'RE STORMBIRDS OF THE WORKING
CLASS ... Christ, cut us up to little pieces. We'll die for
what is right! put fruit trees where our ashes are!" Yet
the strident assertion that life, collectively, will go on is
undercut by Odets' recognition that, individually, it does not.
In Till the Day I Die, just before her last meeting with the
doomed Ernst, Tillie reminisces and foreshadows his death:
"I was a good child. I believed in God. In summer I ate
mulberries from our own tree. In late summer the ground
was rotten where they fell" (7).

In Awake and Sing!, the orange that Moe Axelrod re-
quests from Jacob becomes a microcosm which symbolically
expresses many things: Moe's sensual nature, his anger and
cynicism, and the family's deprivation. Jacob plays a Caruso
record and, as the two sit down to pinochle, Moe says:

>   MOE: Ever see oranges grow? I know a certain
>   place--One summer I laid under a tree and let
>   them fall right in my mouth.
>   JACOB (off, the music is playing; the card game
>   begins): "L'Africana" ... a big explorer comes
>   on a new land--"O Paradiso." From act four

this piece. Caruso stands on the ship and looks
on a Utopia. You hear? "Oh paradise! Oh
paradise on earth! Oh blue sky, oh fragrant
air--"
MOE: Ask him does he see any oranges? (I)

Later, when Moe has taunted Hennie about her forthcoming
marriage to Sam Feinschreiber--"Christ, it's suicide! Sure,
kids you'll have, gold teeth, get fat, big in the tangerines--"
(I)--he once again spits out his sexual frustration in terms
of a fruit image: "What the hell kind of house is this it
ain't got an orange!!" (I).

      Hennie Berger (whose first name signals her procrea-
tive role in the play), after she has given birth to her unwanted child, is jokingly promised "a little nest egg" by
Uncle Morty when he dies. He adds, "You like eggs? Ha?"
(II, 1). At the play's end, she rejects this distant prospect
and runs off for present happiness with Moe, who says:
"Mom can mind the kid. She'll go on forever, Mom. We'll
send money back, and Easter eggs" (III). Murray has linked
this line to the resurrection motif in Awake and Sing! and
noted how it "reveals a high degree of verbal unity in the
play."24 But he has failed to include an earlier blistering
exchange between the lovers:

      HENNIE: Why don't you lay an egg, Axelrod?
      MOE: I laid a few in my day, Feinschreiber.
      Hard-boiled ones too (II, 1).

It is this alternation of ironic tone and associative imagery
that gives the play its rich texture and organic unity. At
the end of Awake and Sing!, Odets can even impart a plaintive note; Myron encounters Hennie, who is departing, and
Ralph, and says, "No fruit in the house lately. Just a lone
apple. "

      In Paradise Lost, we find still another technique Odets
uses to enhance the fertility symbolism: it is Clara Gordon's
famous tag line, "Take a piece of fruit, " which she says
twice to Gus and once to Mr. Pike and Julie. Though she
is the most practical character in the play, Clara is also
the archetypal mother, dispensing food and largess and,
symbolically, representing the Life Force that Leo invokes
in his optimistic closing speech: "Heartbreak and terror are
not the heritage of mankind! The world is beautiful. No
fruit tree wears a lock and key. " In contrast to Clara, her

daughter Pearl is an ivory-tower artist who, after her sweetheart Felix leaves her, retreats into musical isolation. Mr.
Pike makes her sterility apparent to us, though not to Pearl,
when he taunts her by using a variant of the fertility image:

> PIKE: ... There she is alone in her room with
> the piano--the white keys banked up like lilies
> and she suckin' at her own breast.
> PEARL: You must be crazy! What are you talk-
> ing about?
> PIKE: You liar and traitor to your own heart's
> story! You! Lay awake dreamin' at night.
> Don't you know it ain't comin', that land of
> your dreams, unless you work for it?
> PEARL: I'm not sex starved, do you hear? I'm
> not! (II)

A comic variant of the fertility symbol in Golden Boy
emerges from the relationship between Siggie, the cab driver,
and his wife, Anna. Her repeated cries of "Come to bed,
Siggie," and his "What the hell's so special in bed?" are in
counterpoint to Mr. Carp's disdainful "Women ... the less
we have to do with women the better. As Schopenhauer
says, 'Much ado about nothing ... the comedy of reproduc-
tion'" (I, 2). It is not surprising that this cab-driving Bene-
dick calls his Beatrice "Anna-banana" (I, 5).

Cleo Singer exudes sensuality in the heat-soaked office
of Dr. Ben Stark in Rocket to the Moon. Mr. Prince informs her: "You're a girl like candy, a honeydew melon--
a delicious girl.... I'm talking to you from the roots up!"
(II, 1). But her blend of vulnerable naiveté and romantic
aspiration inspires the scholarly dentist to a lyrical allu-
sion--"How green you are and fresh in this old world" (II,
2)--lines spoken by Pandulph in Shakespeare's King John.

Without metaphorical language, Odets foreshadows the
sexual relationship of Earl Pfeiffer and Mae Wilenski in
Clash by Night with Earl's comment: "So this is Staten
Island! It smells like the country out here--fulla trees and
bushes" (I, 1). Later, Kress (Jerry's uncle, who is depicted
as a Father Coughlin follower, a bigoted harbinger of Fascism) goads Jerry into avenging himself violently on the
adulterous pair, saying: "Two bawdy thieves! As for you,
it's simple--tossed off like a sucked-out orange!" (II, 2).

In the mouths of sexually aggressive characters, the

fruit imagery sometimes conveys a torrid lust: Kewpie tells
Libby, "You and the soft juicy body, like a mushmelon"
(Paradise Lost, I); Moody tells Lorna, "Push your mouth
over...." " (Golden Boy, I, 1), as though it were an edible
on the table. Cleo's thawing of Stark's "iceberg" exterior
is shown by Odets without recourse to metaphor but in sear-
ingly explicit stage directions: "Now they move in on each
other. Everything else gone, they are together in a full,
fierce embrace, together in a swelter of heat, misunderstanding, loneliness and simple sex" (Rocket to the Moon, II,
2).

It is remarkable how often the fruit and flower images
appear in Odets' plays whenever he wants to stress the power
of the life cycle. In Night Music, Steve Takis even attributes
such imagery to George Washington: "What this man said--
(Pointing to Washington's statue) Apples and bread for every
man, a flower for his girl! Whatta you think of that?" (II,
4). Charlie Castle's answer in The Big Knife might be
favorable except that, as he cynically informs Coy about the
Hollywood scene, "California, think of it--a place where an
honest apple tree won't grow.... " (II).

In The Country Girl, the fertility images virtually
disappear, possibly because Georgie Elgin's relationship with
Frank is a sterile one; she is resigned to her role as ser-
vant and guardian of Frank's fragile ego:

> GEORGIE: I haven't felt like a woman in ten years.
> FRANK: I suppose that's my fault.
> GEORGIE: Summer dies, autumn comes, a fact of
>   nature--nobody's fault (I, 4).

Only once is Georgie's sexual nature rekindled. This occurs
in the highly charged scene when Bernie Dodd "kisses her
fully on the mouth. " The Stage Directions tell the story:
"She seems to come out of sleep" (II, 2).

But if the fertility symbolism is muted in The Country Girl, it breaks out in lush abundance in The Flowering
Peach. From the title on, the entire play abounds in frequent references to procreation: the gathering of the harvest,
the purchase of seed for replanting after the Flood (the mysterious Kazan cucumber seed), [25] the co-mingling of the animals on the Ark, the lovers' encounters before the Flood
and aboard ship, the flowers that adorn Esther's forlorn hat,
the green leaf in the mouth of the dove, and the final landing

beside the blooming tree, with Noah's three daughters-in-law big with child. At the end, Japheth breaks off a small branch of the tree and hands it to Rachel, who gives "The precious gift" to Noah:

> RACHEL: Now we are a story--a legend.
> JAPHETH: What's ahead, Poppa?
> NOAH (holding up the bloom): This is ahead ... a fruitful world ... the people need happiness (9).

The fertility symbol clusters often merge with a yearning for transcendence. Noah's last speech to the Lord is a good example: "You know what I want, Lord. Just like you guarantee each month, with a woman's blood, that men will be born ... give such a sign that you won't destroy the world again ... " (9). If the fertility symbols demonstrate an immutable cycle of life and death, Odets' plays also exhibit a symbolic cluster of images and allusions to resurrection and rebirth, embodying a poet's hope that somehow the forces of darkness will not prevail over man's spirit. We must not think of this pattern as eschatological, however. Often it is used in an ironic sense, and sometimes it merely reveals the secular playwright's reliance upon orthodox allusions to make a point. For example, the episode in which the producer's stenographer equates The Communist Manifesto and Revelations in The Young Actor scene in Lefty (omitted by Odets from the Modern Library edition)26 is decidedly ironic. Taking pity on the jobless Philip, the stenographer offers to lend him money and educate him:

> STENOGRAPHER: One dollar buys ten loaves of bread, Mister. Or one dollar buys nine loaves of bread and one copy of The Communist Manifesto. Learn while you eat. Read while you run....
> PHILIP: Manifesto? What's that? What is that, what you said ... Manifesto?
> STENOGRAPHER: Stop off on your way out--I'll give you a copy. From Genesis to Revelation, Comrade Philips! "And I saw a new earth and a new heaven; for the first earth and the first heaven were passed away; and there was no more sea."

Soon after (or perhaps before) he had written these propagandistic lines, Odets depicted a symbolic parallel to Christ's passion in Awake and Sing!, where Jacob is the

Christ-figure who achieves a symbolic resurrection after his
suicide through his influence on the revolutionary consciousness of young Ralph. Ralph's conversion is couched in terms
that remind one of the suddenness of Saul's conversion on the
road to Damascus:

> Did Jake die for us to fight about nickels? No!
> "Awake and sing," he said. Right here he stood
> and said it. The night he died, I saw it like a
> thunderbolt! I saw he was dead and I was born!
> I swear to God, I'm one week old! ... (III)

The passage from Isaiah that Jacob had quoted--"Awake and
sing, ye that dwell in dust"--is Old Testament rather than
New; it reenforces the idea that the Bergers live in economic
squalor and the life-in-death of mental torpor. But the context of the scriptural passage suggests that redemption only
comes when the false idols are smashed and the one God wor-
shiped--here, obviously, the idols are those of the market-
place, and the God is Marx.

Christ-figures abound in Odets' early work: Lefty
can so be regarded; after all, he is a martyr found in a
kind of stable--the car barns--with a bullet in his head. It
seems ironic that this God of radical action never appears,
and his work must be done by disciples like Agate, who
spread the new religion. In Till the Day I Die, Tillie, in
bearing the martyred Ernst's child, achieves his symbolic
rebirth also: "Let us hope we will both live to see strange
and wonderful things. 27 Perhaps we will die before then.
Our children will see it then. Ours!" (5). Yet another side
of Odets is willing to risk a flippant denial of the resurrection motif; Moe, in Awake and Sing!, remarks: "If there's
reincarnation in the next life I wanna be a dog and lay in a
fat lady's lap" (II, 2).

Similar ambiguities exist in later plays. Leo, in
Act III of Paradise Lost, intones: "Emerson was a great
man. He promised men they would walk the earth like
gods"--to which Paul, the homeless man, retorts: "Then he
was a goddam liar!" And in Golden Boy, Moody, in a jubilant mood, tells Lorna: "Call it intuition: I feel like the
Resurrection" (I, 3)--a prediction which turns out to be
patently false. It seems clear that Odets avoided the orthodox imagery of resurrection in his later plays but that the
theme of rebirth through love--a very American kind of secular redemption--took its place. What, after all, are Cleo

and Ben Stark, Earl Pfeiffer and Mae Wilenski, Marion and
Charlie Castle, Georgie and Frank Elgin, even Steve Takis
and Fay Tucker, striving to achieve but a spiritual rebirth,
a new life, a second chance? Fay even hints at this when
she describes Steve to Rosenberger: "But he's sweet--sweet
... like a hard-boiled Easter egg" (II, 4).

The poet in Odets would like to believe in life-after-
death, but he always stops ironically short. Just before as-
cending the stairs to kill himself, Charlie Castle asks Marion
to play some music on the phonograph. Echoing Shakespeare's
Cleopatra, he first asks for "Something immortal" and then
"wryly" changes his mind: "Anything that's on the machine"
(III, 2). Even in the miraculous union of Bernie Dodd and
Georgie to resurrect the spiritually dead Frank Elgin, there
is loss to balance gain; Bernie Dodd, perhaps because the
ingredient of genuine, giving love is missing from his make-
up, must pay the price of loneliness. And in The Flowering
Peach, where God in His mercy saves an entire family from
the Flood, Esther must die before she reaches the promised
land and there is no sentimental suggestion of a heavenly
reunion with Noah. Nevertheless Odets' trembling on the
brink of revelation is inherent in his singing lyricism; "I
pray a beautiful soul shall enter your boy ..." (9), Noah
tells Rachel, and it makes a powerful affirmation to offset
the negative clusters of drowned world and sleep and death
images.

Between the Hell and the Heaven of Odets' Earthly
Paradise, there lies a purgatory in which men struggle before they are engulfed and doomed by the one or achieve the
serenity of the other. This is the Darwinian world of "fang
and claw" in which, as Bessie Berger knows, "when one
lives in the jungle one must look out for the wild life" (Introduction, Stage Directions, Awake and Sing!). Odets liked
this phrase so much he had Kewpie, a prime example of a
predator, repeat it verbatim in Act I of Paradise Lost. A
colorful assortment of animal types inhabits this metaphoric
jungle in Odets' plays! Merely to survey some of the
creatures Odets finds akin to man demonstrates the range
and force of his social criticism. Sid and Florrie find life
frustrating "for the dogs which is us," and Edna is "a sour
old nag" in Lefty, a play saturated with references to ver-
min, rats and other rodents, mainly of the capitalist variety.
In Awake and Sing! Hennie calls Moe "Gorilla"; Jake sadly
sees himself as an "old horse for hire"; Sam is described

as "a man like a mouse"; Uncle Morty admits his penchant
for goose (although his speech tic is "Quack, Quack"); Moe
says during the war he was "clapped down like a bedbug."
Small wonder that Ralph cries out, "It's like a zoo in this
house" (II, 2), and concludes, "Let me die like a dog, if I
can't get more from life" (III).

It should be clear that Odets seeks the appropriate
metaphor to illuminate a character's essential trait, just as
he attaches symbolic names to characters such as Katz,
Carp, Pike, Drake. In Paradise Lost, Mr. Pike calls Kewpie "a bantam rooster," which he resembles in his mindless
copulation; Kewpie reminds Libby, "You're a little squab, and
you laid right down in the sand with me" (I). Clara calls
Mr. Katz "a wolf," but Odets in his stage directions says
he prowls up and down like "a bitter lion." The circular
motion inside the Gordon home prompts Clara to cry: "My
children walk around the house like wild animals" (II), a
comment she repeats to Julie at the end of Act II.

In Golden Boy, Roxy Gottlieb, despairing of Joe's
reluctance to hit with his full strength, declares: "I got a
right to say it: a mosquito gives out better!" (I, 3), but
later Joe is "like a cat" under the influence of the killer
Fuseli, who drifts around on "cat's feet" (Stage Directions,
II, 1).

In Rocket to the Moon, the perfect metaphor for Stark
is Cleo's: "He stands there like a big shepherd dog" (I),
while Frenchy, who resents Cleo's flirtation with Ben, calls
her both a spider and a moth (II, 2). When she shows some
sign of striking back at those who patronize her, Mr. Prince
warns: "You work here in an office--a regular insect so-
ciety--so don't act like a tiger" (I).

To merely catalogue Odets' colorful animal imagery
would be pointless if we did not understand that he uses
these images to make moral judgments: Willie Wax in Rocket
pompously says, "I'm a lone wolf--" (II, 2), and Frenchy
immediately deflates his pretentiousness by saying, "Bow
wow!"; and in Clash by Night, Earl recalls his ex-spouse,
"Take my wife, she had the morals of a hop-toad" (II, 1).
Animalism does not always have a negative connotation, however. In Night Music, Fay notices early in the play, "You're
like some sort of wild animal, Mr. Takis" (I, 4), but by the
play's finale she has penetrated his outer shell of toughness
and remarks, "You're as proud as a swan, Steve" (III, 2).

It can also be used for comic effect as, in the same play,
when Rosenberger categorizes the lounge at the Hotel Algiers
(where whores congregate) as "a nest of fine-plumed birds"
(I, 3), and Steve, in an obscure metaphor, complains, "I
feel as low as whale dust!" (I, 4).

What Odets was doing with his animal metaphors was
not merely to suggest the jungle world, which novelists like
Dreiser, London, and Crane used to depict man as victim;
Odets believed man had a chance, but only if he did not allow
his brute impulses to dominate what he called "the human"
element. In a letter to John Mason Brown, Odets said: "I
want to find out how mankind can be helped out of the animal
kingdom into the clear sweet air."[28] Thus in Lefty, in contrast with the decadent and boorish producer who insults the
young actor and worries over an operation just performed on
his pet Russian wolfhound, there is the stenographer's kindness to the stranger:

> PHILIP: You treat me like a human being.
> Thanks....
> STENOGRAPHER: You're human!
> PHILIP: I used to think so.

And in Rocket, Cleo protests indignantly to Frenchy: "Sometimes you act as if you're talking to an animal!" (II, 1).
But as long as man fails to achieve his human potential, to
open his heart and act out of compassion and love for his
fellow man, he is metaphorically back in the jungle. The
violence which destroys three lives in Clash by Night may
be traced to misguided judgments of one another by two human beings. There is Earl's condescending estimate of
Jerry: "a baby hippo on two feet!" (I, 2), and Mae's dissatisfied definition of what a "comfortable" man should be to
his woman: "Today they're little and nervous, sparrows!
But I dream of eagles ... I guess I'm cuckoo!" (I, 2).

With such failures of humanity the later plays are concerned, and the images become particularly violent and viru-
lent. Charlie Castle alludes to himself as "a capering
mouse," but the cruelest images are reserved for Coy and
Hoff. One of the nastiest lines in Odets is Coy's description
of his encounter with Dixie Evans: "I turn around and there
she sits, cute as a skinned, parboiled ham" (II). In Coy's
vicious company Charlie ironically remarks: "Catch me a
few moths, Smiley. I wanna burn 'em with matches" (II).
For Hoff, about whom Charlie asks, "Don't I get a chance

to gaff this monster?" (III, 2), Odets uses a lizard image;
but he reserves a better description for the stage directions
in III, 2: "HOFF stands, white and swolen, a veritable puff
adder." This description of the egotistical movie mogul is
rivaled only by Charlie's vision of Patty Benedict, the gossip
columnist: "She keeps coming at me with those great big
lobster claws, and Mr. Castle, he don't like it!" (I).

From the rapacity of Hollywood Odets turns to the
vindictiveness of Broadway drama critics in The Country
Girl: Unger, the playwright, remarks after Frank's bad Boston notices: "Man is to man as the wolf" (II, 1). Frank
Elgin, despite his "nice guy" facade, thinks of manipulating
others as though they were less than human. He tells Bernie of Georgie: "But I know how to handle her now--back-
wards, like a crab" (I, 3). Georgie, too, sees herself as
a fish, but somewhat differently. She tells Bernie: "He's
taught me to be a fish, to swim in any direction, including
up, down, and sideways" (II, 1). Yet at the same time
Frank is frightened that Georgie will stay behind in New
York--"a city full of wolves"--and not accompany him to the
Boston try-outs. This complex man also has the ability to
project his own animalism into the characterization he is
creating on stage. He gives Bernie his impression of the
judge in the play: "A fox--that's the image. Nimble. Quiet.
On the alert, but nothing shows--a rigid face. A concrete
slab for a face ..." (I, 3). Perhaps the progress of Frank
in the real play can best be gauged by his sudden wild spurt
of inspiration on opening night, when he lashes out at the
ingenue, changing from a fox to a lion. As he explains to
Bernie:

> I'm sorry, kid, forgive me--it just came out that
> way! That's what he should do there, the Judge--
> no one wants him, not even his grandchild! And
> suddenly I got the image--they're caging a lion--
> like you shove him in the face! Like they do in
> the circus, with chairs and brooms! And I couldn't
> hold it back ... (II, 3)

If we reflect about The Flowering Peach, we can realize
that the recurring images of animals in Odets have all been
figures of speech by which man measures his quintessential
humanity. For the birds, beasts, and fowl that converge on
Noah's rude home are all equally innocent and deserving of
salvation (although, with Japheth, we can hear the bleating of
the puzzled sheep, most of whom will die). Still, they will

board the Ark two by two, and none of their qualities exclude them. One thinks of Mr. Pike's remark: "Spring! Flowers buddin', birds twitterin'--south wind--and only Man is vile!" (Paradise Lost, III). The voyage of the Ark will demonstrate yet again the purgatorial nature of Odets' jungle: Noah will drink, in Esther's words, "just like a pig" (1); Shem will quarrel with Japheth and shout, "I'll gore him like a bull!" (3); Ham will sidle up to Goldie, call her "snake" and say, "Well, what's up mouse, looking for a cat?" (6). And Noah will address the Almighty and point out: "... a little bitty of an eagle like me ... But you have shrinked away his wings ..." (4), and implore the gift of strength. God miraculously grants him that strength. As his awed family watches, he is metamorphosed into a young man of fifty and "his eyes are eagle-bright" (4). But strength must be both physical and moral and, as always in Odets, the question is whether Man can retain it in some earthly paradise where, as Rachel says, "the world looks washed" (9).

There is another symbolic cluster in Odets' plays which requires examination: those images of cars, planes, boats, and trains that figure centrally in his work and offer an important clue to his psychic landscape. Like other writers during the past 100 years, Odets had to reconcile the machine's awesome power and efficiency with its potential for the dehumanization and enslavement of its very creators. And, like many of his predecessors, Odets was ambivalent in his feelings about the progress of industrialism. Sometimes, like O'Neill in The Hairy Ape, he was pessimistic about its effects on the individual: at other times, like Whitman, he could optimistically incorporate scientific progress into his hope for man's future.

This ambivalence was evident in his early plays. Edna's metaphor in Waiting for Lefty--"We're stalled like a flivver in the snow"--superbly captures the paralysis of gigantic industrial forces during the Depression. Yet Odets has Uncle Morty boast in Awake and Sing!, "My car goes through snow like a dose of salts" (III). He also stresses the airplane's flight across the Bronx sky as a symbol of hope. In the climactic colloquy in III of Awake and Sing!, Ralph says to Bessie: "There ... hear him? The air mail off to Boston. Day or night, he flies away, a job to do. That's us and it's no time to die. " But the ensuing stage business makes Ralph's statement seem equivocal--"The airplane fades off as MYRON gives alarm clock to BESSIE which she begins to wind. " Per-

haps only youth's naiveté can see such a vision; Bessie's
timepiece reminds us of death.   Yet earlier, Ralph had told
Jacob:

> When I was a kid I laid awake at nights and heard
> the sounds of trains ... far-away lonesome sounds ...
> boats going up and down the river.   I used to think
> of all kinds of things I wanted to do.   What was it,
> Jake?   Just a bunch of noise in my head?   (II, 2)

This lyricism perhaps suggests only Ralph's restless ambition
and desire to get away, but it is also reminiscent of Dos
Passos' young man who must meet all the trains and catch
all the buses in U. S. A. --where the dynamic force of a mechanized America is also regarded ambivalently.

In Paradise Lost, Gus' motorcycle becomes an important symbol.   The foolish jester-philosopher's get-rich-
quick schemes are as ludicrous as the dirty white aviator's
helmet and gloves which he wears; in Act III his shiny, beloved
motorcycle lies rusted and discarded in the junk-heap of the
Gordons' few remaining possessions.   In this play, industrialism and its products are seen as useless because the economic system that supports them is in decay. [29]

Joe Bonaparte's Deusenberg in Golden Boy is a mark
of material success that ultimately becomes its purchaser's
coffin.   His death is foreshadowed by Moody's remark about
one of his fighters "who got himself killed in a big, red
Stutz" (I, 1).   But the Deusenberg is also a symbol of raw,
mechanized power correlative to the brutal, almost murderous
drive that characterizes the prizefight world.

> JOE: Those cars are poison in my blood.   When
>   you sit in a car and speed you're looking down
>   at the world.   Speed, speed, everything is
>   speed--nobody gets me!
> LORNA: You mean in the ring?
> JOE: In or out, nobody gets me!   Gee, I like to
>   stroke that gas!
> LORNA: You sound like Jack the Ripper.   (I, 4)

The parallel between automotive power and the boxer's drive
is also seen in Roxy Gottlieb's taunting remark: "Figure it
out--where would you be in a traffic jam?   You know how
to reverse--but to shift in second or high?--nothing!" (I, 3),
and even in his seemingly offhand comment, "I think I'll run

across the street and pick up an eight-cylinder lunch" (I, 3).
The images relating to cars in Golden Boy are all negative
and destructive.

But in Odets' next play, Rocket to the Moon, he
characteristically uses the symbol ambiguously. Mr. Prince
tells Ben Stark: "Iceberg, listen ... why don't you suddenly
ride away, an airplane, a boat! Take a rocket to the moon!
Explode!" (I). The very fact that Odets titles his allegory
of the search for love with a rocket metaphor underscores
his ambivalence. Actually, the lines most relevant to the
title concern building rather than flying, and express a rueful paradox of the aging process. Stark says to Prince:
"Yes, a certain man once said that in our youth we collect
materials to build a bridge to the moon; but in our old age,
he says, we use the materials to build a shack" (I). Perhaps not so coincidentally Ben and Belle are living in a summer dwelling which is described as "a shack at the beach."
At the play's end, Ben presumably recognizes that even a
shack has its conveniences.

In Night Music, Odets continues to regard industrial
power images with guarded optimism. Steve Takis tells Fay,
"Look, I'm an eighty octane guy--Ethyl in my veins--and
I'm sore as hell!" (I, 2), but this is part of his habitual
bluster. Most important in this play is the closing scene,
set at a New York City airport, Steve's point of departure
both from the city and Fay. Odets' description of the scene
at first is almost lyrical:

> The airport on a brisk windy day. Overhead are
> the rich sounds of airport traffic coming and going.
> In the field left, beyond a wire fence, a transport
> plane is warming up: twentieth-century music. A
> bustling sense of excitement is in the air. (III, 2)

But suddenly the mood changes as Steve learns that he has
been fired and is no longer needed, and the plane departs.
"As the plane turns and begins its run down the field, STEVE
and FAY are showered with a miniature typhoon of dust,
gravel and dead leaves, a final indignity" (III, 2). It is only
when Steve and Fay and Rosenberger join hands and march
off to face the future confidently that the optimistic note
returns. Odets' final stage direction before the curtain is:
"Overhead the airplanes are zooming and singing" (III, 2).

The moral, then, is plain. Industrial power is

regarded as a projection of man's inner nature, and whether
it works for good or evil will depend on the uses to which
he puts it.   For example, if we construe the movie projector
as a complicated mechanism related to the other machine
images we have been tracing, then the final scene in Clash
by Night makes Odets' darkening, ambivalent attitude apparent.
Since, as Charlie Castle states, "This whole movie thing is
a murder of the people" (The Big Knife, III, 2), the description of the projection booth is apt: "The interior of the projection booth is lighted with a typical bluish glare; the projection machinery hums and buzzes: altogether, a veritable
picture of some minor hell!" (Clash by Night, II, 3).

   In The Big Knife, this idea is pursued in thematic,
not imagistic, terms, and in The Country Girl--Odets' most
psychologically inward play--there are no machine symbols;
here the theater itself becomes a metaphor for man's inner
life.   But, as is repeatedly the case with these clusters,
The Flowering Peach gathers up and summarizes a major
symbol's meaning.   Here the construction of the Holy Ark
offers a vehicle for a chosen family to escape the flood.   It
is carefully built by cunning hands, mainly by Japheth, although it is a communal effort.   Noah insists that the family
ride out the flood by placing absolute faith in God's ability to
guide them to safety.   But Japheth had insisted that a rudder
be built, and when Noah is in drunken despair and the ship
is in danger of foundering, Japheth steers them all to safety
despite his father's objections.   No construct of man's brain
and hands--even though it be divinely inspired--can be left
to the winds of chance but must be guided and controlled by
human effort.   As Noah had said, "Now it's in man's hands
to make or destroy the world" (9).

   Odets claimed in an interview: "A good composer was
lost when I took up writing";[30] he collected classical records
all his mature life and, according to Mendelsohn, "identified
himself closely with Beethoven until his death in 1963."[31]
With so avid an interest in music, it is no surprise that
Odets used a fiddler-hero both in Golden Boy and in Humoresque, one of his better screen plays.   He tried to orchestrate
entire plays such as Night Music and Paradise Lost; there is
not one of his eleven plays that does not contain music, and
many have references to musical works, instruments and musicians.   I shall examine a few examples of his use of music
that have so far escaped notice.

   Most critics have seen Jacob's identification with

Caruso's recording of L'Africane as a projection of his disillusionment and his yearning for rebirth in a Utopia.[32]   What
no critic has remarked is that, after he has protested the
ensnarement of Sam Feinschreiber and been rebuked like a
child by Bessie near the end of Act I, Jacob puts on a different Caruso record--the lament from The Pearlfishers--
in keeping with his shift in mood.   Nor is music a matter
of the ear, solely, in Awake and Sing!: twice it is evoked
metaphorically.   Moe sees in Hennie's eyes "Ted Lewis playing the clarinet--some of those high crazy notes!" (II, 1),
and later tells her, "Say the word--I'll tango on a dime" (III).
Music enters the play also through a tragicomic announcement of Sam about Hennie: "She said I'm a second fiddle in
my own house" (II, 2), to which Bessie responds, after she
has calmed the worried husband down and he has left, "Second
fiddle.   By me he don't even play in the orchestra" (II, 2).

A technical and effective use of music occurs in Lefty
when the separating lovers, Sid and Florrie, dance to "a
cheap, sad, dance tune" played on a small portable phonograph.   "The music stops, but the scratching record continues to the end of the scene. " Odets rasps at the audience's nerves as the tense and expectant Florrie waits for
Sid to say goodby.

Musical metaphors came easily to Odets.   However,
in Paradise Lost his purpose seems to have been more ambitious: to make Pearl's piano playing symbolic of the bourgeois, sterile values of the Gordon clan, and at the same
time, to let the music she plays complement the varying
moods of the action and characters.   Pearl's piano playing
is interrupted only at critical moments in the first two acts:
twice to allow her to make brief stage appearances "down-
stairs" with the family and to see Felix, and once when she
is drowned out by the blare of patriotic music coming from
the radio.   In Act III, she is finishing a piece of music at
the opening, after which she comes down to learn that her
piano is being repossessed.   Kenneth Burke thought that
"the correspondence between this music [Pearl's] and other
contents might be got by looking for some common quality
of action or speech that runs through all the events on the
stage concurrent with the playing offstage (including entrances
and exits of characters, a kind of break that often supplies
significant cues). "[33] My search has turned up no common
quality of speech or action, but rather indicates that Odets
provided verbal cues similar to those that mark the score
of the accompanist in a silent movie.   For example, is it

accidental in Act I that Pearl begins to play Für Elise--the
only piece of Beethoven's that might be called banal!--pre-
cisely when Libby remarks about Ben, "He might even go in
the movies" (I)?   Near the end of Act II "PEARL begins to
range over the keyboard in light fleet exercises," but when
the tragic news of Ben's death becomes apparent, she "passes
into a furious section of the sonata [Beethoven's] as the curtain falls." Again, it does not seem coincidental that her
piece ends in Act III, precisely when we learn Julie is to be
taken to the hospital.   Somewhere there undoubtedly exists
the original musical score for Paradise Lost.

In Golden Boy, Odets' unflagging interest in music is
enunciated by Mr. Bonaparte with an Italian version of "music
hath charms"; as he puts it, "Music is the great cheer-up in
the language of all countries" (I, 2).   In I, 3, Joe and Lorna
talk on the park bench, with carousel music and traffic noises
nearby, as well as a blinking traffic light.   This scene has
been acutely analyzed by Edward Murray as one with many
symbolic referents--the carousel music here reminding us of
Joe's desire to play the violin. 34

Murray also has an excellent analysis of music as "a
symbol of the good life" for Cleo in Rocket to the Moon, 35
though he does not note Mr. Prince's remark about his
money, "... maybe I'll leave it to Jascha Heifetz" (I), which
would seem to support his thesis, nor the voice of the radio
crooner heard from the Hotel Algiers at the opening of Act
III, which circumscribes the good life symbolism with a
suggestion of exotic sin and reminds us of Ben's infidelity.

Though there are good discussions of Night Music by
Murray, Mendelsohn, and Weales, I think the artistry with
which Odets set about to write a tone poem of New York
City still has not been sufficiently appreciated. 36   Steve's
and Fay's misadventures on the island of Manhattan during
one weekend are so arranged that there is a fusion of
rapidly changing set locales (eight in all), a lyrical score
by the composer Hanns Eisler--used primarily to bridge
scenes but also "to heighten the sound and feel of the city,"37
and the on-stage musical interludes and verbal arias.   The
latter are strategically placed and connected to the play's
theme of homelessness.   For example, in I, 4, when Steve
discovers the broken-down harmonium in Fay's bedroom, he
begins to improvise a tune which Odets describes as "the
music of a lost boy, gloomy, apprehensive, lonely." The
words are plaintive, anticipating Bob Dylan and other folk
singers, but would not have succeeded then on Tin Pan Alley:

> Move over, Mr. Horse. Gimme room in your
> stall. How are the oats, Brother Horse? Gimme
> room in your stall. Didn't you ever wish you was
> dead? Brother Horse, giddiap, Brother Horse!
> I got those nobody-nothing blues! I'm feelin' like
> the King of the Jews! Oh, you Brother Horse,
> eating oats by the peck. Brother Horse, Brother
> Horse, send a dish over to me. How's your father?
> How's your mother, Brother Horse? Got no
> mother, got no father, anywhere! Some fun,
> Brother Horse!

Odets mocks commercial music in II, 5, by introducing
Rosenberger's song-plugging brother-in-law, Al, who impro-
vises on the same harmonium "a new popular ballad"--a
dreadful clichéd number about "Feeling ever so blue/Up, up
in my penthouse built for two...." And, in the same act
and scene, Steve reveals his love and need for Fay, not in
words but by unpacking his clarinet from his suitcase and
playing while she listens in the adjoining bedroom--"Whatever his pride and fear of repudiation prevented him from
saying to the girl he is now able to express in his music"
(Stage Direction). Thus the brave speech Fay makes at the
World's Fair, which has been anticipated musically, sums
up the play's optimistic credo:

> Crickets are my favorite animals in all the world.
> They're never down in the mouth. All night they
> make their music.... Night music.... If they
> can sing, I can sing. I'm more than them. We're
> more than them.... We can sing through any
> night! (II, 4)

The jazzed-up optimism, the sentimentalizing of character in
Night Music, will remain subjects of critical censure, but
the felicity of the basic musical metaphor will not. The
play does not fail in its technical execution, but rather because of the forced nature of its uplifting conclusion.

One could linger over other examples of Odets' use
of music which convey a symbolic point--the father's playing
of an old Polish folk song on his concertina in Clash by
Night "about the little old house, where you wanna go back,
but you can't find out where it is no more ..." (I, 1); or
the phonograph at curtain rise of The Big Knife which is
playing "a snatch of French operetta, a love duet by two
eminent Parisian players" (Stage Direction), perfectly

capturing the opéra bouffe quality of the world Charlie Castle
inhabits and wishes to escape. But Odets' happiest invention
was surely the mythical "gitka" which mysteriously appears
in scene 2 of The Flowering Peach and "is heard singing a
wordless, sad and delicate song" (Stage Direction) as the
animals gather. Noah makes a special pet of it, and it sings
at the opening of scene 6 (which opened Act II when the play
was produced originally); and again at the end of scene 8,
when Esther dies, it lifts its little falsetto voice in a mourning song. Then, in the final scene, after the Ark has reached
land, it is entirely ignored. It is as though Odets uses the
gitka to symbolize the singing lyricism and idealism which
he felt most men capable of, and without which men would
perish: the gitka is the living vessel within the Ark in which
is transported the sacred gift of poetry.

I shall turn now to Odets' use of scenic properties to
enhance the "realistic symbolism" which was his characteristic
technique. As a poet of the theater Odets revealed again and
again his mastery of making the visual emblem evoke more
than words could say. A few selected examples from early
and late plays will be sufficient to demonstrate this point.
In Lefty, Fatt, the corrupt union boss, smokes a cigar during
the "present" scenes and blows smoke frequently over the
lighted circles in which the flashback episodes are played
out. Robert Warnock has commented: "The retention of the
background characters who frame the flashback episodes represents visually the interrelationship of the two time levels.
Fatt's cigar, which cuts across the levels, symbolizes his
selfish prosperity through his sinister power over the
others. "[38] And he might have added that it may possibly
symbolize the smokescreen of lies with which Fatt habitually
hides the truth from the men.

Mary McCarthy, in her essay "The American Realist
Playwrights," remarked of Awake and Sing!: "I can still
see the bowl of fruit on the table, slightly to the left of
stage center, and hear the Jewish mother interrupting who-
ever happened to be talking, to say, 'Have a piece of fruit.'
That bowl of fruit, which was the Jewish Bronx, remains
more memorable as a character than many of the people in
the drama. "[39] Miss McCarthy evidently had confused the
earlier drama with Paradise Lost. It is surprising that she
makes no reference to the other prominent visual symbol in
this play--the statue Ben received for running in the Olympic
games, which symbolically reflects the attitudes of several

characters: Gus' admiring salute as he mutters "How like a
god!" (I); Ben's self-disgust, registered by spitting on it;
and Kewpie's homosexual love, revealed by wiping it clean
with a handkerchief (II). But the main significance of the
statue emerges when Julie, having just observed Ben's and
Kewpie's actions, asks Leo: "Who was it had the wooden
horse, Poppa? The Trojans?" (II), to which Leo, oblivious
to the irony, replies: "The Greeks. They made a beautiful
civilization. " Ben's statue, like the Trojan horse, is also
hollow, since the bourgeois values it represents are phony
and, in Odets' view, will not lead to a beautiful civilization
but to a second fall of Troy.

Another favorite Odets scenic symbol was the Hotel
Algiers, which figures in both Rocket and Night Music. It
is first evoked obliquely when Mr. Prince observes it from
the window of Ben Stark's dental office, and remarks:
"Hmmm, I know a bookie in there. What must go on in
those rooms at night ... " (Rocket, I). And in I, 3, of
Night Music, Odets brings us into its lobby, where we discover the hotel is "as unsavory as its name ... a haunt
where questions are seldom asked and rooms are rented
sans luggage or marriage ring. " It has a "jazz-record
machine" and a "nickel gambling machine. " It is presided
over by Mr. George, whose "character feeling is that of
the old song In the Good Old Summer, " Teddy, the Italian
hotel "Strong Man, " and Marty, the bellboy, an artful dodger--
"his pockets are full of amatory supplies" (Stage Directions).
All in all, it is Odets' middle-class Inferno, and every prop
in the mise en scène, from a telephone booth to a pinball
game, is utilized to juxtapose the innocent lovers against a
background of seedy decadence.

There is one other scenic property that Odets employs symbolically in The Country Girl which is vital to the
play. This is the pier glass in Frank's dressing room.
Although the main theme of The Country Girl is redemption
through love, an important motif in the play is deception--
the lies we tell each other--and the consequent difficulty of
distinguishing illusion from reality. The pier glass mirrors
the deceit and distortion that characterize Frank Elgin's
world--a topic that is introduced in the first act when Frank,
doing a "runthrough" for Bernie from the play-within-a-play,
reads: "You said when you'd grow big I'd grow small.
Children have that delusion, don't they?" (I, 3). This observation about the daughter in the rehearsed play is an
analogue to what has happened between Bernie Dodd and

Frank Elgin in the real play, and the quoted lines signal the
central polarity of truth vs. illusion. The pier glass before
which Frank postures in I, 5, is a silent mirror to the lies
and half-truths and evasions he employs in presenting an un-
ruffled surface to Bernie, Phil, Unger, and the others, while
revealing his real worries and insecurities to Georgie. Then,
in II, 1, it becomes significant as Nancy, the ingenue, dressed
in bouffant evening gown, enters and preens herself before the
glass. Nancy, to whom "life is a long, delicious time"
(Stage Direction), makes Georgie aware of her frustrated
womanhood and, as the two females, arms about each other's
waist, look into the glass together, Nancy wonders if she will
ever grow up, while Georgie, who confesses to being ". . . On
the dim, mysterious side of thirty, " tells her to cherish her
puppy fat--"It is a passport to the best of life. " After Nancy
leaves, Georgie takes off her glasses and begins to dance to
the radio music "as if it were possible to waltz herself back
to a better time" (Stage Direction). In this scene the pier
glass has become a reflector of truth from which even Georgie
must turn away to seek release in fantasy. Then, at the
scene's end, after his quarrel with Georgie, Frank stands
before the pier glass, angrily trying to construct an image
of himself as the victimized husband, but he needs a full
bottle of cough syrup to do it. Only then can he finish knot-
ting his tie and sneer bitterly at the pier glass: "Helpmate!
Sweetheart! Country Girl!" In the next scene (II, 2), the
morning after his binge, lights go on and Frank sees his
drunken, disheveled self revealed in another glass as he
slumps before the make-up shelf. The truth emerges in-
exorably as the others enter--even his slashed wrists (scars
of the suicide attempts he had attributed to Georgie) are un-
covered--and Bernie Dodd sees him in all his naked help-
lessness and agony. Finally, in II, 3, there is another large
mirror installed over the make-up shelf in Frank's stage
dressing room on his triumphant opening night. It is in this
mirror that Georgie places the supposed congratulatory wire
from Unger's aunt and the other phony telegrams sent by
Bernie. But Frank, having survived his ordeal, is strong
enough now to look directly into the mirror and feel pleased
with himself. Finally, Georgie ends the play by going to the
mirror, taking Sue's telegram down, and, after considering
quickly, crumpling it into a ball and throwing it into a trash
basket. The last vestige of falsehood--and, incidentally,
Georgie's ruse to pass Frank on to another woman--has been
disposed of. There are no longer any distortions and the
mirror reflects only an empty room.

2. Dialogue

Even Odets' severest critics admit that he wrote good
dialogue.   Joseph Wood Krutch has said, "His dialogue is
often brilliantly suggestive,"[40] and Murray Kempton allowed
that "his talents were of the ear rather than the vision."[41]
When we move down the scale of severity, we find encomiums
enough: Downer writes, "... in at least one element of the
drama he has been unequalled in the modern theater: he has,
or had, an absolute ear for human speech";[42] Block and
Shedd call him "a master of dialogue";[43] William Gibson
flatly states that the playwright's Golden Boy contains "the
best dialogue ever written by an American."[44]   Though they
might dislike aspects of his plays, throughout Odets' career
reviewers like Atkinson, Stark Young, and Gassner found
redeeming qualities in his dialogue;[45] most would agree with
Joseph Mersand's statement: "Odets' language merits special
attention.   It is unlike that of any other dramatist in America."[46]

So it is surprising that in the only book written on
this subject, Ruby Cohn's Dialogue in American Drama, we
find the following statement:

> In preparing the reader for the contents of this
> book, I find myself forced to begin with conclusions.
> Having read through (and often seen) plays of Max-
> well Anderson, Philip Barry, S. N. Behrman, Lil-
> lian Hellman, Sidney Howard, Sidney Kingsley, even
> Clifford Odets, Elmer Rice, Robert Sherwood, I
> concluded that their language does not deserve ex-
> tensive analysis.   In spite of a plethora of words
> on stage--and a few atypical plays such as Hell-
> man's Little Foxes, Kingsley's Dead End, Odets'
> Awake and Sing!, Rice's Adding Machine--most
> twentieth century American dramatists followed
> their predecessors in writing genteel, anonymous
> English.

The statement is an outrageous oversimplification which permits Cohn to do what she wants to do--write extended analyses of the plays of O'Neill, Miller, Williams, and Albee,
the only American dramatists "whose dialogue achieves a
recognizable style," and complete her book with a study of
the admittedly poor and ephemeral products of American
novelists and poets-turned-playwright "in a kind of might-

have-been spirit. "[47] At the beginning of her chapter on
Miller, Cohn throws a qualified sop to Odets:

> In phonographic fidelity to colloquial speech, Odets
> moved a step onward from O'Neill by recording
> urban Jewish-American--both syntax and vocabulary.
> Where O'Neill had gone to books, Odets went to
> voices. O'Neill had lived through his sea voyages
> and bar periods before he began to write; Odets
> began to write because of his immerson [sic] in the
> "hangdog, ratty, and low. " With success and
> celebrity, however, Odets lost his ear for this
> idiom. But Arthur Miller, also a product of a
> Jewish urban environment, responded to Odets'
> Awake and Sing! just as he was beginning to write.
> As Odets took from John Howard Lawson a blend
> of lofty morality and city slang, so Miller took
> them from Odets. And made them distinctively
> his own. [48]

Again half-truths and oversimplifications are used to justify
the arbitrary scheme of Cohn's book. Elsewhere I shall
deal with the charge (made by others) that Odets "lost his
ear, " but I must immediately point out that "phonographic
fidelity to colloquial speech" is a misleading and ambiguous
term, implying as it does a lack of artistic selectivity, a
merely literal transcription, and an unimaginative approach
to language--qualities which are totally uncharacteristic of
Odets' dialogue. As for Cohn's accurate statement that
Odets was influenced by John Howard Lawson, [49] it tends to
suggest a qualitative scale from the minor efforts of Lawson
to the major works of Miller, with Odets somewhere in the
middle. Yet, in my estimation, Odets was a more poetic
writer than Miller, had a better ear for the living language
of human speech, and a lightness and quickness of tone that
the gravely portentous author of All My Sons, After the Fall,
A View from the Bridge, and Incident at Vichy rarely attains.
(Compare The Flowering Peach and what Miller did with
language in the abortive The Creation of the World and Other
Business.) In fact, it is questionable whether Miller would
have achieved the speech rhythms of Death of a Salesman,
or the early plays of Tennessee Williams would have been as
free in their southern colloquialisms if there had not been
the prior example of Odets' artistic dialogue.

I cite these passages from Cohn's otherwise interesting book not only because I believe she has been unfair to

Odets, but also because she represents a segment of drama specialists who cannot regard Odets' dialogue as poetic and find it instead dated, overstrained, crude if not vulgar--in a word, prosaic. Nor is this notion confined to drama specialists alone; recently, a friend, who likes Greek dithyrambs and the metaphysical cocktail dialogue of T. S. Eliot's late verse plays, snorted in disbelief when I conjoined the words "Odets" and "poet."

I believe such attitudes are not based solely on literary snobbery and a taste for the precious (though they are partially so), but rather on a misunderstanding of the task of a dramatic poet, especially a middle-class poet who is trying both to reflect and criticize the values and aspirations of a whole class--the dominant one in America. Odets had to conceive a new, rich kind of dialogue that would accomplish that task. In his youth he was anything but unambitious. He had read Emerson, [50] and he would remember Emerson's words:

> For it is not metres, but a metre-making argument that makes a poem--a thought so passionate and alive that like the spirit of a plant or an animal it has an architecture of its own, and adorns nature with a new thing.... The poet has a new thought; he has a whole new experience to unfold; he will tell us how it was with him, and all men will be the richer in his fortune. For the experience of each new age requires a new confession, and the world seems always waiting for its poet. [51]

And, like Emerson's disciple, Whitman, Odets created in his work a barbaric yawp (he uses the word "yawping" in The Big Knife) that was original and distinctive enough to express his individual impressions of urbanized twentieth-century America--a rhythmic utterance that was capable of conveying both major and minor chords that Lawson's play Success Story had only hinted at. Harold Clurman has attempted to describe this new kind of theater dialogue: "It was a compound of lofty moral feeling, anger, and the feverish argot of the big city. It bespoke a warm heart, an outraged spirit, and a rough tongue." [52] But so brief a description can only suggest some of the qualities that we find in the poetic idiom Odets invented. Odets' variation of tone--for example, his use of lyrical passages alternating with taut, cynical dialogue--is of the highest importance in his overall achievement.

In the dialogue of his eleven plays, the following character-
istics, in addition to the symbols, metaphors and image clusters already shown in great detail, are prominent:

      1.   It is Yiddish in its inflections (sometimes even
when he is writing about goyish milieux), and contains Yiddish-
English expressions.

      2.   It is lyrical and rhetorical, sometimes success-
fully, sometimes not.

      3.   It is tough, often witty, and exploits the wise-
crack and epigram.

      4.   It is colorful and hyperbolic and makes use of
clichés, often with a fresh twist.

Yiddish-English

      The first breakthrough in Odets' invention of a living
memorable dialogue was his discovery of the resources of
Yiddish-English and his willingness to seriously represent,
not caricature, the speech rhythms and inflections of the
American Jew on the stage. His parents had been rapidly
Americanized and spoke no Yiddish at home, [53] but his aunt
and uncle were older, less acculturated, and in the enclaves
of Philadelphia and the Bronx where he grew up, Odets had
ample opportunity to listen to the conversation of immigrant
Jews. What he heard he remembered, and when he came to
write of the Berger family--and, to a lesser extent, of the
cabbies and their wives and sweethearts in Lefty--he naturally
turned to a language that would make the characters he wished
to depict believable.

      But to say it this way is to ignore the historical
and cultural factors that made Odets' use of Yiddish idiom so
startlingly original. His was no Abie's Irish Rose crossed
with The Goldbergs' idiom, as Gerald Weales, who compared
the dialogue of the latter with that of Awake and Sing!, makes
clear:

> [The Goldbergs contained] verbal humor at the
> expense of a real language, and it is used, per-
> haps unintentionally, to destroy any suggestion
> of validity in the characters and the situation.
> Odets manages to find the humor in the language
> and retain the psychological truth of the family. [54]

The reception accorded the Group Theater's production of Awake and Sing! and the double bill of Lefty and Till the Day I Die was a historic dramatic event. Before analyzing examples of Odets' idiomatic innovations, I should like to cite Alfred Kazin's description of the tremendous liberating effect of Odets' plays on a Jewish intellectual:

> ... for it seemed to me, sitting high up in the second balcony of the Belasco Theater, watching Julie Garfield, J. Edward Bromberg, Stella and Luther Adler and Morris Carnovsky in Odets's Awake and Sing, that it would at last be possible for me to write about the life I had always known. In Odets's play there was a lyric uplifting of blunt Jewish speech, boiling over and explosive, that did more to arouse the audience than the political catchwords that brought the curtain down. Everybody on that stage was furious, kicking, alive--the words, always real but never flat, brilliantly authentic like no other theater speech on Broadway, aroused the audience to such delight that one could feel it bounding back and uniting itself with the mind of the writer. [55]

Kazin's phrase, "the life I had always known," suggests how deeply Odets' language and the characters who spoke it evoked the Jewish experience. In Robert Warshow's interesting essay, "Clifford Odets: Poet of the Jewish Middle Class," we find the author reacting similarly:

> For the Jew in the audience, at least, the experience is recognition, a continuous series of familiar signposts, each suggesting with the immediate communication of poetry the whole complex of the life of the characters: what they are, what they want, how they stand with the world.
>
> It is a matter of language more directly than anything else. The events of the play are of little consequence; what matters is the words of the characters--the way they talk as much as the things they say. Odets employs consistently and with particular skill what amounts to a special type of dramatic poetry. His characters do not speak in poetry--indeed, they usually become ridiculous when they are made to speak

"poetically"--but the speeches put into their
mouths have the effect of poetry, suggesting
much more than is said and depending for the
enrichment of the suggestion upon the sensibility
and experience of the hearer. [56]

What are these familiar poetic "signposts" that Warshow sees and which allow Odets to give a "truthful description" of the facts of Jewish life and, in turn, the entire immigrant experience and process of acculturation of New York
City Jews?   The historical and cultural artifacts of this ex-
perience--the shtetl, the East Side tenements and the move
to the Bronx, the struggle to make a dollar in the garment
industry, the snatching of a laugh or a good cry at the thriv-
ing Yiddish theaters or from the Forward's "Bintel Brief"
column, the revolt of the young against parental tradition and
respectability--Bessie Berger: "I raise a family they should
have respect" (Awake and Sing!, I)--all these nourish and en-
rich Odets' early plays.   He was both influenced by them, in
the sense that he drew upon them for sources and prototypes, [57] and critical of them, in the sense that he was aware
of the limitations and ironies imposed by what Warshow describes as "the three imperatives" of Jewish life: "be secure,
be respected, be intelligent."   But, difficult as it is to disagree with so perceptive a student of the sociological implications of Odets' work as Warshow, I cannot agree with his
statement that "The characters [in Awake and Sing!] are di-
minished as human beings in favor of their function as instruments of poetic evocation....   The responses called forth
by the play are responses to the life of the Jews, to the
psychological roots of one's own life, never to the individual
lives of the people on the stage."

I think what Warshow overlooked is that Awake and
Sing! is a play with universal appeal, since it evokes the immigrant experience of the variety of ethnic groups in our
pluralistic society.   Furthermore, in the breathlessly urgent
pace of Odets' plays, there just is not time to build characters into three-dimensional human beings via the conventional
routes of exposition and onstage change and growth.   Odets,
remembering the Aristotelian dictum that dialogue reveals
character, begins with a type and rapidly individualizes him
or her through extraordinarily rich and allusive language.
Who can testify that Bessie Berger is not an individual when
she says, "They threw out a family on Dawson Street today.
All the furniture on the sidewalk.   A fine old woman with
gray hair" (I)?   Or when, after disapproving of Myron's

gambling, she buys an Irish Sweepstake ticket from Moe, saying, "Say, you can't tell--lightning never struck us yet. If they win on Beck Street we could win on Longwood Avenue" (I)? Or Myron, reacting to Hennie's announcement of her pregnancy: "It's like a play on the stage...." (I)? Or Sam Feinschreiber, softly musing, "Sometimes I think there's something funny about me" (II, 2)?

Where Warshow is on target is in his recognition of the special tone of the play: "It is as if no one really listens to anyone else; each takes his own line, and the significant connections between one speech and another are not in logic but in the heavy emotional climate of the family."[58] The illustrative lines selected by Warshow from Act I are so apt that I will include them here:

> RALPH: I don't know.... Every other day to sit around with the blues and mud in your mouth.
> MYRON: That's how it is--life is like that--a cake-walk.
> RALPH: What's it get you?
> HENNIE: A four-car funeral.
> RALPH: What's it for?
> JACOB: What's it for? If this life leads to a revolution it's a good life. Otherwise it's for nothing.
> BESSIE: Never mind, Pop! Pass me the salt.
> RALPH: It's crazy--all my life I want a pair of black and white shoes and can't get them. It's crazy!
> BESSIE: In a minute I'll get up from the table. I can't take a bite in my mouth no more.
> MYRON: Now, Momma, just don't excite yourself--
> BESSIE: I'm so nervous I can't hold a knife in my hand.
> MYRON: Is that a way to talk, Ralphie? Don't Momma work hard enough all day?
> BESSIE: On my feet twenty-four hours?
> MYRON: On her feet--
> RALPH: What do I do--go to night clubs with Greta Garbo? Then when I come home can't even have my own room? Sleep on a day-bed in the front room!
> BESSIE: He's starting up that stuff again. When Hennie here marries you'll have her room--I should only live to see the day.
> HENNIE: Me too.

In this arrangement of indirect dialogue, Odets has the ear of a musician for the sharp turns and counterpoints of a verbal fugue.

But what of the jumble of Yiddish-English syntax and expressions poured into the verbal mix--what exactly are they and what do they contribute to the emotional tone? As Gerald Haslam has shown, an expression such as "I should live so long"--generally regarded as a Yiddish-English phrase forty years ago--today is an American cliché. [59] But Yiddishisms that today are colloquialisms were unfamiliar then, and the prepositional changes and omissions, inverted sentence order, and verb variations Odets employed were alien to non-Jewish (or non-Germanic) members of the audience. Examples from Awake and Sing! are:

> BESSIE: You were sleeping by a girl ... ? (I)

> BESSIE: You gave the dog eat? (I)

> BESSIE: Ralphie, bring up two bottles seltzer from Weiss. (II, 1)

> JACOB: ... give me for a cent a cigarette. (I)

> JACOB: It needs a new world. (I)

> SAM: Once too often she'll fight with me, Hennie. (II, 2)

> SAM: I won't stand he should make insults. (II, 2)

> MORTY: Bessie--sweetheart, leave me live. (III)

Then there are the word borrowings from German or Slavic tongues: Examples are:

> the ubiquitous "Noo," which is Germanic

> "boychick," a Slavic coinage

> "shtupped," which means "slipped money under the counter," but is derived from a dialectical German word meaning "to give a gentle reminder"; and in vulgar Yiddish means to fornicate

> "delicatessen," standard English now, but Germanic then

154 / Clifford Odets

"knish" and "kishkas, " Jewish foods.

Merely to list these examples of Yiddishisms cannot begin to convey how they function within the play and their cumulative effect on an audience. Odets consciously attempted to create an art-language from Yiddish roots, [60] and to do this he needed a profound knowledge of the psychology of Yiddish as a language. In addition, he had to be aware of its effect on a mixed audience of Gentiles and Jews (many of whom were second-generation sons and daughters of immigrants), and to avoid the extreme of heavy Yiddish dialect which would make his plays unintelligible or ludicrous. He solved the problem by seizing on the exact moment in the history of the Berger family (and later Noah's family, and individuals in other plays) when it was sufficiently acculturated to speak urban-Yiddish-English--an admixture which looks backwards to the dialect of the shtetl and forward to Americanized urban slang. Here Odets brought into play his sensitivity to the psychological implications of words and phrases for both the older generation and the younger.

Some examples will help demonstrate the verbal signposts by which old and young in Awake and Sing! "give themselves away" (Warshow's phrase). When Bessie asks Jacob "You gave the dog eat?" and he replies, "I gave the dog eat" (I), an entire complex of understandings is involved. On the dramatic level, we know that Bessie regards her father as a ne'er-do-well and relegates him to menial tasks in the household. But, on an additional level, Jews would appreciate Bessie's concern for feeding the animal, remembering the biblical and talmudic injunctions for the care and nourishment of cattle and sheep, which is an ancestral memory of a formerly nomadic people. Linguistically, Bessie's query and Jacob's reply in almost the exact words have a ritualistic quality to which an audience accustomed to incantations applied even to the slaughter of animals would respond. However, there is irony in the fact that Bessie's concern is for a pet dog. In the shtetl, dogs and cats as pets were unheard of--that was a goyish custom--and Jewish children played with a young calf or ewe. No proster Yid (common Jew) would own a dog, although perhaps a grosser gevir (very rich man) might acquire a watchdog to guard his house and land. Thus, Bessie's concern for Tootsie is a sign of her Americanization; she, above all the others, has accepted the status symbols of the new land. Her excessive pride is evinced moments later when she defends her pet to Schlosser, the janitor: "Tootsie's making dirty? Our Tootsie's making

dirty in the hall? ...   Tootsie walks behind me like a lady
any time, any place" (I).

Bessie's Yiddishisms also point up another psycho-
linguistic effect of the language which Odets exploited for
serio-comic overtones, namely, the Jewish tendency to identify verbally intense anguish and emotion with the digestive
process.   In the passage I have previously requoted from
Warshow, Bessie says: "In a minute I'll get up from the
table.   I can't take a bite in my mouth no more. "   In Amer-
ican-English, the equivalent phrase probably would be--"I'm
leaving any minute.   This is making me sick to my stomach. "
But the Yiddish-English expression is psychologically more
acute because the specificity of "bite in my mouth" is tied
up with hunger and underscores the preciousness of eating
against a background of frequent famine and deprivation in
"the old country. "   This would be apparent even to the younger Jewish members of the audience, who had heard this
phrase from their parents; Gentiles could also appreciate its
idiomatic verve.   (They might even understand why the Bergers are constantly eating in this play.) Similarly, in the
pregnancy-revelation dialogue with Hennie, Bessie exclaims,
"My gall is bursting in me, " and later, growing angry at
Jacob, she says, "Your gall could burst from such a man. "
Bessie is translating her emotional state to a bodily state,
but the interesting bit of synecdoche in which gall bladder is
omitted and the secretion is stressed, is emblematic of the
intensity with which Jews express anguish and anger.   In the
verbs "bursting" and "bust, " one can hear the echo of the
Yiddish plotz, as in : "His heart will plotz from such suffering. "[61]

Finally, Bessie reveals linguistically a rather desperate effort to assimilate into her vocabulary words and
phrases picked up from the mass media--"Another county
heard from" (I, and again in II, 1)--and "A graduate from
the B. M. T. " (II, 1)--show the sarcastic usages by means
of which Americanisms could be rendered into Yinglish, and
Bessie's class-consciousness is demonstrated by her acidu-
lous reference to Hennie as "Our society lady ... " (I).

That Yinglish in Odets' plays involves a reciprocal
relationship between young and old is evidenced by the fact
that Hennie and Ralph, though for the most part they speak
straight urban English, are influenced by the speech patterns
of their parents and grandparents.   In the scene where she
is "put down" by Bessie as "Our society lady, " Hennie rejects

her mother's suggestion that she marry Sam Feinschreiber: "I'm not marrying a poor foreigner like him. Can't even speak an English word. Not me! I'll go to my grave without a husband." A finely attuned ear would detect something foreign sounding in her last sentence, slyly mocking the sentiments she expresses. Instead of saying "I'd rather die than marry that mockie" (a pejorative meaning "greenhorn" or foreigner, which Hennie uses earlier to describe Sam), she will go to her grave without a husband. The sentence is formalized, and its concrete specificity suggests Yiddish rather than English, an outcry from Tevye the Milkman, or a phrase that Hennie might have picked up from some other melodrama at the Yiddish theater.

In the same way, Ralph's speech is overlaid by patterns learned from his family. The opening line of the play, "Where's advancement down the place?" contains an elision and prepositional omission that are typical of Yinglish. Even more significant is his use of the word "place" rather than "shop" or "factory." Here, the German word platz connotes a much richer meaning since it is tied in with the Jewish idea of the value of having a place of work--not merely in the physical sense, but in the moral sense of the need to attain a position, a vocation, a useful status in society. Amusingly, Ralph mixes this Yiddish idiom with the very American word "advancement," which establishes at once an ironic link to the theme of a family in economic and linguistic transition. Yet in II, 1, Ralph reverts automatically to Bessie's emotional body language; describing Blanche's home, he says, "Every time I go near the place I get heart failure."

Yet another source of Yiddishisms in the play is Jacob, who represents the intellectual, bookish tradition of Judaism: "I'm studying from books a whole lifetime" (II, 1). He is the melamed, the unworldly teacher, and his words have a prophetic biblical cadence which Odets mixes with a smattering of Marxist-English diction Jacob probably picked up at the Arbeiter Ring (Workmen's Circle) on Manhattan's Lower East Side. Sometimes Jacob's mixed-up English is exploited for broad comic effect, as when he warns Ralph about the family's probable attitude toward Blanche: "Boychick ... It's no difference--a plain bourgois prejudice-- but when they find out a poor girl--it ain't so kosher" (I). More often, there is a pathetic side to Jacob which, linguistically, is expressed by the juxtaposition of poetic prophecy with the cant Marxist terms which represent his process of acculturation. In a moving speech in II, 1, Jacob tells the assembled family:

So you believe in God ... you got something for it?
You! You worked for all the capitalists. You har-
vested the fruit from your labor? You got God!
But the past comforts you? The present smiles on
you, yes? It promises you the future something?
Did you found a piece of earth where you could live
like a human being and die with the sun on your
face? Tell me, yes, tell me. I would like to
know myself. But on these questions, on this
theme--the struggle for existence--you can't make
an answer. The answer I see in your face ... the
answer is your mouth can't talk. In this dark corner you sit and you die. But abolish private property!

The last sentence is totally incongruous and destroys
the poetry by its platitudinous, soap-box quality. The audience would see the irony of a scholar who speaks Hebrew
and quotes Isaiah being taken in by the cant terms of a then
popular Americanized political philosophy. (It could be assumed that Jacob had become a Marxist in the old country,
but that is hardly possible since, in Act III, Ralph examines
his Marxist volumes and discovers "the pages ain't cut in
half of them. ") We should remember that a subsidiary
meaning for melamed is "an incompetent, " and Jacob himself
is aware that he is "a man who had golden opportunities but
drank instead a glass tea" (II, 2). The poignancy of that
image is difficult to translate unless one has childhood memories of elderly Jews carefully lifting steaming glasses of hot
brew to their mouths and smacking their lips in an almost
obscene surrender to the exotic and sensually stimulating
beverage. Although he is a failure, Jacob's role in the play
is not to point the way to some Communist panacea for social ills (insofar as he does this, he is comic and pathetic),
but to stand for older traditional Jewish values in opposition
to Bessie and her cohorts. In II, 1, he tells Morty: "In
my day the propaganda was for God. Now it's for success. "
Linguistically, Jacob's Yinglish reminds one of the moral
authority and hortatory quality which was carried over syn-
tactically into Yiddish-urban-English. One should not be
told that one should make success. One should remember the
words of Hillel: "If I am not for myself, who will be for me?
And if I am only for myself, what am I? ... And if not now--
when?"

It is remarkable how often Jacob uses the obligatory
construction "it should. " Examples: "So long labor lives it

should increase private gain" (II, 1) [used ironically]; "My
insurance policy. I don't like it should lay around ... " (II,
1). Both moral stricture and putative hope are expressed in
his language. By contrast, the more assimilated characters
in the play have lapsed into vulgar Yiddish: Uncle Morty
says, "We'll give them strikes--in the kishkas [guts] we'll
give them" (III); and in the same act, Moe Axelrod informs
Ralph: "The insurance guy's coming tonight. Morty 'shtupped'
him. " The vulgar materialists in the play add their minor
notes to what I have referred to as a verbal fugue but, to
continue the metaphor, the major counterpoints in the fugue
are Jacob's Yinglish versus Bessie's--a contrast which Odets
later would repeat in the language of the patriarchal, world-
weary Noah and his practical, down-to-earth wife, Esther.

The overall effect of these foreign inflections and idiomatic phrases was threefold. For Gentiles (and even many
Jews) it imparted a comic twist of fractured English that
amused and provided some relief from the grim and gritty
world of some of his plays. Indeed, Awake and Sing! proves
Blake's adage: "Excess of sorrow laughs, " and stands as
the progenitor of Jewish "black humor" found in the works of
dozens of later Jewish-American writers. 62 Second, the
Yiddish idiom conveyed a sense of family solidarity despite
the family's conflicts and arguments, and the "feel" of a
social unit moving "up. " Third, by this marvelous alchemy
due to the addition of symbolic and metaphoric language and
ironic, abrasive, cynical lines to the rhythmic, foreign inflections, Odets transforms Yiddish-English into a rich poetic
tongue. Many years ago Eleanor Flexner said of Awake and
Sing!: "His dialogue displays what is little less than genius
for sharp vivid phrasing which is unrealistic while it is still
lifelike and human, a poetizing of speech that is nevertheless
more realistic than poetic. " And she added, "These [phrases
from the play] are the poet's transformation of a commonplace idiom into literature. "63

There are several anomalies in the quartet of plays
by Odets staged in 1935 which bear on his use of Yiddish-
English and Jewish characters. In Lefty only one character
is nominally Jewish--Dr. Benjamin (in The Young Interne
episode), who is fired from his hospital job because of anti-
Semitism. Most of the others--Joe, Edna, Sid, Florrie,
Irv, even Fatt and the Stenographer--sound Jewish. For
example, Fatt asks a typical Yiddish rhetorical question:
"Where's Philly? A thousand miles away?" And the Stenographer calls hungry actors "Phony strutting 'pishers'--that's

French for dead codfish!" In Till the Day I Die, Major
Duhring, who is partly Jewish, explains that he married into
an old German family, "Nordic from the year one" (4); perhaps his inflection is understandable, but a telltale Yiddish
slip shows when Odets has Trooper 2 of the Brownshirt thugs
say: "To me you can't talk like to your snotnose friends!"
(3).

The nonsense that the Gordons of Paradise Lost "were
not definitely Jewish, like the Bergers of Awake and Sing!, "64
was at least nominally accepted by some critics; and it is true
that Odets had announced that "The hero ... is the entire
American middle class of liberal tendency, "65 and pointedly
set the play not in New York but in an unspecified "American
city. " Obviously he was trying to widen his literary horizons.
But Sam and Mrs. Katz, Gus Michaels, Clara and Leo Gordon
(despite the Anglicized name) are obviously Jewish. Their
city could be west of Brooklyn, but only metaphorically so.
The only difference between them and the Bergers is that
they come from the upper middle class, and my guess is that
they are German-Jews, not Eastern Europeans. (Gus says
he is German in Act I.) This makes a vast difference not
only in the way they speak but in their attitudes, as readers
of Stephen Birmingham's Our Crowd will be aware. The
German-Jews, who arrived during an earlier wave of immi-
gration than the Russians and other Eastern Europeans, tended
to look down on the latter, were more quickly assimilated and
economically secure, and regarded themselves as more cultured than the later Jewish arrivals. Thus, the Gordons
adopt a mock formality in their Yiddish cadences and have a
more extensive English vocabulary. For example, Leo: "My
dear, don't you trust anyone?" Clara: "My dear, I wasn't
born yesterday. " Yet Clara has a broad Yiddish speech tic:
"Do yourself a personal favor: don't trust him for a nickel!"
(I); "Do yourself a personal favor, listen to me ... In our
whole family you alone will be a success" (I); and "Do yourself a personal favor--go home!" (II). And for fractured English, we can depend on Gus Michaels: "I'm dumbfound! Just
dumbfound!" (I), he says, and "No one takes me serious" (I).
Nor is it likely that a Gentile in the mid-Thirties would have
followed Leo's lead in giving away a canary solely because it
was German and he wanted to protest Hitler's actions. For
irrefutable proof of the ethnic origin of the Gordons, we can
rely upon the greeting which the Irish politician, Phil Foley,
gives on entering their home: "Sholom Aleichem, Gus!" (I).

When he moved on from the family-trap plays with

their ensemble casts, it was only natural that the frequency
and specificity of the Yiddish idiom in Odets' dialogue would
diminish. In Golden Boy, he made use of a different dialect,
Italian-American. He could not have felt at home with it,
and Mr. Bonaparte's dialect--"The mosta golden present for
his birthday ... " (I, 2)--has always struck me as stage-
Italian. However, almost as though he could not bear desert-
ing his former milieu, he included in the cast three Jewish
characters--Mr. Carp, Siggie and Roxy Gottlieb--and their
speech rings true. Mr. Carp says, "You think you got worries? Wait, you're a young man yet" (I, 2), and Siggie complains: "I'm worried. I don't sleep. It's my Jewish dispo-
sition" (I, 2). Roxy Gottlieb, the fight promoter, is a lin-
guist's delight. My favorite sample of his fractured English
is: "He leaves us here standing in our brevities!" (II, 1).
Even Lorna Moon, a shikse if there ever was one, tells Joe:
"You want your arm in gelt up to the elbow" (I, 4). Odets'
Yiddishisms cross ethnic lines.

I shall bypass for the present the Yiddish-English
cadences of Rocket to the Moon as they are intermingled with
wisecracks and epigrams, which I shall examine soon. Here,
it is sufficient to note that all of the characters but Frenchy
are Jewish, and that this is the only play of Odets' that explores all three of the Jewish imperatives mentioned by Warshow: Be secure! Be respected! Be intelligent! By now,
in the paradigmatic journey of the Jew through the process
of acculturation, we are listening to the speech cadences of
a professional man--a dentist--and the epigrams of Mr.
Prince, one of the most intelligent characters in Odets' canon.

In his next two plays, Odets deliberately underplayed
Yiddish-English almost as though he was making a conscious
effort to leave his cultural roots behind him. But as in Golden Boy, like a cautious man who keeps one foot on dry land
while trying out the waters, he retains Jewish characters in
gentile milieus. Though the hero of Night Music, Steve Takis,
is a Greek-American from Brockton, Massachusetts, and Fay
Tucker is a WASP from Philadelphia, the presiding deity on
the island of Manhattan is Detective A. L. Rosenberger, who
is a student of language--"An interesting figure of speech.
You made it up?" (II, 4)--and given to pompous utterances,
such as: "Be cheerful, young man ... God is where He was
before" (I, 1), and "I'll tell you a secret ... All the dead
and living are cheering for you when you are a good person"
(II, 4). Rosenberger is a little better when he waxes colloquial and folksy: "In your whole life you never had a pretzel"

(II, 5), and "Why should two bald men fight about a comb?"
(II, 5).

In Clash by Night, there is an almost unrelieved linguistic line of straight proletarian English, except for the
father who speaks only a few lines in a Polish accent.   At
the last minute Odets inserts Horowitz, Earl's fellow-pro-
jectionist, who is an epitome of middle-class Jewish respectability and source of pithy Yiddishisms.   He tells Earl:

> ... One son will be a doctor in three years.   The
> other studies an engineering profession.   The girl
> is already married to a dear boy in Brooklyn.   My
> wife an' me, we planned everything like that.   (II, 3)

Still, we are aware in these two plays (which I have listed
among Odets' failures) of a diminution of tonal resources, of
a reduction of the richness and density of the language, and
one of the reasons may be the relative scarcity of the Yiddish-
English dialect.

We must deal, then, with Ruby Cohn's charge against
Odets that while his early plays showed a fidelity to colloquial
speech and urban Jewish-American syntax and vocabulary, his
later plays lacked accuracy and bite.   "With success and
celebrity ... Odets lost his ear for this idiom."[66]   Such a
charge is manifestly untrue of The Flowering Peach, where
Odets returns to Jewish-American speech patterns quite successfully.   However, it must be considered in connection with
The Big Knife and The Country Girl.   Here Odets is no longer
writing out of his immersion in the "hangdog, ratty and low,"
but is dealing with success and failure in the upper echelons
of Hollywood and Broadway.   His characters are the power
brokers and their minions, the glamorous and the not-so-
glamorous of the upper middle class and the very rich.   Did
his ear fail him when depicting these characters?

I would answer No, but I would qualify my answer with
the argument that Yiddish-American dialect took a new turn
when it went Hollywood and incorporated a strain of what
Charlie Castle called "phony cathedral eloquence"; it also
took a positive pride in its fractured English when such expression as Sam Goldwyn's "Include me out" passed for wit.
The Big Knife reflects this linguistic upward mobility.   Nat
Danziger, Charlie Castle's agent, has "all the qualities of
the president of a synagogue" (Stage Description, I), though
he is still capable of inverted Yiddish sentences and verb

variants, such as "Her I'm gonna talk to again" and "a million dollars is got an awful big mouth" (I). His speech tic, "dear sir and friend," reflects the formality and grandiloquence that had overlaid the racy Yiddish idiom of Awake and Sing! As we listen to the cadences of Marcus Hoff's lengthy speech in Act I about his former wife's supposed treachery, we notice three things: the rhythms are, by turn, interrogatory and choppy--not too far from the Yiddish inflections of past plays; the speech itself is studded with chichés and religiosity, e.g., "Son, you're gonna be one of the biggest stars in this business," "as sure as God made the green earth," "as God is my witness above," "The woman I called my wife for almost thirty years"; and Hoff injects literary, rolling phrases, e.g., "I saw, by a revelation of pain," "the multiplicity of a great career," and, a bit later, "I solemnly adjure realism." The speech is a parody of what Yiddish-English had become, not only for a particular movie mogul but for a certain type of ambitious Jew.

In The Country Girl, there is little that smacks of Yiddish-English. Phil Cook, the producer, may be of Jewish origin but his speech patterns may be termed "Broadway wise guy" variety. It was probably a mistake for Odets to have Georgie answer Bernie's question about why Frank went to pieces, with the words: "It needs an Einstein to tell you that" (II, 2). But the play does not suffer from its lack of Yiddishisms; it has linguistic compensations which I will deal with shortly. The lack of such language, however, may help explain why Odets always ranked the play so low; here he had dropped two of his favorite roles: the outspoken social critic and the specialist in Yiddishkeit.

He made up for the latter omission in The Flowering Peach. I am not going to belabor the obvious by citing examples of the broad Yiddish-English of Noah and his family; here we have everything from word borrowing--Esther addressing her daughters-in-law as tuchter--to inverted word order and verb variants in practically every other sentence. Rather, I am going to address myself to two controversial points relevant to the Jewish language used in the play. When the work was first produced, there was criticism of the many anachronisms. For example, Noah says to Japheth: "Go get him. It's Friday today? Shem should be here tonight, before shabbos, before sundown" (1). And, in an infamous example, Shem tells Japheth: "If Momma didn't like to have you around the house, I swear I'd get a court order and sell you into Egypt!" (2). To some it seemed sacrilegious to put

such a wisecrack into a biblical drama. This brings me to
the second point. To others it seemed altogether questionable
to place a family talking the dialect of Bronx Jews nurtured
in the shtetls of Eastern Europe on board Noah's ark.

Anachronisms are pardonable; even Shakespeare fell
prey to them, and he never tried to deal with a prehistoric
fable. But the deeper criticism is a question of decorum
and it seems to me to miss entirely the intention of Odets'
strategy, a strategy which should be obvious in a period when
one of Shakespeare's comedies, Two Gentlemen of Verona,
has been converted into a rock-and-roll wingding. Odets
was writing a comedy--not a serious drama like Awake and
Sing!--and what better prototypes could be found for "Noah
and his troupe ... assorted clowns and acrobats" (Stage
Direction, 2) enacting the human comedy than his Bronx Jewish family. In words of one syllable, why not? Would it
have been better to use the intricate poetic line of MacLeish
in J. B. , or the clichéd, fake-Bible language of Cecil B. De-
Mille? It is true that some of the bite and cynicism of the
Yiddish idiom of Awake and Sing! has disappeared from The
Flowering Peach; Ham, the erring son, is a poor replace-
ment for Moe Axelrod. But the play is a comedy with serious
overtones, and in it Odets' lyricism reaches new heights, re-
placing the irony of Awake and Sing! with something rich and
strange.

Lyricism and Rhetoric

"It is easier to recognize an Odets line than to characterize one," Gerald Weales declares, and then proceeds to
cite a barrage of examples from Lefty and Awake and Sing!
illustrating Odets' various strategies and crudities side by
side. [67] He manages to convey quite successfully that Odets'
dialogue is a fusion of the rough and the smooth, banalities
and inspired verbal inventions. That totality of effect is difficult to analyze under separate rubrics, and I would not want
the reader to assume that although I praise Odets for his lyricism, I have not winced more than once at some strained
metaphor like "Christ, Baby! I get like thunder in my chest
when we're together" (Waiting for Lefty, The Young Hack and
his Girl episode), which so annoyed Otis Ferguson. [68] Yet I
believe that Odets' "barbaric yawp" is ultimately poetic and,
like Whitman's, was not merely flung together haphazardly
but was composed with a deliberate and artistic purpose. For
the most part, as I shall show, he succeeds through the use

of verbal juxtaposition and a complex alternation of the poetic
and the banal--so much so that even some of the clichés have
a positive function and add sauce to the mix.

Having mentioned the tendency of Odets toward metaphoric overkill and occasional grotesqueries, I wish to emphasize that Odets wrote prose-poetry in depicting the depths
of his characters' emotions, and that a lyrical quality in his
dialogue was present from the first. Even in so uninspired
a play as Till the Day I Die, there are isolated memorable
lines: about Ernst, "Children will jeer him in the darkest
streets of his life!" (6); or about the future Germany Ernst
envisions, "In that dizzy dazzling structure some part of me
is built" (7). I have already cited the lyrical uplift of Leo's
final speech in Paradise Lost and Agate's in Lefty. But
these speeches are marred where they shade off into mere
rhetoric; at these times Odets insists on preaching a revolutionary sermon, and all his lyrical fervor cannot conceal
threadbare political slogans. In Ernst's peroration about the
future, referred to above, we find: "Brothers will live in
the soviets of the world! Yes, a world of security and freedom is waiting for all mankind!" (7). As I have mentioned
previously (See above, p. 38), Odets later regretted these
forced conclusions and blamed them on the atmosphere within the Group Theater at the time. In Awake and Sing! he
was less strident in his didacticism because he found apt
metaphors. For example, Jacob says, "In this boy's life a
Red Sea will happen again. I see it!" (II, 1); and Ralph's
optimistic "Coletti to Driscoll to Berger" speech near the
end of Act III functions effectively because of the baseball
imagery. Yet it cannot be denied that the poet in Odets
sometimes gives way to the rhetorician and that even the
later plays are marred by purple patches.

Odets' lyricism, nevertheless, was consistently successful when he dealt with the lyric's favorite topic--love.
Most critics deride Ralph's attempt to convey his feelings
about Blanche to Jacob: "Boy, I'm telling you I could sing!
Jake, she's like stars. She's so beautiful you look at her
and cry! She's like French words!" (I). Most of the speech
is banal, an inarticulate youth struggling to express the in-
effable and arriving at sentimental bathos, except for the
simile "like French words, " which is as close a comparison
as Ralph's high school memories can conjure up for charm
and beauty. It is the heart's palpable message that Odets
communicates--Jacob: "Do what is in your heart and you
carry in yourself a revolution" (II, 2)--and he is especially

poignant in lines where lovers reach toward one another. Joe
Bonaparte pleads: "Oh, Lorna, deep as my voice will reach--
listen!! Why can't you leave him?" (Golden Boy, II, 2), and
Moody says: "I don't need crowns or jewels. I take my girl
and we go sit by the river and it's everything" (II, 3). In
The Country Girl, Bernie speaks low to Georgie: "Lady,
lady, close to you this way ... " (II, 3). This unabashed
sentimentality would be unacceptable if it were not balanced
by lines such as Lorna's "Go to hell! ... But come back
tonight" (Golden Boy, I, 1), or Moe Axelrod's "Baby, if you
had a dog I'd love the dog" (Awake and Sing!, II, 1). It is
the fusion of sentimentality with the abrasive street talk that
permits us to empathize with emotional expressions we might
normally reject.

The poet in Odets also responded to the changing
seasons and nature and beauty in the city: Joe: "The city
is full of girls who look as if they never had parents" (Golden
Boy, I, 4); and Moody tells Lorna he resents Joe's looking at
her "As if he saw the whole island of Manhattan in your face"
(II, 3). Even in the stage-Italian of Mr. Bonaparte, Odets'
lyrical emotion comes through:

> The streets, winter a' summer--trees, cats--I
> love-a them all. The gooda boys and girls, they
> who sing and whistle--(Bursts into a moment of gay
> whistling)--very good! The eating and sleeping,
> drinking wine--very good! I gone around on my
> wagon and talk to many people--nice! Howa you
> like the big buildings of the city? (Golden Boy,
> I, 2)

Yet he recognized the subjectivity of such an emotion; Cleo
Singer might be answering Mr. Bonaparte when she says:

> Madison Avenue! No more! I don't care to think.
> Sometimes I wish I didn't have a head. Last night
> I didn't have a wink of sleep. Nobody loves me!
> Millions of people moving around the city and nobody
> cares if you live or die. Go up a high building and
> see them down below. Some day I'll fall down on
> them all! (Rocket to the Moon, II, 1)

Detective A. L. Rosenberger in Night Music wishes to "celebrate the city" and tells the Lieutenant, "The evening is here.
The lights of the city go on.... It gives me a kind of heartbroken feeling" (I, 1), and later says that the real criminal

to catch is the winter wind, "... it comes into New York and nobody stops it" (I, 2).

Odets has the ability to write a tightly controlled tone poem in dialogue form, and nowhere is this more apparent than in Mr. Prince's speech on the theme of day-to-day monotony. The cadences are rhythmic, and the images perfectly chosen for the subject.

> A life where every day is Monday. There used to be a week-end, but now it's always Monday. Awnings up, awnings down, coat on, coat off. Sweat in summer, freeze in winter--a movie, a bridge game, an auto ride to Peekskill. Gas is twenty cents a gallon, worry about the bills, write a budget--the maid is too expensive--you bought a pair of shoes last month. You're old, you're getting old--she's old. Yesterday you didn't look in my face. Tomorrow you forgot I'm here. Two aspirin pills are good for headaches. The world is getting ... so dull, let me sleep, let me sleep! You sneeze, you have a cold. No, that was last month. No, it's now. Which is now and which is then? (Rocket to the Moon, I)

Yet when he attempted to give Fay Tucker a speech on the same subject in I, 5, of Night Music (the "nothing happens in Philadelphia" aria), it has an unintentionally flat effect and fails to move the reader. The truth is that Odets began to repeat his linguistic speech patterns in both Night Music and Clash by Night, and the poetic texture of the language thins out (though isolated symbols and metaphoric content are still interesting). Jerry Wilenski's semi-articulate apostrophes to the moon and stars above Staten Island in Clash by Night are hardly lyrical, and we find in both plays long rhetorical speeches that are windy and unconvincing. (Examples: Steve's speech in II, 4, which ends, "... those harmony boys who mighta been! Make this America for us!" and, in Clash by Night, Joe W. Doyle's speech in II, 2, about "the anti-picnic facts. ") In both cases it is as though Odets is verbally revving himself up for an oratorical flight. (Joe actually begins his speech by saying: "You listen to me.... Here's where Volcano Joe throws off sparks again. ")

This tendency toward mere rhetoric is also found in The Big Knife; in fact, it is never entirely absent from Odets' plays. He believed in the magical power of words to stir an

audience and perhaps he came to feel that the big aria was
expected of him.   Certainly it is a flaw in The Big Knife
that he manufactures a climax with an emotional verbal tor-
rent in which the content seems not to matter.   At the end
of Act II, Charlie launches into a long speech, essentially a
counterattack against Marion, saying that--aside from his
rottenness--Marion is bargaining with her own nature by rejecting him.   "The merchant psychology" is in her blood because she implies that she will love him if he only "meets
a certain price and conditions. "   Charlie points out that
though coarsened, he is still struggling.   If she stays, she
must fight him if he is wrong.   But one of his conditions is
"SILENCE! ...   Oh darling, how we need silence and
thought ... in this noisy grabbing world!"   The speech is
weak, contradictory, and unintentionally ironic; its virtues
are eloquence and passion.   As Marion recognizes, "You
can talk.... How you can talk, when you're Charlie Cass!"
Apparently, Odets believed that a poem was in truth a myth-
making argument, and that sincerity could be attained by
shouting figuratively at the top of one's voice.   Not for him
T. E. Hulme's "hard and dry" modern classicism; in this
he was a thoroughgoing romanticist.

In contrast with this rapid rhetorical flight, Odets was
in perfect control when he circumscribed his rhetoric with a
touch of irony, as he did in the speech in which Hank, Charlie's sophisticated author-friend, characterizes the suffocating
atmosphere of Fifties America:

> I don't want Marion joining the lonely junked people
> of our world--millions of them, wasted by the
> dreams of the life they were promised and the
> swill they received! They are why the whole world,
> including us, sits bang in the middle of a revolu-
> tion! Here, of course, that platitude carries with
> it the breath of treason.   I think lots of us are in
> for a big shot of Vitamin D: defeat, decay, depres-
> sion and despair.   (III, 1)

When he had a stronger conception of character, Odets
was able to display the value of restraint and understatement.
Georgie Elgin, "The Country Girl, " is such a character--
laconic, intelligent, lyrical.   When Bernie meets her as she
is suffering from a toothache, she tells him, "All of autumn's
in this tooth" (I, 2).   Later, she describes her longing for
peace as the need for "the fiesta of a quiet room" (II, 2).
Standing on the almost empty stage in I, 3, she utters one

of Odets' most beautiful lines: "Nothing is quite so mysterious and silent as a dark theater ... a night without a star ..." Her answers to Frank's anxieties are simple and lucid:

> GEORGIE: People don't go back to the same life, Frank. They go above it or below it, but they don't go back.
> FRANK: But do I still have the country girl?
> GEORGIE: Here I am.

Although there are few terse Georgies in Odets' surging, passionate plays, lyricism does not necessarily give way to rhetoric, as illustrated by The Flowering Peach. Noah's soliloquies usually work because he is the embodiment of the patriarch: pious, yet earthy and emotional, in touch with both the human and the beatific. He holds the tiny gitka in Scene 2, and whispers: "Shhh, gitka, shh.... She breathes in my hand like a heart," and tells Japheth in Scene 3: "The Lord is good for anybody an' everybody, at all times! He was wonderful for the world in the old days an', blessed be His name, He will be for the new days to come! ..." And, in Noah's masterly closing soliloquy, Odets reveals a new gift of simple lyricism which caused so many critics[69] to regard Noah as a projection of Odets himself:

> But what I learned on the trip, dear God, you can't take it away from me. To walk in humility, I learned. And listen, even to myself ... and to speak softly, with the voices of consolation. (9)

Wisecrack and Epigram

The wisecrack was the hallmark of the Thirties--its calling card and safety valve. In the Twenties it had been smart to be flippant, and Vanity Fair and the wits of the Hotel Algonquin (Dorothy Parker, Alexander Woollcott and others) represented a literary sophistication that laughed at America's provinciality and small-town Puritan mentality. But the Thirties did not utilize the wisecrack for the same purpose. In an era of hard times and the struggle to survive it seemed necessary to cultivate an outer toughness, a protective shell that would insulate one against the horrors encountered daily in the newspaper and the streets. The wisecrack lost its literary veneer and became an adjunct to character--the rough response hiding the soft inner core of feeling, the sally that kept you sane, the response that un-

leashed the head of steam you had been building up all day.
You saw it in a hundred movies, It Happened One Night or
a Cary Grant-Irene Dunne film, and you recognized that the
wisecrack had passed from the intellectual to the common
man.

Odets was instrumental in this transition, and his
plays caught the contemporary idiom of irony and developed
it into a genuine art. It is in this form, if anywhere, that
the "Odetsian line" was produced. At first it emerges in
roughhouse metaphors in Lefty: Joe's crude comments,
"That Wop's got more guts than a slaughterhouse," and "It's
plain as the nose on Sol Feinberg's face we need a strike."
Here, too, we find what I call the evasive pattern, in which
a character responds to an unwanted question with a non-
sequitur: Sid: "What's on your mind?" Florrie: "The
French and Indian War" (The Young Hack and his Girl episode).

In Awake and Sing!, the same pattern emerges:

> BESSIE: Tell me what happened....
> HENNIE: Brooklyn Bridge fell down.
>
> BESSIE: Who's the man?
> HENNIE: The Prince of Wales. (I)

And later--Sam: "Why should you act this way?" Hennie:
"Cause there's no bones in ice cream. Don't touch me"
(III). (As late as Clash by Night Odets was still using the
evasive pattern. Earl: "What's furrowing your brow,
cookie ...?" Mae: "The bankers of America ..." I, 3).
Also, in Awake and Sing!, we listen to Moe Axelrod, cynic
par excellence, as he bandies wisecracks with Uncle Morty:

> MORTY: I saw it happen Monday in my building.
> My hair stood up how they shoveled him to-
> gether--like pancake--a bankrupt manufacturer.
> MOE: No brains.
> MORTY: Enough ... all over the sidewalk. (II, 1)

And later with Bessie:

> BESSIE: ... I never saw conditions should be so
> bad.
> MORTY: Times'll change.
> MOE: The only thing'll change is my underwear.
> (II, 1)

Though these exchanges are relatively simple examples of "black humor," Thirties style, we also find in Awake and Sing! Odets' tendency toward the terse and epigrammatic. Moe says, "What this country needs is a good five-cent earthquake," and a bit later on the subject of war, "Nothing good hurts," while Jacob pronounces a judgment on the American way: "Don't live, just make success" (I, 1).

Why we laugh at these remarks that seem funny and startling to us cannot easily be explained. They elicit a wide range of psychological and perceptual responses, some of which have been analyzed by Bergson and Freud. Moe's remark about the "five-cent earthquake" follows precisely one of Bergson's general rules: "A comic meaning is invariably obtained when an absurd idea is fitted into a well-established phrase form." Throughout Awake and Sing! there is a great deal of self-deprecatory humor, such as Myron's "My scalp is impoverished," and his "The moment I began losing my hair I just knew I was destined to be a failure in life ... and when I grew bald I was" (II, 2). Statements like these evoke laughter because, according to Bergson, they suggest mechanical rigidity in the speaker which, coupled with absentmindedness, evoke a comic response. "Suppose we imagine a mind always thinking of what it has just done and never of what it is doing, like a song which lags behind its accompaniment."[70] Myron is exactly like this.

Moreover, Odets' witticisms are characterized by verbal irony, such as Hennie's angry retort to Bessie when Bessie asks where she is going: "For my beauty nap, Mussolini. Wake me up when it's apple blossom time in Normandy" (I). Though there is an element of self-deprecation here, Hennie is saying one thing and meaning another. She knows that her lover has skipped town, leaving her pregnant, and that the sweet, sentimental atmosphere connoted by the popular ballad can never reappear in her life if, in fact, it ever had. There is also the blatant incongruity of Bessie as Mussolini, and the notion of a beauty nap being taken against a dictator's wishes.

For the most part, Odets eschews the comic and farcical in favor of quick ironic witticisms. Freud stressed "the peculiar brevity of wit," which he also characterized as a form of "developed play" which originates in the foreconscious. "Wit is made, while the comical is found."[71] Such mental alacrity may be demonstrated by Clara's retort to Mrs. Katz's plea, "Please, he'll make good." Clara says,

"With what--chiclets?" (Paradise Lost, II). Or by Frank
Bonaparte's explanation about how he learned of his brother's
fighting from the newspaper: "Truth is cheap. We bought
it for two cents" (Golden Boy, I, 2). While such remarks
are hardly hilarious, they point up what my later citations
will reveal: that Odets' ironic humor revolves around the
basic concerns of love and money, and that his verbal juxta-
positions often evoke a moral world turned topsy-turvy; e. g. ,
Joe (to Lorna): "And what does your soul do in its perfumed
vanity case?" (Golden Boy, I, 4).

    While it is difficult to trace to their sources all the
verbal strategies Odets employs, we should remember that
he is interested in both the witty and the comic. Bergson
tried to draw a distinction between the two, but he found that
they overlapped:

> A word is said to be comic when it makes us laugh
> at the person who utters it, and witty when it makes
> us laugh either at a third party or at ourselves.
> But in most cases we can hardly make up our minds
> whether the word is comic or witty. All we can
> say is that it is laughable.... [72]

    In Paradise Lost, Gus Michaels is the vehicle for some
of Odets' choicest malapropisms, which become witticisms by
default. Gus says, "I guess failure's gone to my head" (I),
and in Act III, after selling his last valuable possession, he
cheerfully anounces: "Last of the Mo-higgins!" And yet Gus
is capable of sardonic introspection; he says of his son-in-law,
Ben: "He don't like me, but it's all right--I don't like myself" (II). In this play Kewpie continues the wisecracking
role of Moe Axelrod; he describes Ben bitterly to Libby:
"Good in the receiving department, but lousy in the shipping"
(I), but later gets his comeuppance when Ben discovers his
relationship with her: Kewpie: "Who the hell are you to
make me uncomfortable?" Ben: "I'm the guy who slept with
Mrs. God!" (II).

    Later, in Golden Boy, Odets used a variation of this
gag for an ironic moment that defines the relationship between Tom Moody and Lorna Moon. The harried fight manager is in his office with his mistress when the telephone
rings. He shouts:

> MOODY (of the ringing bell): If that's for me, tear
> it up. I ain't in, not even for God.

> LORNA (answering): Hello? ... (Putting her hand
> on the mouthpiece.) It's Mrs. God--your wife.
> (I, 3)

Joe and Lorna, too, release their share of venom in the
scene where, temporarily estranged, they meet just before
Joe's fight. In this encounter, Joe gets the decision:

> JOE: Moody's right for you--perfect--the mating
> of zero and zero!
> LORNA: I'm not sorry to marry Tom----
> JOE (scornfully): That's from the etiquette book--
> page twelve: "When you marry a man say you
> like it!" (III, 1)

And when Joe is about to stalk off, he flings a verbal knock-
out punch at the girl he loves: "I wouldn't look at you twice
if they hung you naked from a Christmas tree!" (III, 1).

Still another entry in the verbal sparring match in
Golden Boy is Roxy Gottlieb. He loftily tries to explain to
Lorna why the ring crowd does not like Joe's scientific box-
ing:

> Excuse me, Miss Moon. In the prizefight ring the
> cash customer don't look for stoodents. Einstein
> lives in a college--a wonderful man in his line!
> Also, while I think of it, a woman's place is in
> the hay, not in the office! (I, 3)

Roxy is elated when Joe begins to mix it up with his oppo-
nents, but it is he who labels Moody "Frankenstein!" at precisely the moment when Eddie Fuseli saunters onstage to
join Moody in the process of creating a moral monster. The
two men begin to bargain over Joe's contract:

> EDDIE: I thought it over, Tom. I like to get a
> piece of that boy.
> MOODY (angrily): I thought it over, too--not for
> sale. In fact I had a visitation from Jehovah.
> He came down on the calm waters and He said,
> "Let there be unity in the ownership. "
> EDDIE (with a dead face): I had a visit, too. He
> come down in the bar and He ate a pretzel.
> And he says, "Eddie Fuseli, I like you to buy
> a piece!" (II, 1)

Whenever I hear this dialogue, I get a delicious chill of evil,

comparable to what one might feel observing two graverobbers
arguing over a cadaver. [73] And I understand why Mordecai
Gorelik designed all the sets for Golden Boy "as if each scene
were set up in a prize ring, as if a gong rang for the start
and finish of each scene, as if the actors came toward each
other from opposite corners each time. "[74] The entire play
is a succession of verbal fisticuffs, a Manichean struggle for
the soul of Joe, and the dialogue consists of a series of
punches and counterpunches in which the wisecracks strike
the most telling blows.

In 1942, Odets thought the first act of Rocket to the
Moon was his most effective piece of writing, [75] and part of
the reason is the dialogue he invents for Mr. Prince, the
most epigrammatic of Odets' characters. When he enters
wearing an old panama hat, a fine Palm Beach suit, and
sporting a malacca cane, bearing himself with "the dignity
and elegant portliness of a Jewish actor" (Stage Direction,
I), he fires off a series of bon mots which succeed in impress-
ing Cleo as well as the audience:

> In my opinion the universe is governed by a com-
> mittee: one man couldn't make so many mistakes.
>
> Everything that's healthy is personal.
>
> Every woman wants to convert a man to the gospel
> of herself. Fact? Fact!
>
> Always address your elders with respect. They
> could leave you a fortune.

And later he tells Stark: "There are two kinds of marriages,
Benny--where the husband quotes the wife, or where the wife
quotes the husband. Fact? Fact!" Mr. Prince confesses
to Cleo, "I like to make people laugh. My daughter calls
me a clown. The two of them, my wife included--with their
bills they ate holes in me like Swiss cheese, but I was a
clown!" (I).

Not only is this self-styled Yiddish King Lear witty in
himself, but he is the cause of wit in others. His epigrammatic flair certainly rubs off on Cleo, who repeats his remarks verbatim to Ben, and perhaps Odets' success with
Prince induced him to place similar phrases in the mouth of
Phil Cooper, the hapless tenant in Ben's office. "In my
younger days I was inclined to poetry. In my older days I'm

inclined to poverty, " says Cooper, and worrying over the
fate of his family, he says, "I don't know what I'll do with
my boy--Children are not like furniture--You can't put them
in storage" (I).   Cooper, despite his woes, has a flair for
the ironic phrase; drinking from the water cooler, he exults,
"Municipal champagne!" (I).   But the self-pitying Cooper--
"Diphtheria gets more respect than me!" (II, 1)--is no match
for the aristocratic Prince, who says, ". . . in my whole life
one sensible woman came to my attention--she killed herself.
She left a note, 'I am a pest'" (I).   Prince's misogyny is
echoed by Frenchy, the chiropodist, in a devastating line.
Stark says, "A man would be a mad idealist to want a honey-
moon all his life. "   Frenchy retorts: "No, he'd be a woman"
(I).   And when he is warning Cleo against enticing his friend
into an affair he will regret, Frenchy makes a juxtaposition
which I find interesting: "I know the difference between love
and pound cake" (II, 2).

Nor are the females in the play entirely without verbal flair.   Belle Stark reminds her husband: "A place is
not a place.   A place is who you're with!" (II, 2).   And even
Cleo, describing her crowded home, where she shares one
room with her sister who is keeping company, delivers a
riposte: "I have all the inconvenience of love with none of
the pleasure" (II, 1).

In Rocket, Odets lifted the wisecrack to a new height
of verbal dexterity and wit.   R. Baird Shuman said that after
the play opened, "Another critic called Rocket to the Moon
an exercise in dialogue ... and accused Odets of suffering
'... from the belief that an epigram is a thought. '"76   But
I find this typical of the "damned if he does and damned if
he doesn't" attitude with which certain critics approach Odets.
The epigrammatic lines in Rocket to the Moon were not intended to be the equivalent of the maxims of La Rochefoucauld,
but like all of Odets' dialogue, to reveal character.   The test
of their merit lies in the fact that they make Mr. Prince a
marvelously real character; we believe in him and like him.
To a lesser extent, the same is true of Frenchy, Cooper,
and Cleo.   Because their language is intensified and heightened by Odets, they become important and meaningful to us.
When Odets does not like a character, he puts pompous
platitudes in his mouth.   For example, Willy Wax expostu-
lates: "Movies! They're what started me off on my path of
painless perversion. ...   Do I glisten with arrogance ...?"
and "You're living in the city of the dreadful night: a man
is coarse or he doesn't survive" (II, 2).   And this, in turn,

also reveals character. The only character in Rocket who
does not have a knack for a turn of phrase is Ben Stark, who
utters only one epigrammatic statement:

> "Marriage is the only adventure open to the coward,"
> a certain man says. He made a mistake; you have
> to be a hero to face the pains and disappointments.
> (III)

More frequently, he is given to pedantic remarks, such as,
"Your aberration grows by the minute!" (III).   And the reason
for his slow-witted responses is supplied by Mr. Prince:
"What can he say?   He's as mixed up as the twentieth century!" (III).

In later plays Odets never composed so accomplished
a series of epigrams as he did in Rocket, but it is a mistake
to suppose that the wisecrack and epigram disappeared from
his dialogue.   In Night Music and Clash by Night, both weave
in and out of the rich mixture of his dialogue, defining character and establishing mood.   Steve Takis in Night Music says:

> I'm good on the wisecrack, the tough crack--offen-
> sive and defensive.   That's how I cheer myself up.
> But suppose I try to make the love crack--here's
> a nice girl--it ain't in my sample case! (II, 4)

Rosenberger's epigrams have a magisterial air, befitting his
Jehovah-like role in the play.   He tells Fay's father: "The
function of the parent is to make himself unnecessary.   Un-
fortunately, only animals and birds know it" (II, 3), and
rallies Fay's spirits: "To fall, Miss Tucker, is permitted.
But to get up is commanded" (II, 3).   Rosenberger admires
Steve because "he understands that life is no half-way business....   Only the living can cry out against life" (II, 4).
And when Steve claims that he is a big-shot in Hollywood,
Rosenberger remarks, "Lying is a certain form of cheering
yourself up" (II, 5).   Later, when his mask is stripped away,
Steve tells Fay: "Don't you know T-bone steak's the first
law of preservation?" (III, 2).

In Clash by Night, Mae's relationship with Jerry is
defined by one of her opening remarks to her carpenter-
husband: "... you talk too much, Jerry.   You jump on
everything like it's a plank and you're gonna saw it in half!"
(I, 1), and after they have taken in Earl as a boarder, she
shrewdly comments: "You impress me as one of those who

needs a new suit or a love affair, but he don't know which"
(I, 2), to which Earl replies, "You can't make me any
smaller ... I happen to be pre-shrunk. " Even Peggy, who
fears and yet wants to marry Joe, has an epigrammatic
flair: "Do you want my history in four words? Great ex-
pectations, great disappointments" (I, 2). Then there are
the cracks about money in this play about "how the poor
live ... " (Mae, II, 3). Both Earl and Mae answer the cliché
"Money isn't everything" with "It's ninety-nine point nine of
everything!" (I, 3). And in this play, where Hollywood is
called to account as a pernicious dream factory, we find the
following flippant exchange:

> EARL: They're not happy, those movie people,
> none of them.
> JERRY (awed): Yeah, all that money an' cars an'
> chauffeurs, an' what have they got?
> MAE (dryly): They've got money, cars and chauf-
> feurs ... (I, 1)

It was second nature for Odets to invent aphorisms,
but a favorite stragegy of his was to attribute them to others.
Thus, from Awake and Sing! on, he habitually prefixes a
maxim with the words "A great man said it ... " or "As a
famous historical character says ... " or "A certain man
says ... " However, in Clash by Night, when Vincent Kress
remarks, "A great man said it, social justice for all" (II, 1),
the effect is ironic: the great man was Father Coughlin, the
fascistic radio priest of the Shrine of the Little Flower. It
is curious how Odets can place an aphorism in the mouth of
even a minor character and have it linger in the memory.
Earl asks his fellow worker in the projectionist's booth:
"Say, Abe, what makes a happy marriage ... ?" and Abe responds: "Three children and a wife who can bake bread"
(II, 3).

It should be apparent by now that most of Odets' wisecracks and epigrams have to do with husbands and wives, the
vicissitudes of marriage and family life, and the deprivation
to the spirit caused by lack of money. He was the poet of
middle-class life, and what I have been calling epigrams
sometimes seem only a step removed from the wisecrack and
gag--an epigram being witty and pointed, while a wisecrack
is merely smart or facetious. All of Odets' sayings in this
category are pervaded by the folk wisdom of the middle-class
mind and are based on received moral assumptions. One
should not read them as one reads the aphorisms of Kahlil

Gibran--a poet who has great appeal for the young, but who is singularly uninterested in what Samuel Johnson called "the bread and tea of life."

In The Big Knife, a bitter play, Odets found more incisive epigrams and wisecracks to illuminate characters and a way of life that was, at that point in time, abhorrent to him. Early in the play, Charlie Castle remarks: "We're homesick all our lives, but adults don't talk about it, do they?" (I). He is not merely sickened by Hollywood's slick facade but by the money-grubbing disease that is infecting the whole country. He tells Nat, his agent and friend:

> How do we know that America isn't dying of trying to please its clients? ... What I mean ... don't you feel it in the air? Don't you see them pushing man off the earth and putting the customer in his place? (I)

I do not know whether the wisecrack he gives Patty Benedict-- "Divorce is as common as the ordinary head cold" (I)--originated with Odets, but the sentiments of Marion about marital fidelity have the Odetsian ring: "Nowadays, to be faithful ... it gives you that loony, old-fashioned moral grandeur of an equestrian statue in the park" (I). Marion is particularly good at cutting through linguistic clichés:

> CHARLIE: Come on now, be yourself....
> MARION: That's another good local remark: "Be yourself," which means, "Be just like me, don't be yourself!" (II)

Again, even the minor characters are given heightened, epigrammatic insights. Nat says, "... never underestimate a man because you don't like him" (I), and when Charlie tells him, "Every way is a way to die," he replies, "I'm older-- every way is a way to live" (I). And the villains also are given character-revealing wisecracks. Hoff says unctuously when bargaining with Charlie, "So you see, Charlie, I'm like a girl in a summer-time canoe--I can't say no!" (I), and Smiley advises Charlie, "Ideals, kid? Nowadays? A lost crusade.... (Smiling) Don't study life--get used to it" (II). As the plot mounts to its climax, Charlie, aping Claudius and Polonius, asks Hoff: "Were you never told the embroidery of your speech is all out of proportion to anything you have to say?" (III, 1). Coy succinctly remarks, "A woman with six martinis can ruin a city," and Charlie backs off from Coy's bloody plans, saying, "Murder is indivisible, Smiley.... Like chastity, there's no such thing as a small amount of it" (III, 1). Coy's farewell line to Marion is the epitome of his slimy nature: "I'd never forget your kindness for forgetting anything I'm ashamed to remember" (III, 2). This was undoubtedly the type of line that Joseph Wood Krutch was thinking of when he wrote: "... even the most vulgar of his villains rises to the dignity of the tortured ... "77

The Big Knife, an underrated play, is richly wrought with verbal inventions; Odets' ear was never better, and even the characters listen. Charlie says to Marion: "Okay, you win! Famous husband remarks--you win!" And moments later she says to him: "I know you deeply, darling ... I've had you with my morning coffee" (I). Remarks like these are not wisecracks or epigrams by strict definition, but the playful pun on sexual as well as mental intimacy points up an ironic contrast for the perceptive.

In The Country Girl, most of the ironic exchanges occur in the tautly dramatic encounters between Bernie Dodd and Georgie; often the dialogue ranges from the wisecrack to the epigram. When Bernie broaches the touchy subject of Frank's alcoholism--"Does Frank still drink?"--Georgie snaps back: "Just like us--one mouth and five fingers on every hand" (I, 2). Bernie disbelieves Frank's claim that Georgie sacrificed a big career to marry him: "What career? Marriage doesn't suit women any more--they don't want a home: the only piece of furniture they'll touch is the psychoanalyst's couch!" (I, 3). His distrust of Georgie is partially based on his bitterness over his ex-wife: "Five months ago she invented a phrase, 'The Perennial Bachelor,' and went to Reno to patent the invention!" And a moment later, he claims: "My wife was so twisted, 'I hope your next play's a big flop!' she says. 'So the whole world can see I love you even if you're a failure!'" (I, 3). When Bernie, deceived by Frank's lies, announces his judgment--"Lady, you ride that man like a broom! You're a bitch!"--Georgie, "after a long moment," says: "You have a very lyric and lurid opinion of me" (I, 5). Then, in II, 2, Georgie gets in some licks of her own:

> BERNIE: ... I'm interested in theater, not show business. I could make a fortune in films, but that's show "biz" to me.
> GEORGIE: What do you call this play, Literature?

And in the same scene, when Frank's hypocrisy has been

exposed and Bernie realizes that he both owes Georgie an apology and needs her help with Frank, she at first puts him off:

> BERNIE: I must ask you several questions ...
> GEORGIE: Michael on angel wings couldn't talk
>   to me with your face.

When Frank has been miraculously salvaged for his triumphant first night, Bernie capsules the role of a director: "... On an opening night, the world's most useless man" (II, 3). Unger, the playwright, had defined the writer's role earlier: "Loneliness is the badge of the writer's profession. It's ruined more good writers than every other reason combined" (II, 1). And Georgie dispatches the would-be lover of "The Country Girl" with some sage and sad advice: "Wrestle, Bernie, You may win a blessing. But stay unregenerate. Life knocks the sauciness out of us soon enough" (II, 3).

Thus it can be fairly stated that verbal irony, the flippant crack, and the philosophic aphorism remained part of Odets' poetic idiom throughout his career. There is some question about The Flowering Peach, where the bite and cynicism lessen and the humor becomes broader; even in this play, familial wisecracks are plentiful, though they are in keeping with the Sholom Aleichem-like, gemütlich tone that defines Noah's family. An example would be Esther, the perennial mother-in-law, remarking of Shem's wife, Leah: "She married the richest boy in the neighborhood, that's her trouble" (2); or Noah and Esther's exchange after Japheth has brought Goldie back from town:

> NOAH: Such a boy, so strange, what could he offer
>   a decent girl?
> ESTHER: He could offer her a nice boat ride. (3)

The wisecracks in this play sometimes have a Second Avenue ring. Take Japheth's admiring put-down of Noah:

> JAPHETH: ... but I love you, Poppa, and I always
>   will. You're the only master in my life--you
>   taught me everything I know. I respect and
>   revere you like you were dead.
> NOAH (dryly): Thanks ... (3)

And there is the vaudevillian twist in Noah's protest that there are no snails on board the Ark, and the exchange that follows:

> JAPHETH: We have one, the murmox snail.
> NOAH: But what good is one?
> NAPHETH: With snails the he is a he AND a she.
> NOAH (astonished): He's a she? A he AND a
>   she? Lucky person! (6)

Or of Noah's worried comment to Esther: "God didn't speak to me in a big long time. I'm worried, but no news is good news" (6). We might wonder with Japheth: "Is Poppa a saint or a fool? Now I know he's half of each ... but I never know which half is operating" (7). Yet Noah in his wrath can be terrible in his judgments; he tells Shem: "The whole world stinks of ruined bodies an' rotten grass. And today, Shem, on this sacred wood, your head's fulla business ... ?" (6). Japheth, the idealistic son, can be curtly critical. When Rachel asks, "Where did the wind come from suddenly," he replies: "From the bosom of God's infinite mercy ... " (5). And Esther can be contradictory and ferocious. After months of sailing, she and Noah are at odds:

> NOAH: Whatever you're saying, all of you, it's a
>   thing I hate it as well as I hate murder! The
>   ark is a holy temple!
> ESTHER: No, it's a stable--around the clock a
>   Turkish bath for animals! People are wore out
>   from work an' misery! (6)

So we respond to The Flowering Peach not only in the spirit of its shtetl humor but also to the dramatic irony of the happenings on board. We enjoy the mocking tone of Ham's offhand comments and the lyricism of Noah's soliloquies with God, which are not unmixed with humor. When Noah tries to beg off by claiming he knows nothing about boats: "... a pickle is a pickle, a knife is a knife--but boats?" (1), the stage directions read "Noah's slyness is reproved by a brief but angry thunger roll." Finally, we respond to our sheer enjoyment of its verbal rhythms and inflections. This is what Eric Bentley meant when he said in his review of the play:

> I left the theatre in a glow of pleasure and admira-
> tion; that perhaps is the main thing to say. And
> the source of the pleasure? In some degree, it is
> just that a play has been written--that is to say,
> set down in living language.... The real merit of
> this author, as of O'Casey and De Filippo, is a
> matter of the imaginative use of dialect, which in

turn is a matter of the poet's inner identification
with the poeple who speak that dialect.

I call these writers poets with only one poetic genre
in mind: the poetry of the theatre, a poetry of the
spoken word, the acted word, the word held up to
the light to be stared at by a crowd, the word flung
across footlights by actor-marksmen aiming straight
at the heart of an audience. And I have in mind
that when Mr. Odets' plays were presented in London during the Marxist decade "a well-known English novelist and playwright" dared to question the
reality in Mr. Odets' realism. "Practically every
scene is jazzed up, given more punch and excitement and noise than it should have, without reference to reality at all. " If he had added "and a
good thing too, " I should have agreed with him.
Not that I want to defend "noise, " which, for that
matter, Mr. Odets, in his new play, does without.
But there was always more jazz and punch in Mr.
Odets than there was "socialist realism, " less of
Karl, than of Harpo, Marx.

All of which is to repeat that he is a poet and of
the theatre. [78]

Cliché and Verbal Strategy

To end this survey of Odets' dialogue with Eric Bentley's tribute is tempting, but it would not be honest. It ignores the criticism of the English reviewer cited by Bentley,
and there have been others like it on this side of the Atlantic.

In his initial review of Golden Boy, Brooks Atkinson
noted:

His dialogue is the best and the worst of his talent.
It is the best instrument in his expression because
it is vigorous, crisp and salty and because it gets
at the truth of characters by indirection.... But
Mr. Odets's taste is unsettled. In fact, his dialogue is by turns so genuine and so counterfeit that
he can almost be said to have no taste at all.
Especially in the first act ... he writes with a
braggart's want of discrimination--joining cheap
cleverness and Broadway flippancies to genuine

182 / Clifford Odets

> improvisations. In his eagerness to avoid a dull
> statement of a situation Mr. Odets sounds like a
> medley of popular songs; he echoes all the brassy
> bits of argot he has ever heard. [79]

This is a rather severe statement in a review that was generally a rave ("one of his best plays"), and one wonders how
it is possible for estimates of the playwright's language to
fluctuate so widely among astute critics, many of whom admire his plays. I suppose that some sensibilities simply reject Odets' hyper-realism in dialogue. Even when they understand what he is doing and why, critics such as Hunt[80] com-
pile lists of gaucheries and clichés, and where I will find a
line surprising and delicious, they find that same line flatu-
lent and obvious. The principle de gustibus operates even
in the most closely and logically constructed analyses.

Still, I began the section on lyricism by stating that
Odets' Whitman-like "barbaric yawp" was emitted consciously,
that it was composed with deliberate artistic purpose, and
that, for the most part, it succeeds. I can prove this to
my satisfaction, though it may matter not a jot to Messrs.
Atkinson and Hunt. In examining the plays' language, I have
come across several specific strategies Odets uses when revealing character through dialogue.

One is the placing of a metaphor or image in the
mouth of a character who might logically be expected to use
it by virtue of his trade or occupation. In Lefty, Edna, a
housewife, in exhorting Joe to strike with the other hackies,
tells him, if the others will not fight, "let them all be ground
to hamburger!" She tells Joe: "Sweep out those racketeers
like a pile of dirt!" and exhorts him, "Get brass toes on
your shoes and know where to kick!" (Ironically, she had
just been worrying about having her daughter's shoes soled.)
In Awake and Sing!, Moe, a gambler all his life, pronounces
Hennie's soubriquet: "Paradise," Pair-a-dice. In Paradise
Lost, Kewpie, a cab driver, tells Libby that Ben is "A burnt
out spark plug" (I), and Ben, an athlete, uses imagery from
sports: after announcing his sudden marriage, he urges his
family to celebrate, saying, "Let's make it a real field
day ... " (I); when Clara asks him, "How's business?" he
replies, "Swimming without my water wings by now" (II).
In Rocket, Ben, a dentist, tells Belle: "We're like two exposed nerves!" (III). Mae Wilenski, another housewife, tells
Jerry, "The season's over for us. I can't help it ... everything's in camphor" (Clash by Night, II, 1). In The Country

Girl, Cook, the financial backer, says, "I wish I could lay
myself away in a safety deposit box for a few months!" (I,
1), and Georgie describes herself to Frank in a moment of
anger: "Old waffle iron ... ! The mop behind the door ... "
(II, 1). And Esther, in The Flowering Peach, tells Japheth:
"Ham likes her very much ... a tested recipe by now ...
and Rachel knows it" (5). These metaphors and images,
while they are far from startling and original, seem perfectly
natural in the mouths of the characters who speak them.

Odets' problem as a middle-class dramatist was to
find fresh ways of expressing familiar thoughts. The people
who inhabit the family plays--clerks, cabbies, housewives,
fruit store owners--and the upper middle-class professionals
of later plays--dentists, Broadway and Hollywood show people--
would tend to speak in clichés. Short of giving them idiosyncratic speech tics and endowing them with unusual eloquence
(both of which tactics he tried), how could he avoid the flattening out of their speech patterns into dreary platitudes and
bromides? If he was to avoid a reputation as master of the
cliché, he had to master the cliché itself. This is a second
strategy I have noted: Odets' tendency to take a tired phrase
and infuse it with fresh energy, or follow it rapidly with an
original juxtaposition that banishes the curse. Sometimes it
is simply a matter of a changed inflection or a variation in
syntax.

Jacob, in Awake and Sing!, says, "... new lessons ...
not for an old dog" (II, 2). Combining two maxims, Uncle
Morty advises Bessie, "In the long run common sense is
thicker than love" (II, 1), and Ralph tells Jacob, "Two can
starve as cheap as one!" (II, 2). In Paradise Lost, after
Gus' tragicomic account of his arrest for supposedly molest-
ing a woman on the subway, he states pontifically: "Yes,
yes ... believe me, the sanctity of human dignity, " and is
interrupted by Clara: "You'll eat some supper, Gus--pot
roast" (II). Or take the rapid juxtaposition of Ben's exclama-
tions to his brother and sister: "Orphans of the storm! We
are low enough to crawl under a snake! Julie, Pearl, rise
and shine!" (II). The ironic "rise and shine" echoes hollowly
the lyric cry to "awake and sing" in Ralph's conversion speech
and Agate's curtain speech.

Often the unadorned cliché is voiced by ignorant or un-
sympathetic characters. Fatt's opening speech in Lefty is
typical--"It's the trend of the times. " Uncle Morty, a firm
believer in the American Dream, says: "This is Uncle Sam's

country. Put it in your pipe and smoke it" (<u>Awake and Sing!</u>,
II, 1); and Libby tells Gus: "See you in the funny papers,
Pop!" (<u>Paradise Lost</u>, I). In contrast, Odets attempts to
rescue the colorful or interesting character from linguistic
limbo via the unexpected twist or unusual juxtaposition. In
<u>Golden Boy</u>, Roxy Gottlieb says, "Wine, women and song, to
make a figure of speech. We offer him <u>magnitudes</u>! ... "
(I, 3), and later he congratulates Tokio: "I gotta give the
devil his dues" (II, 1). When an intelligent character like
Mr. Prince lapses into a clichéd wisecrack, Odets redeems
him by the originality of his next sentence. For example:

> STARK: I feel sure she wants to bury the axe.
> PRINCE (<u>cynically</u>): Certainly.... Right in my
> head! I have a certain respectable mania for
> the truth--we don't like each other. (<u>Rocket to</u>
> <u>the Moon</u>, I)

Few platitudinous phrases are allowed to stand alone. They
are either introduced--Prince: "Last night I fell asleep and
dreamed the secret of the world. It is not good for Man to
live alone" (III)--or they are given metaphoric reenforce-
ment--Prince: "A dear true friend is more than love--the
serge outlasts the silk" (III).

Odets sometimes went to incongruous lengths to avoid
the naked cliché. In <u>Night Music</u>, Steve Takis tells the Lieutenant, "I hear you like water off a duck's back" (I, 1), and
later Steve abruptly terminates a familiar literary allusion,
saying: "Fay, you're a thing of beauty. You're delicate....
I don't know how to say it.... You're flowers on the hill,
morning on the river ... but I'd puddle you up in a month"
(III, 2).

In <u>Clash by Night</u>, Earl launches into a familiarly trite
expression, which swerves unexpectedly: "A man's just a
bum without a woman, a foul tip ... " (I, 1). In general,
though, <u>Clash by Night</u> is Odets' least rewarding play linguistically. For every good line--Earl: "I don't enjoy my
life ... I enjoy only the dream of it" (I, 3)--there are two
bad ones--Joe: "We wear our love like a mustard plaster,
don't we?" (I, 2); and Mae's final curtain speech to Peg and
Joe: "Go on, the fist of God is in your back! Now get out
of here" (II, 3). The latter is my choice as the most overstrained and unconsciously comic line in Odets.

In later plays Odets continued to employ the cliché-cum-witticism. Nat Danziger, in The Big Knife, soothes his angry and anguished client: "Charlie, for once I'll tell you shut up. Stop wringing your mental hands" (III, 2). In The Country Girl, Frank is addicted to outright clichés because he affects a deceptively casual air to the outside world; the clichés suggest his hypocrisy. But Georgie employs a trite metaphor to administer a home truth:

> GEORGIE: ... We're at the bottom--
> FRANK (stoutly): But we'll be at the top!
> GEORGIE (correcting him): But one rung at a
> time, separated by quiet, healthy sleep. (I, 4)

In The Flowering Peach, the same process is repeated. Goldie, the visitor to the Ark, tells Noah about the townsfolk: "They're just killing time. And time is killing them" (4). Noah, in an antic mood, can say: "What! I'm a loaf of bread. Don't butter me, Shem" (7). And then he can intone a traditional prayer to the Lord that might seem humdrum, except for the unexpected colloquialism with which it ends:

> Oh, Lord above us, are we no more to see peace
> an' good in our day ... ? This is a serious
> game ... Give the people time to repent! Look
> in your pocket to forgive them ... (2)

There are some scenes in Odets where the clichés figure in still another way, as a kind of fugal counterpoint with no verbal twist or unexpected juxtaposition; they exist to point up ironies or underlying symbols. In II, 3, of Golden Boy, where Lorna defaults on her promise to Joe to leave Moody, there are a half-dozen clichés. Moody's pathetic appeal for her loyalty--"What the hell's all this struggle to make a living for if not for a woman and a home?" (II, 3)--is followed by Lorna's "I oughta burn. I'm leaving you...." Next Joe enters and tells Moody Lorna loves him, not Moody, and asks, "Is it so impossible?" "About as possible as hell freezes over," Moody replies. Then, after Joe has stalked off angrily, we get the last of this deliberate series of clichés:

> MOODY: What's wrong, Lorna? You can tell me....
> LORNA: I feel like the wrath of God.
> MOODY: You like that boy, don't you?
> LORNA: I love him, Tom.

The redeeming effects of all these banalities are the symbolic hellfire that forges many of the phrases and the dramatic irony apparent to the audience, as Lorna vacillates between truths and half-truths and total lies. These may not justify the language for everyone--it did not for Brooks Atkinson-- but, nevertheless, this scene works.

The architectonics of Odets' poetic constructions de- serve careful analysis. On the whole, Odets' dialogue suc- ceeds more often than it fails because it functions on deeper levels than the audience at first surmises. I have been con- cerned so far with demonstrating the range and variety of his dialogue, but many individual lines have poetic resonances and components that my survey has only hinted at. A few examples will serve here to indicate what I mean.

Moe's remark to Hennie in Awake and Sing!--"Say the word--I'll tango on a dime" (III)--is one of them. In its immediate context, the line is a passionate appeal for love, and is followed by a popular ballad-like reenforcing line that is more blatant--"Don't gimme ice when your heart's on fire!" A scanning of this line reveals a syncopated one-two- three rhythm which evokes a Latin American dance beat. Moe, who is about to launch into his "break-out" speech, is using every possible means to convince Hennie. The irony of a one-legged man who is willing to attempt the tango be- cause of the intensity of his passion has a seriocomic effect.

But the resonance of the line extends further. The audience presumably would remember the conclusion of II, 1, in which Ralph receives a phone call from Blanche, while the rest of the family, excluding Jacob, is eating in the din- ing room. To cover his clandestine talk, Ralph asks Jacob to turn up the radio, and "Music comes in and up, a tango, grating with an insistent nostalgic pulse" (Stage Direction). Ralph's disillusionment when he learns that Blanche's family is sending her out West parallels Moe's ill-concealed chagrin when Hennie is married off to Sam Feinschreiber. The radio tango symbolizes Ralph's undiminished passion as, later, the word "tango" symbolizes Moe's.

There is a further connection between Moe's phrase and two major motifs of the play--sex and money. The very fact that Moe is willing to "tango on a dime" suggests that passion and money are closely related in his mind. Actually, the phrase probably derives from Moe's familiarity with the taxi dance halls of the period and their ten-cents-a-dance hostesses; he may be implying that he is willing to become a male prostitute if only he can convince Hennie to leave her husband. In any case, the phrase conjures up the desperation and moral laxities of the Depression period.

There is yet another component to the phrase which relates it to "The Family Trap" theme. A tango is a highly stylized dance, characterized by stiff restraint of the upper torso while the legs perform intricate, wide-ranging movements; it is a sinuous, sultry dance, but one filled with highly artificial poses. The fact that Moe is willing to figuratively perform this dance on the smallest of coins suggests both the pressures and restraints felt in the Berger household, where there exists "a struggle for life amidst petty conditions" (Preface Notes). Moe has, in fact, been playing a role, hiding behind his wise-guy cynicism, holding back from declaring his true feelings. But now, despite his bravado, he is willing to accept the risks and financial obligations which a break-out with Hennie would involve. The restrictiveness of the metaphor impresses Moe less than its sensuous implications.

All of this would not be at once apparent to an audience, but the associations of a phrase such as Axelrod's build toward an allusive ambience that enriches a major theme. Hoff's wisecrack in The Big Knife--"So you see, Charlie. I'm like a girl in a summer-time canoe--I can't say no" (I)--is another such line rich in allusive possibilities. It capsulizes the conflation of sex and money, which is the Hollywood scene. It is precisely this combination which has corrupted Charlie Castle. The remark in its immediate context is made by the studio head who is trying to inveigle his star property into signing a ten-year contract which would prostitute his talents, by offering the lagniappe of a cash bonus. That is only one of its ironies. The phrase reminds us of Marion's earlier remark about Charlie's "occasional girls, " and looks forward to the conclusion of Act I, when Charlie "can't say no" to the tempting Connie Bliss and staggers drunkenly upstairs to bed her. In the same way, the remark foreshadows the fate of Dixie Evans, who tries to say no to Marcus Hoff and then floats perilously on the Hollywood tide until she is killed by a car while drunkenly crossing the street. Above all, the metaphor is applicable to Charlie's boxed-in status as he is blackmailed and pressured into signing the contract he had promised his wife not to sign. "Nolo contendere: I do not contend" (II), Charlie tells Marion, and this is, and has been, his tragedy.

Even a casual remark like Roxy Gottlieb's in Golden

Boy--"I think I'll run across the street and pick up an eight-cylinder lunch" (I, 3)--works on several levels. Not only does it reenforce the negative and destructive symbol of Joe's Deusenberg in which he dies (see above, p. 137), but it suggests the false values of power and prestige which have lured Joe away from his career as a violinist. Roxy, who gorges himself on others, thinks of an eight-course meal as a casual luxury, but the metaphor he uses reenforces the play's moral concept that success obtained by mechanical, unnatural means is grotesque. Further, the speed necessitated by a competitive, brutal society turns a civilized pause in the day into an orgiastic, potentially sickening eating bout. That such an interpretation was intended by Odets can be seen by examining in context Moody's next line to the departing Roxy. He tells his not-too-bright, greedy partner: "Sprinkle it with arsenic. Do that for me, for me, sweetheart!"

Further instances of the resonances which individual lines possess might be cited, but one cannot deny that Odets' images are sometimes trite, and that his "poetry" is occasionally banal. That this is true of many modern dramatists from O'Neill to Albee certainly does not mitigate the lapses in a playwright I have consistently called poetic. Though banal lines exist, sometimes even the banality, in the context of other pressures of language, is raised to a level of genuine intensity. In Clash by Night, where the working class milieu makes bromides inevitable, Mae's definition of her ideal man begins and ends with clichés: "Today they're little and nervous, sparrows! But I dream of eagles ... I guess I'm cuckoo!" (I, 2). The "Today ... " sentence is flat, merely accurately "realistic" speech. The same is true of "I guess I'm cuckoo!" But between these two banalities one finds: "But I dream of eagles." Here, Odets is consciously reaching for grandeur and nobility, consciously elevating his language, deliberately eschewing the flat-realistic for the more artificial, stylized rhetoric of poetic utterance. Rubbing banality against "poetry." That mixture of tones allows his audience to move rapidly from the unavoidably banal to the romantically sublime. With a sudden throb of empathy, we realize that the submerged passions of the Mae Wilenskis of this world are our passions.

The process can work in reverse. I have cited previously (page 185) Noah's humble appeal to God in The Flowering Peach to postpone the catastrophe and give the people time to repent. Since much of this speech is imitative of biblical diction, it would be intoned by the actor at

a high level of emotional intensity. The tone would be for-
mal-poetic, a phony striving for Miltonic grandeur. But
what does Odets do? He has Noah remind God that "This
is a serious game," and urge, "Look in your pocket to for-
give them ..." The oxymoron and the idiomatic phrase
combine to deflate what could have been merely pompous.
And we who read or listen are touched by the humanity of
this none too saintly figure pleading with an anthropomorphic
God to save his fellow humans from catastrophe. It is because of Odets' willingness to take verbal risks, and his
superb ear for tonal qualities that his dialogue is unique and
deserves the adjective--poetic.

There are other strategies Odets employs in his dialogue: for example, his tendency to give his characters
identifying tag lines and speech tics, which has been amply
covered by Weales and Dusenbury. [81] I have already discussed Odets' use of allusions both to literature and popular
culture in my chapter on "The Family Trap" and described
how they function (see above, pp. 40-42). It is important to
recognize that Odets did not confine these allusions to the
family plays but kept up a running satiric commentary on
mass circulation anodynes and popular songs in Golden Boy,
Rocket to the Moon, Night Music, Clash by Night, and all
of his post-war plays. Even The Flowering Peach has Noah
referring to the Flood in terms that remind one of the editor
of a tabloid daily--"A story like this, big as Adam--bigger
maybe--such a story you put yourself against?!" (4). Ralph
Willett has said: "Odets realizes that, however corny the
images of beauty and contentment circulated by popular culture, they at least provide a language through which the inarticulate can express their desires."[82]

Odets' use of slang terms deserves some mention
here, but not as much as one would think. My survey of
slang terms that have actually dated, such as "Marvellousy"
and "Carbolic," indicates that the percentage of such terms
is much lower than one might expect, considering that his
last play, The Flowering Peach, was written more than 20
years ago. But, even now, having delved into syntax and
strategies, I keep remembering Weales' statement that "It
is easier to recognize an Odets line than to characterize
one," and think of Cummings' lines, "since feeling is first/
who pays any attention/to the syntax of things/will never
wholly kiss you." I hope that I have adequately conveyed the
raciness of Odets' dialogue. Odets' hyperbole, though it can
be obtrusive, nevertheless has the power to transfix his

audience. I think of Sid telling Florrie that they must break
their engagement: "The answer is no--a big electric sign
looking down on Broadway" (Lefty, The Young Hack and His
Girl), or Belle insisting that Ben Stark owes her "certain
common courtesies, " and then when he asks her what, shouting: "The truth! The truth! The truth!" (Rocket to the
Moon, III). What one finally remembers in Odets' dialogue
is its sheer exuberance: Moody saying, "I'm up to the throat
in scandal, blackmail, perjury, alimony and all points west!"
(Golden Boy, I, 1); Frank Elgin, in an ebullient mood, recalling their former life to Georgie: "There's so much to remember of living together--all the winters and summers ...
And the fights, snarling and yipping--settling blue murder
with an hour in the bed ... " (The Country Girl, I, 3). And
its lyrical, quiet moments: Esther telling Noah: "This time,
I won't take your part against the boys--you'll sail alone, my
sailor, on the lonely deep, " and his answer: "Lonely times
is nothing new to me ... " (The Flowering Peach, 1).

I suppose that Odets' dialogue can only be summed up
by a critical cliché (with a twist): the whole is infinitely
greater than its parts, the mix better than any single ingredient. It seems ironic to cite T. S. Eliot's "disassociation
of sensibility" theory here, for the New Critics would despise
Odets' language for its uninhibited embrace of the banal and
the racy, and its refusal to let form and control always
balance emotion. But Odets' dialogue exhibits a fusion of
thought and emotion that is not metaphysical like Donne's--
hardly that complex and sophisticated--but it has comparable
significance for its own time and place. For the poet in
Odets knew the middle-class myths and assumptions intellec-
tually, he felt them intuitively, and he fused thought and
emotion in a richly earthy and profuse dialogue that begins
and ends in a folk idiom--nourished in the urban ghetto atmosphere where a large part of the middle class first grew
and flourished.

NOTES

[1]Burke, The Philosophy of Literary Form (Baton
Rouge, 1941), pp. 430-31.

[2]Burke, pp. 33-35.

[3]Quoted in Clurman, Fervent Years, p. 139.

[4]Quoted in Rabkin, p. 186.

[5]Krutch, American Drama, p. 271.

[6]Quoted in Weales, Clifford Odets, p. 94.

[7]Lawson, Theory and Technique, pp. 249-55; see Blankfort, quoted in Weales, Clifford Odets, pp. 102-3.

[8]Phelan, pp. 590-91.

[9]In addition to Weales, Clifford Odets, pp. 102-3, see Himelstein, pp. 166-76, passim.

[10]"Center Stage," May 1963, p. 74.

[11]Wagner, p. 65.

[12]"Center Stage," May 1963, p. 76.

[13]Murray, p. 33.

[14]Weales, Clifford Odets, pp. 47-49.

[15]Lawson, Theory and Technique, p. 254.

[16]Nathan, pp. 291-92.

[17]Goldstein, Political Stage, p. 321.

[18]Introduction to Night Music, p. xii.

[19]Odets, "On Coming Home," p. 1.

[20]Agee on Film (New York, 1958), I, 197.

[21]The Moral Impulse (Carbondale, 1967), p. 107.

[22]"Center Stage," June 1963, p. 30.

[23]The symbolic opposition between light and darkness is worth noting in this speech. Odets uses it elsewhere; for example, Esther in The Flowering Peach dies with the sun in her face.

[24]Murray has a good discussion of both the orange and egg images as they relate to the procreative theme and the Hennie-Moe relationship, pp. 48-50.

[25]Weales, Clifford Odets, p. 30, alludes to Odets'

habit of inserting the off-stage names of Group directors in his plays, such as the Mrs. Strasberg who minds Hennie's baby in Awake and Sing!, and the Dr. Clurman who looks after Julie in Paradise Lost as an "affectionate joke." Weales regards the reference to the Kazan seed as a continuation of this private joke. But Kazan had already "sung" before HUAC in January of 1952 (see Kanfer, p. 173), alienating many of his old friends in the profession. The reference in scene 3 is put in the mouth of the materialistic son, Shem, who admires the cucumber's size and texture: "It's the Kazan seed--it's an early grower, without rain." His wife makes a note as she customarily does "for anything which suggests possible gain" (Odets' Stage Directions). This does not sound complimentary to me, and hardly "affectionate."

[26]Mendelsohn, "Center Stage," June 1963, p. 29, questioned Odets about the omission of this scene in the Modern Library version of Waiting for Lefty in Six Plays. Odets claimed that the scene had been dropped because "it seemed to me so untypical to include an unemployed actor and a casting agent, that I simply dropped it for that reason." When Mendelsohn pressed him for further details explaining its omission from the printed version, Odets was uncommunicative.

[27]Parenthetically we should note that once having found a good line, Odets was reluctant to let go of it. Leo, in Paradise Lost, says, "We will live, my darling Clara, we will live to see strange and wonderful events" (II). The line from the Preface Notes to Awake and Sing!, "She knows that when one lives in the jungle one must look out for the wild life," is uttered verbatim by Kewpie (Paradise Lost, I). Ben Stark in Rocket to the Moon, tells Cleo, "All I can offer you is a second-hand life" (III), which is the same phrase for a humdrum existence Fay Tucker uses (Night Music, II, 3). A key line in The Big Knife is Hank Teagle's, "If you wrestle, Charlie, you may win a blessing" (III, 1), and this turns up as Georgie's advice to Bernie Dodd at the conclusion of The Country Girl: "Wrestle, Bernie. You may win a blessing."

[28]Quoted in Weales, Clifford Odets, p. 188.

[29]Gus has also sold his beloved stamp collection to assist his friends. Parenthetically we might note that Odets had a fixation about postage stamps, emblems of official success which he regards as worthless. For example, in Till

the Day I Die, Tillie tells Carl, "He's your brother, " and
he responds: "That won't sell a postage stamp!" (2); in
Paradise Lost, Ben says, "What did I want? To be a great
man? Get my picture on a postage stamp?" (II); and in The
Country Girl, Bernie tells Georgie: "I'm ambitious--I wanna
get my picture on a green postage stamp, too.... I know I
won't--the idea is talented but phony" (I, 5).

[30]"White Hope, " p. 45.

[31]Clifford Odets, p. 5.

[32]Mersand sees a parallel between the character's
joy when he sights land in L'Africane with Jacob's remembered
joy "when he beheld the shore of America, " p. 65. Other
critics stress the irony of his wistful hope in the face of im-
potence and failure.

[33]Burke, p. 35.

[34]Murray, pp. 68-69. There is another thorough discussion of this scene in James H. Clay and Daniel Krempel,
The Theatrical Image (New York, 1967), pp. 69-71, which
includes part of a sound-and-lighting plot.

[35]Murray, p. 80. His discussion of the radio music
in Act I of The Country Girl and the radio's subsequent identification with Georgie is perceptive, a brilliant piece of work,
and can be consulted for further proof of Odets' artistic use
of music, pp. 189-91.

[36]I know I have listed this among Odets' failures, and
it does read like a bad play, but it remains curiously vivid
in one's memory. Clurman gives some cogent reasons for
the failure of its revival in 1951 in "Around Night Music, "
New Republic, 124 (30 Apr. 1951), 22, but I should like to
see it staged once more because I suspect it is one of those
plays that must be heard and seen--not read.

[37]Weales, Clifford Odets, p. 143.

[38]Warnock, p. 554.

[39]On the Contrary (New York, 1961), p. 303.

[40]Krutch, American Drama, p. 272.

[41]Kempton, p. 186.

[42]Alan S. Downer, Fifty Years of American Drama (Chicago, 1951), p. 61.

[43]Haskell M. Block and Robert G. Shedd, eds., Masters of Modern Drama (New York, 1952), p. 646.

[44]Gibson, Golden Boy, p. 10.

[45]See Atkinson, rev. of Golden Boy, New York Times, 21 Nov. 1937, Sec. 11, p. 1; Young, quoted in Mersand, p. 73; John Gassner, Masters of the Drama, 3rd rev. ed. (New York, 1954), p. 692.

[46]Mersand, p. 72.

[47]Ruby Cohn, Dialogue in American Drama (Bloomington, 1971), pp. 5-6.

[48]Cohn, pp. 68-69.

[49]Odets admitted his debt to Lawson--particularly to the latter's Success Story--in Mendelsohn's interview, "Center Stage," May 1963, p. 76.

[50]Mersand, p. 63, quotes an interview with Odets from the New York World Telegram, 19 Mar. 1935, in which Odets acknowledges a debt to Emerson.

[51]Alfred Kazin and Daniel Aaron, eds., Emerson (New York, 1958), p. 238.

[52]Clurman, Fervent Years, p. 140.

[53]Shuman, "Clifford Odets: A Playwright and His Jewish Background," South Atlantic Quarterly, 71 (1972), 228.

[54]Weales, Clifford Odets, pp. 76-77.

[55]Kazin, Thirties, pp. 80-81.

[56]Warshow, The Immediate Experience (New York, 1962), p. 58.

[57]It is not my intention to trace these historical and cultural influences here, but for those interested, they are documented in Judd L. Teller, Strangers and Natives (New York, 1968); Rhoda Silver Kachuk, "The Portrayal of the Jew

in American Drama Since 1920," Diss., Univ. of Southern
California, 1971; Richard H. Goldstone, "The Making of
Americans: Clifford Odets' Implicit Theme," Proceedings
of the IVth Congress of the International Comparative Literature Association, 1966, 654-60; Shuman, "Jewish Background,"
pp. 225-33.

[58]Warshow, pp. 60-65.

[59]G. W. Haslam, "Odets' Use of Yiddish-English in
Awake and Sing," Research Studies of Washington State University, 34 (1966), 161-64, passim.

[60]"Of American Jewish writers, only Clifford Odets,
whose original voice is now unrecognized (probably because
it is assumed that all Jews talked this way during the Depression), took the same pleasure [as Malamud] in creating
this art-language from Yiddish roots." Alfred Kazin, Bright
Book of Life (Boston, 1973), pp. 141-42.

[61]Leo Rosten, The Joys of Yiddish (New York, 1968),
p. 292.

[62]Morris Freedman in Introduction to Mendelsohn,
Clifford Odets, p. xiii.

[63]Flexner, p. 299.

[64]Mersand, p. 82, and Shuman, Clifford Odets, p. 71.

[65]Odets, "Some Problems of the Modern Dramatist,"
New York Times, 15 Dec. 1935, Sec. 11, p. 3.

[66]Cohn, p. 68.

[67]Clifford Odets, pp. 79-80.

[68]"Pay-off on Odets," New Republic, 100 (27 Sept.
1939), 216.

[69]See Gassner, Crossroads, p. 155, and Mendelsohn,
Clifford Odets, pp. 80-81.

[70]Henri Bergson, "Laughter," in Comedy, ed. Marvin Felheim (New York, 1962), p. 216.

[71]Sigmund Freud, "Wit and Its Relation to the

Unconscious," in Comedy, ed. Marvin Felheim (New York, 1962), p. 231.

[72]Bergson, p. 225.

[73]For an entirely different view of this passage, see Albert Hunt, "Only Soft-Centered Left," Encore, 8 (May-June 1961), 10.

[74]Gorelik, in Clay and Krempel, p. 139.

[75]See Odets' letter in Whit Burnett, ed., This Is My Best (New York, 1942), p. 786.

[76]Shuman, Clifford Odets, pp. 99-100.

[77]Krutch, American Drama, p. 272.

[78]Bentley, "Poetry of the Theater," pp. 210-11.

[79]Atkinson, rev. of Golden Boy.

[80]Hunt, passim.

[81]See Weales, Clifford Odets, p. 48, and Dusenbury, pp. 99-100.

[82]Willett, "Clifford Odets and Popular Culture," South Atlantic Quarterly, 69 (1970), p. 74.

CHAPTER IV

THE SUM AND THE SUBSTANCE

> ... here's me and there's that miserable
> no-good, lonely world out there ... hurts
> me.
>   --Noah, The Flowering Peach

Now that more than a decade has passed since Clifford
Odets died of stomach cancer at the age of 57 in Cedars of
Lebanon Hospital in Los Angeles, it is possible to understand
why he has remained so persistently an underrated dramatist.
There was first his youthful flirtation with Marxism and his
trumpet-tongued early plays, which blared out "the birth-cry
of the Thirties" and both identified and stereotyped him as
the Depression playwright.   Next there was his seeming ex-
emplification of the Hollywood sell-out, his self-flagellation
in plays of his own devising.   Then there was his failure to
produce a serious play on Broadway during the last decade
of his life--nothing from The Flowering Peach in 1954 until
he died in August, 1963, at work on a musical version of
Golden Boy.   And, finally, there was the domination of the
New Criticism and the emphasis on existential philosophy
during the Fifties and Sixties, both of which contributed to
his neglect.

Given the strengths of his prose-poetry, his gallery
of characters, and his thematic consistency, we may understand all these factors and still wonder why he was relegated
to a minor role in the literary histories and in many works
of dramatic criticism.   Now we can see that critics were
inclined to emphasize his weaknesses instead of his strengths.
Because he wrote personal plays which objectified his subjective experience, critics tended to confuse the man and his
plays and made Clifford Odets a character in an Odets drama.
Both the man and his plays are fused in his work, but it is
necessary to recognize that Odets used himself as a microcosm of American experience.   In this respect the British,

who greeted both his early and late plays with warm critical enthusiasm, were wiser than we. Robert Whitehead has remarked:

> I think that one of the reasons for Odets's importance to the American theatre is that his work reflects so strikingly certain American national characteristics: rebelliousness, virility and violence coupled with tenderness, sentiment, and humor. Perhaps this is the very reason Odets has been so successful in England, where other important American playwrights seemingly have not been understood. The English probably find some fascination--perhaps it is a repulsive fascination-- in this simple, robust, naked emotion of his, so directly in contrast with their polite expression.
>
> It is interesting to me that Odets's earlier works, sometimes charged with being limited by their topicality, all possess the same underlying general theme--the need and the search for responsibility and self-respect that can help generate the finest nature in man. [1]

This confusion of the man and his plays was no doubt responsible for the intense response to Odets' death. The obit writer for The New York Times set the tone; in his piece he referred to failure seven times, and commented:

> Scarcely a year went by without a promise of a new play, a new Broadway repertory company, a new film that he would make his "personal" contribution to the artistically developing movie industry.
>
> Frequently, he kept his promises--but the artistic potential everyone expected to materialize was somehow never quite fulfilled. [2]

A host of friends sprang to Odets' defense and amid the tributes to a warmhearted, sensitive human being, there were explanations of why there had been so great a falling off. Odets had been traumatized by a series of events in the Fifties: his divorce from his second wife, Bette Grayson, and her death soon after, leaving him with two children to rear; his inner revulsion at his public humiliation before HUAC in 1952;[3] the monetary failure of the critically success-

ful The Flowering Peach and the Columbia University trustees'
refusal to accept the Drama Committee's recommendation to
award a Pulitzer Prize to that play (it was given to Williams'
Cat on a Hot Tin Roof instead). [4] "The Theater Did Not Want
Clifford Odets," j'accused William Gibson in The New York
Times, [5] and Max Lerner rhapsodized over his friend whom
time "had left ... like a lonely sea creature stranded on the
beach by a receding wave. "[6]

Undoubtedly all these events had wounded Odets and
made him wary of charging the front lines of Broadway again
(a conversation with Mendelsohn indicates as much). [7] But
what the apologists forgot was that during the height of these
several pressures Odets had turned out the flawed but vibrant
The Big Knife and two excellent plays: The Country Girl and
The Flowering Peach. Moreover, during his decade of
silence he never ceased to write and plan and continue his
critical onslaught on all that he thought was phony and wrong
in America. In 1963, shortly before his death, a physically
haggard but verbally resourceful Odets appeared on a half-
hour TV interview show entitled "The Sum and Substance. "
When asked what would be his crucial commitment and what
he would communicate in a play at this time, Odets replied:

> I would want to talk, in our country particularly,
> about the fulfillment of each individual human being.
> I would want to make a statement, as definitive as
> I was able--let me say, at the age of 75, knock
> on wood. I would like to make a statement about
> what, in our American world, develops, or the in-
> herent possibilities of each man and woman, and
> what holds them back, what stymies them. Con-
> comitantly with that I would like to make a state-
> ment in the same work about innocence versus ex-
> perience. I have the play picked out, I have the
> materials picked out, and I don't think it's a play
> that I will write until I am really 10 or 15 years
> older. I find our American world today, I find it
> lacks innocence; I find it lacks the conviction of
> innocence; I find that as quickly as we can, we
> are taught, we pick up from the air, we pick it
> up from the movies or the magazines, we pick up
> those techniques in which we are richest, and those
> are the techniques of conciliation and ingratiation,
> the techniques of selling yourself, of getting across,
> which necessarily means that innocence goes, and
> experience perhaps shrivels our souls. I would

> include, in a final statement in a play, a need and
> feeling for human sympathy as I once said, but
> human sympathy and cooperation always within a
> context of personal integrity. [8]

Later, as he inveighs against success in this country, one
realizes that Odets was still vibrant and alive, still plugged
into the nervous currents of American life and thought: "The
newspapers, magazines beat down your door. They want interviews. They want to give you publicity. They must be
hep. They want to be in the know. They want to get the
news first. So that the buildup works always. "

It is, of course, sad to think that we shall never see
those roughed-out plays: An Old-Fashioned Man, which he
described to both Wagner and Mendelsohn;[9] and the biblical
drama on Saul and David, in which he seemed intent on re-
mining the ore of Golden Boy:

> I want to show in David, who is pursued by a psy-
> chotic Saul, a young poet. And I want to show how
> the young poet becomes a very successful man--in-
> deed, the most successful in his realm, because he
> becomes the King. And I want to show the life of
> Man from the time he is a poet until he dies an
> old man, unhappy, but somehow still a poet gnaw-
> ing at his soul. I want to turn the various facets
> of his nature around so that you see what happens
> to men of big success and how they meet the con-
> flicting situations of their lives. [10]

These projected plays sound intriguing, but nothing in
Odets' description of them convinces me that they would have
been radically different in theme, characterization, or tone
from the eleven plays he did finish. If my study has convinced me of anything, it is that Odets' obsessive themes
and imagery were present in his earliest work, and that
while he frequently varied his shapes and forms, he could
not become a dramatic chameleon--nor would we have wanted
him to be. For Odets, artistic progress should be measured
not in linear growth but in the geometric metaphor of a
circle. Though he sometimes talked of an artistic break-
through and hoped to emulate Beethoven's late great period,
Odets' plays all grow from his psychological core and contain similar ingredients. The projected plays might have
made the circle larger, but there is a certain aptness in the
fact that, in my judgment, his greatest play, Awake and

Sing!, begins the circle, and his second best, The Flowering
Peach, closes it.

Odets' perspective did not change. He kept hammer-
ing away at the flaws in the American ethos almost until his
final breath. I disagree strongly with those who see a direct
autobiographical parallel between Noah and Odets in The
Flowering Peach, in which Noah feels that he will have to
let the young take over, comically expressing his willingness
to be a "janitor" on the Ark and let the boys run things.
Odets, unlike Noah, had no plans to retire; in fact, he
bristled with ideas and was undertaking new and challenging
projects. The year before his death he had agreed to serve
as story editor and occasional script writer for the NBC
Repertory Theater starring Richard Boone on TV. Here was
another mass medium to explore; my guess is that the for-
mat of presenting a permanent cast in a different play each
week appealed to the veteran of the Group Theater. (Unfortunately, the three half-hour scripts he wrote for the
series turned out to be "occasional pieces"; both Weales and
Mendelsohn find them of little consequence.)[11] And, in an
interview with Time magazine, he did not sound like a man
who had given up on the theater:

> The theater needs new forms. I think audiences
> are hungry for new ideas like they never were be-
> fore.... To hell with the astronauts. To hell
> with the moon. There's a whole sky in your chest
> that's waiting to be explored. [12]

The only thing that did change was his self-concept,
with the awareness which comes to all men that he was
growing older. Just before Peach opened, he told Herbert
Mitgang:

> When you start out, you have to champion some-
> thing. Every artist begins as if he were the first
> one painting, every composer as if there were no
> Beethoven. But if you still feel that way after ten
> or fifteen years, you're nuts. No young writer is
> broad. I couldn't have written "The Flowering
> Peach" twenty years ago. As you grow older, you
> mature. The danger is that in broadening, as you
> mature, you may dilute your art. A growing writer
> always walks that tightrope. [13]

While walking that tightrope, Odets did not hold himself rigidly aloof and jealously avoid the younger men who might succeed him in the American theater. In the early Fifties, he had conducted a class in playwriting at the Actors Studio. He is remembered as an inspiring talker and a generous teacher, patient, willing to share the secrets of his style, and preaching a gospel of stern discipline and devotion to craft. [14] All who attended that class--among them William Gibson, Arnold Schulman, Louis Peterson--profited from it. Peterson's Take a Giant Step was one of the first important plays of middle-class Negro family life written by a black, and it was followed by Lorraine Hansberry's A Raisin in the Sun, both reminiscent of Odets' "family-trap" plays. The dialogue of William Gibson, Paddy Chayevsky, and Arthur Miller owes an immense debt to Odets, a debt that was later warmly acknowledged by Gibson and indirectly by Miller. [15] (Even so, Odets was vexed at Miller's failure to personally acknowledge his influence, and was gratified one night when Marilyn Monroe told him: "Gee, I can't tell you what your work means to Arthur.")[16] In addition, Walter Kerr has stated that "the current ... tendency toward a more poetic realism is really Mr. Odets' invention, and ... both Miller and Williams remain indebted to him."[17] Indeed, Biff's athletic prowess and the golden statue his parents are so proud of in Death of a Salesman might be seen as borrowings from Ben Gordon in Paradise Lost, and Edward Murray has pointed out other parallels in Miller's plays. [18]

Williams' indebtedness is harder to trace, though one can see how the sensitive, wounded, vulnerable characters in his plays derive from Odets, as well as his rich, colloquial dialogue. In fact, we may have an instance of cross-fertilization in Odets' The Big Knife, where the pathetic, rapidly unraveling starlet, Dixie Evans, seems to have stepped out of a Williams drama; e.g.:

> CHARLIE: You're sweet, you little bitch!
> DIXIE: You're the only one who can call me that.
> Really! Because I like you--you've been kind
> and courteous--and that's a very special matter
> in my memory box. (II)

But the legacy Odets left behind him was not a matter solely of style and technique, important as these matters are. We now can see that the body of plays he created stands for much more: a unique individual expression. To borrow yet again from The Flowering Peach, we might recall Japheth's rueful words to Rachel as he surveys the landscape from the hill on which the Ark is being built:

Those roads down there! The patterns they make!
They're not cobwebs, those roads, the work of a
foolish spider, to be brushed away by a peevish
boy! Those roads were made by men, men crazy
not to be alone or apart! Men, crazy to reach
each other. (5)

Odets' plays, collectively, are like those roads, and they are
peopled by men and women filled with passion and loneliness,
desperately reaching out for community. And if we read
them correctly, we can see that far from being merely plays
of social realism, they are poetic visions, purgatorial plays
in which man struggles to achieve fulfillment against the
sinister forces in American life. Nor should we read them
for solutions to our social problems, remembering Hank's
remark to Charlie Castle: "... I can't invent last-act curtains for a world that doesn't have one" (The Big Knife, III,
1). Odets' plays, even those that end sadly, are dramas of
hopeful beginnings, in which men are brought to the threshold
of wisdom by understanding themselves and their world. Nor
are these plays facile in their optimism. For twenty years
Odets looked hard and critically at the myths of American
life--the bourgeois dreams of family respectability, the magical promise of overnight success, the fantasy that love could
save us--and noted how the media mocked us and the past
eluded us. Out of his own tangled, often contradictory responses to these myths, he created dramas that capitalize
on this very ambivalence for artistically satisfying tension
and rewarding insights.

Odets was a socially committed playwright who loved
the middle class he wrote about, and stubbornly refused to
desert it for a plunge into existentialist "nightmares of the
self. " Though he did not seem relevant to the New Critics
of the Fifties and Sixties, time may be on his side, as a
new generation--struggling with the alienating effects of affluence and technology--turns toward communal and nature-
oriented environmentalist solutions. While no new generation
can ever recapture the precise ideological set of an earlier
one, Odets has much to say to us because our social dilemmas have not changed in kind. The middle class has moved
into suburbia, but is still plagued by the disturbing thought
that "life should not be printed on dollar bills. " Odets
speaks even more directly to the insurgent minority groups;
the new black playwrights echo his plays and unconsciously
reflect his influence. [19] Odets has something universal to
say to those who still believe that man, through group action,

is capable of "changing the world. " More important, he has
a universal understanding of the kind of mind capable of such
idealism, and of the environment which nurtures it and the
corruptions that threaten to destroy it.

NOTES

[1]Robert Whitehead, "Odets' Tale for Today, and Our
Time, " Theatre Arts, 38 (Oct. 1954), 25.

[2]New York Times, 16 Aug. 1963, p. 27.

[3]On Odets' revulsion about his appearance before
HUAC, see Kanfer, pp. 174-76, and Harold Clurman, All
People Are Famous (New York, 1974), p. 166.

[4]New York Times, 18 Aug. 1963, Sec. 1, p. 80.

[5]Quoted in Ira Peck, "The Theater Did Not Want
Clifford Odets, " New York Times, 18 Oct. 1964, Sec. 2,
p. 3.

[6]"My Friend Clifford Odets, " San Francisco Examiner,
29 Aug. 1963.

[7]"Center Stage, " May 1963, p. 74.

[8]"The Sum and Substance, " pp. 206-7.

[9]See Wagner, p. 69, and Mendelsohn, "Center Stage, "
May 1963, p. 74.

[10]Mendelsohn, p. 75.

[11]Weales, Clifford Odets, p. 185, and Mendelsohn,
Clifford Odets, pp. 93-97.

[12]"Credo of a Wrong-Living Man, " Time, 80 (14 Dec.
1962), 40.

[13]Mitgang, p. 3.

[14]Gibson, Golden Boy, passim.

[15]See Gibson, quoted in Mendelsohn, Clifford Odets,
pp. 107-8, and Miller, Introduction to Arthur Miller's Collected Plays (1957; rpt. New York, 1973), p. 16.

16Quoted in Mendelsohn, p. 106.

17Quoted in Shuman, Clifford Odets, p. 109.

18Murray, p. 181.

19See the summary of Odets' influence on black playwrights in Doris E. Abramson, Negro Playwrights in the
American Theater, 1925-1959 (New York, 1969), pp. 269-70.
There is an interesting parallel drawn between Odets' themes
and characterizations in Awake and Sing! and Golden Boy and
the plays of James Baldwin in the Sixties, in Vilma Potter,
"Baldwin and Odets," California English Journal, 1 (1965),
iii, 37-41. In addition, it is worth noting that the purchaser
of the movie rights to Joseph A. Walker's powerful The
River Niger felt that "'The River Niger' is one of the most
exciting plays to appear since Clifford Odets was in his
prime." Quoted in A. H. Weiler, "'Niger' Will Flow on
Film," New York Times, 27 May 1973, Sec. 2, p. 11.

APPENDIX

THE SUM AND SUBSTANCE:
A DIALOGUE ON CONTEMPORARY VALUES

with Herman Harvey--
An Interview with Clifford Odets

Harvey: It's difficult to think of Clifford Odets as having worked his way into the American theater. Actually he rocked it within it. In a sense, he detonated it. In his first play, Waiting for Lefty, in the ones which followed-- Awake and Sing!, Golden Boy, Rocket to the Moon--one could see the mark of a man who had probed and examined a large part of his world and, having done so, had no alternative but to protest. When we met he spoke of such things and described what he had come to see within the region of his own life and experience as the sum and substance. Quite frequently Clifford Odets is described as a playwright whose primary concern has been to provide a manner of stimulus for social reform through the American theater. Perhaps there is basis for this. Clifford Odets would like to see a man say what he thinks, to say how he sees life, how he sees the world. For him there is the unquestioned right of the individual for maximum fulfillment, and for him there are ingredients in our contemporary culture which keep this from happening. So it is that he speaks as a critic of what there is around him; but Clifford Odets is not the less critical of what he sees within himself, and his protest is not the less severe nor demanding. When we met we spoke of this and I asked him what he would write if at this time he wanted to communicate what had come to represent his primary value investment, what he would say as a human being who had lived in and sensed the world around him, what there was that--after all had been said and done--proved to be substantial and real and meaningful, what he saw as un-questioned and irreversible commitments.

Odets: I would want to talk, in our country particularly, about the fulfillment of each individual human being. I would

206

want to make a statement, as definitive as I was able--let
me say, at the age of 75, knock on wood. I would like to
make a statement about what, in our American world, develops,
or the inherent possibilities of each man and woman, and what
holds them back, what stymies them. Concomitantly with that
I would like to make a statement in the same work about innocence versus experience. I have the play picked out, I have
the materials picked out, and I don't think it's a play that I
will write until I am really 10 or 15 years older. I find our
American world today, I find it lacks innocence; I find it lacks
the conviction of innocence; I find that, as quickly as we can,
we are taught, we pick up from the air, we pick it up from
the movies or the magazines, we pick up those techniques in
which we are richest, and those are the techniques of conciliation and ingratiation, the techniques of selling yourself,
of getting across, which necessarily means that innocence
goes, and experience perhaps shrivels our souls. I would
include, in a final statement in a play, a need and a feeling
for human sympathy as I once said, but human sympathy and
cooperation always within a context of personal integrity. Or
leaving out our American world, I think that men and women--
particularly men, since women have never had their rightful
place in affairs--that men have always had to fight for personal integrity, and have always had to fight for what I would
call humanistic and sympathetic cooperation. Does what I
am saying make sense?

Harvey: Yes. I'm concerned with one aspect here: your
use of the term innocence. It has come to mean so many
things and I think so frequently it becomes one peculiar
manner of synonym for ignorance. This isn't the way you
mean it, I know. What is this quality of innocence?

Odets: By innocence I mean that quality, that uncorrupted
quality, with which all children are born--what Emerson
called "uncorrupted behavior. " He ended by saying that only
animals and children seem to have it. There is a problem
in America as far back as Emerson, probably a statement he
made let's say in 1860. That quality of uncorrupted behavior,
when nothing outside of yourself influences you, when you are
in command of yourself with honor, without dishonesty, without lie, when you grasp and deal, and are permitted to deal,
with exactly what's in front of you, in terms of your best
human instincts. This is rather what I mean by innocence.
I don't mean, I don't mean--the innocence--although it is
connected--the innocence of a Blake--who as Mrs. Blake
said: "I seldom have his company because Mr. Blake is so

much with heaven. " I don't quite mean that. Sure we have
to, as we grow older, by some of the real techniques we
have to learn, out of reality testing, we must learn to live
in communities, we certainly must be acculturated, house-
broken (to put it more vulgarly), every child. There is, of
course, the agony and a certain crippling in giving up that
takes place with acculturation. With children of course, this
you know as well as I do, chiefly through the parents who've
themselves been acculturated in one way or another. But I
would like to see innocence and uncorrupted behavior kept.
I would like a man to say what he thinks, not rudely. I
would like him to say how he sees life, how he sees the
world. I would fight to the death for him to have the right
to say it. And I see it disappearing. I see the whole Jeffer-
sonian ideal of what an American citizen should be disappearing.

Harvey: Life [inaudible] is getting too great?

Odets: Oh yes, yes. How, in how many cases, does a
man's job depend upon it? Putting it again in, let me say
the parlance, you know, mind your business, keep your nose
clean, keep your mouth shut. The best we get nowadays,
for the most part, the best we get is living in the comfortable middle. That can be living on the uncomfortable fence,
too, and we're ready to jump out of the way. It reminds me
of a story about a school teacher who was called up before
a local school board, and he wanted the job very badly. And
they kind of looked him over, kind of sniffed him over, and
they said, "Well, uh, you're a good teacher?" He said,
"Yes. " They said, "Well, uh, suppose you tell us, Mr.
Jones, " and Mr. Jones, wanting the job, listened very carefully. They said, "Well, suppose you tell us, what about
the world? Is it round or is it flat?" And Mr. Jones said,
"Well, gentlemen, I can teach it either way. " There's too
much of that in this country today.

Harvey: The point you make is well taken. You make it
about the school teacher. May I come back in another way
and say that I have seen it, I think almost without end, in
the creative artist, in the novelist, in the playwright, in
the musician?

Odets: You certainly have.

Harvey: What's happening then?

Odets: I don't know about the musician. The composer does

not have the chances for awards and rewards. The awards and rewards in America are enormous. They do not, and have never existed--except, perhaps, in the days of the Renaissance patron--they have never existed as they do today, but in those arts which are popular arts. So the serious composer who is not a popular artist is not liable to [inaudible] rewards, financial and otherwise, of our creative people today. He, therefore, must stay fairly clean or fairly kosher, so to speak. But when it comes to someone in my field, where there is an enormous demand for that sort of material, the man corrupts very easily. Success in this country is a fantastic experience. The newspapers, magazines beat down your door. They want interviews. They want to give you publicity. They must be hep. They want to be in the know. They want to get the news first. So that the buildup works always. They want to have the hottest news story about you. They want to know all about your personal life. They want to present their readers with fresh news. There gets to be a kind of whole bandwagon psychology. Everybody jumps on you, photographers and what not, including TV men. The man goes on and reads about himself and, before you know it, if he does not try to retain being a simple, working private citizen, but if he begins to believe or be beguiled for one hour by the public image that he has become, that man's on the way to--that's one reason that the man is on his way down.

Harvey: There's another aspect here that frightens me, that frightens me I think to an extreme degree. There are forces, there are pressures, certainly, in all situations, and I always feel comfortable if I can look around and pick out the good guys and the bad guys, the heavily moustached people, the black. Somehow, in an affective sense, I know these are bad guys. The others stand for all the virtues, and we know what they are. But there's a very insidious quality in this where I think, eventually, particularly the creative artist, doesn't even know when he is being dishonest. And I want to ask you, how do you know it when actually you come through with a piece of work? How do you know that you haven't tried in deliberate fashion to match the idiom that will bring forth the greatest acclaim, the greatest overall reward? It's nice to be liked and loved by a society.

Odets: It's a good question that almost makes it necessary for me to put in a disclaimer and say that I have never done that, though I might not be telling the full truth. But I think I would answer that question by dividing it into, dividing the answer into two parts. For the first part, we are still a puritanic America. I'm a writer; I have been a writer for something like over twenty-five years. That means I'm a professional writer. I want to be a professional writer. But in this country, to make this first part only about my medium, I am an honorable writer and an honest writer-- because of what I call the puritanic ethic--I am a writer of integrity only as long as I stay in the American theater. The moment I come out to Hollywood to stay here for one picture or four pictures it is considered, generally, that I have prostituted myself or my talents. Is that a strong word for TV?

Harvey: It has its meaning [inaudible] for your feeling, and it's the word.

Odets: There are pieces written about it in papers, there is gossip that goes on. Let me put it a different way: they say, "Well, Odets has sold out; we thought this man was a wonderful writer. Now, you see, he's sold out." They forget that I'm a technician. They forget that I'm a technician when I write plays on Broadway, they forget that I'm a technician when I write movies or, as I will do later this year, write a series of TV shows with Richard Boone. They will forget that I am also a technician. It is permitted to, really a great artist like Mozart, to write a piece of wedding music one day, an occasion piece--in fact, maybe, a series of occasion pieces for two or three years, as, for instance, Beethoven had a silent period of almost eight years in which he wrote some cheap Scotch and Irish songs, settings for a company named Thompson in Edinburgh. He's a technician. When Mozart turns away from his occasion pieces that he writes for money, bringing his enormous skill to the work, he then sits down and makes a personal statement. There's no ethic involved, no puritanism, there's no contempt for the man because he writes occasion pieces. We are lucky, of course, that they are not all occasion pieces, and that some of his greatest pieces are written out of his own state of being. And that brings me to the second part of my answer to your question. I know that I am functioning at the peak of my talent when I don't construct, I don't build a construction which will please, which is primarily fashioned to please an audience. But I do know that when I sit down to express my own inner state of being that I am working at my best and, whatever depth I have, that will be in that work. I, by the way, think that's the only way that one can be creative; that the creative writer, artist, composer--what

you will--is creative only because his own inner state of
being demands some kind of outward statement. He then has
sufficient technique to, shall I say, gell, solidify, or express
in his given medium that state of being. The state of being
might be--you know, I, the world, something's wrong with
the world, something's rotten in Denmark, I don't feel well,
or I'm lonely, or I feel that men should work together in
harmony as teams (as the technicians are doing here in this
studio at this moment). It appears to me that there is something in contemporary life that makes that very difficult.
What is that? I'm not geared in, I'm not a cog, there's
something larger than myself. I'm not serving some purpose outside of myself. Whatever the state of being is, if
it starts that way instead of with some kind of gag, some
kind of little story, I think I'll write a love story, this will
please an audience. If it doesn't start that way, if it starts
from a state of being, then I, for myself (and I believe, I
believe most other creative men and women) know that they
are on the trail of something real. The something real, if
imperfect, perhaps imperfect, structure-wise, something real
will come out.

Harvey: Your writing, then, is an act of growth for you,
isn't it?

Odets: It's an act of growth, or I referred to earlier--cer-
tainly not in the original phrase--an act of becoming, and
your becoming is expressed in the play you've written. You
say, [inaudible], that's what's been bothering me for two or
three years. That's what's hurt me. Your great artist is
a kind of divine baby. He's wearing a diaper, and he's
screaming, and someone turns him over, or he turns himself, and he finds he's got a big safety pin stuck in his rump.
And, to say it in that light way, the making of the artwork
is the discovery and the removing of that safety pin.

Harvey: When you go back and see your other plays, then,
in a sense you have a psychological history of Clifford Odets
unfolding for you?

Odets: I think so, I think so, yes. I don't always like it
when I look back. I'm not always pleased. And I say well,
if I had it to do over again, I might change it this way, I
think I was unfair, I think I was out of balance. But, by
and large, what you say is true. Again let me talk always
of great artists (I talk so much about musicians because I
like music more than I like even playwriting or plays), we

212 / Clifford Odets

certainly have the spiritual and psychological history of a Beethoven in his sixteen quartets and his famous six sonatas, in
his nine symphonies. There it is, there it is, no secrets,
that is, if the ear is perceptive. You know there are no
secrets.

Harvey: You use this technique to find yourself from time to
time, as you must have me look [inaudible].

Odets: I think maybe one of the main impulses behind cre-
ativity and its functioning in terms of works is that act of
locating yourself, finding yourself. I don't mean the American scare of every day looking for status: who am I, where
am I, what am I doing, gee am I getting ahead, where am I
on the weekly chart, you know, Book-of-the-Month Club,
there's gonna have a book of the hour club you know, and
I'd better be a man of the hour and I'd better be confident
and appear all the time. I don't mean that kind of status
thing. But I mean finding the way you are in terms of growth,
in terms of maturation, quietly, without anxiety, although
anxiety is awfully good; it frequently gives heat to the work;
it gives pressure.

Harvey: You've [inaudible] in all the times, I think as you
mention it. A Clifford Odets play comes out. There's a
review written of it. An audience listens to it and applauds
it more or less. And their reaction to the product is, in a
sense, such a small part of the overall thing which is involved. In a way there's this surplus value of the product
for you that no one ever knows, do they?

Odets: I would think that a few perceptive men and women
know it. They are a very small minority. As for the rest,
they're looking for a good show. They only want a buck's
worth. It's a hard buck, and you've paid it, and you want
a buck for it. I don't call it very human; it's understandable. You've paid your dollar--and nowadays, your five or
six dollars--to see a play, my God. You do want your
money's worth. That doesn't help the creative person; that
never did help an artist. What helps an artist is to look at
his work, play, tune, a novel or two, a musical piece or
two, a painting, a few paintings, see an exhibit, one or two
or more, and decide for yourself, I like that man, I like
what that man says. That man says something that's very
close to me. That man expresses something what I am not
able to express. Therefore, I will commit myself to that
man. I will make a commitment to him and what he stands

for. I will wish him luck, I will wish for his fulfillment, for his success. I will do it by the moment I hear a new play of his has opened, the moment I hear he has an exhibition down in Mr. Cantor's gallery, I will run there to see it. If I had a hundred dollars with which to buy a small drawing, I would do that, because that will help him. I will buy a ticket to his show in advance, before I read what the critics say. I am committed to that man. That is the more human way to treat the writer, the artist, call him what you will. Yes or no?

Harvey: Yes, yes. But, essentially, you're looking for the kind of commitment on the part of the audience that you and I have just been talking about doesn't even exist in the artist.

Odets: The artist is a lonely, cut-off man. He is, however, coming into his own in the United States. A friend of mine, Lee Strasberg, said to me in a recent visit in New York, he said, "You know, there are artists in the American scene are now becoming the new priests. They're looked up to in a strange way. Nowadays, doors fly open, foundations open their coffers the moment they hear the word artist, artist. You see there's something new. It's not like when we founded the Group Theater and had to exist from hand to mouth and from play to play." He was talking of way back in 1930 or '31.

Harvey: And the artist is thinking our world today lacks innocence. It lacks the conviction of innocence. As quickly as we can we learn the techniques of conciliation and ingratiation, the techniques of selling oneself. Then, innocence goes and experience only shrivels our souls. Such was the way that one man in the twentieth century came to view his universe. This man, Clifford Odets.

BIBLIOGRAPHY

Works By Clifford Odets

A. PLAYS

The Big Knife. New York: Random House, 1949.

Clash by Night. New York: Random House, 1942.

The Country Girl. New York: Viking, 1951.

The Flowering Peach. Typescript in my possession. Never
    published.

Night Music. New York: Random House, 1940.

Six Plays of Clifford Odets. New York: Random House,
    1939. (Contains "Waiting for Lefty," "Till the Day
    I Die," "Awake and Sing!" "Paradise Lost," "Golden
    Boy," and "Rocket to the Moon," as well as a Preface
    by Odets and Three Introductions by Harold Clurman.)

"Waiting for Lefty," in Representative American Plays. Ed.
    Robert Warnock. Oakland, N. J. : Scott, Foresman,
    1952. (This is the original version.)

B. ARTICLES

"Boone, Renoir Find Common Ground." Los Angeles Times,
    1 Aug. 1963, Sec. 4, p. 16.

"Democratic Vistas in Drama." New York Times, 21 Nov.
    1937, Sec. 11, pp. 1-2.

"Genesis of a Play." New York Times, 1 Feb. 1942, Sec.
    9, p. 3.

214

"In Praise of a Maturing Industry. " New York Times, 6 Nov. 1955, Sec. 2, p. 5.

"On Coming Home. " New York Times, 25 July 1948, Sec. 2, p. 1.

"Some Problems of the Modern Dramatist. " New York Times, 15 Dec. 1935, Sec. 11, p. 3.

"To Whom It May Concern: Marilyn Monroe. " Show, 2 (Oct. 1962), 67, 136.

"The Transient Olympian. " Show, 3 (April 1963), 106-7, 130-33.

"Two Approaches to the Writing of a Play. " New York Times, 22 Apr. 1951, Sec. 2, pp. 1-2.

"When Wolfe Came Home. " New York Times, 14 Sept. 1958, Sec. 2, p. 3.

"Willem de Kooning. " The Critic, 21 (Oct. -Nov. 1962), 37-38.

C. MISCELLANY

Beals, Carleton, and Clifford Odets. "Rifle Rule in Cuba. " New York: Provisional Committee for Cuba, 1935.

"I Can't Sleep, " in The Anxious Years. Ed. Louis Filler. New York: Capricorn, 1964.

"None but the Lonely Heart, " in Best Film Plays, 1945. Ed. John Gassner and Dudley Nichols. New York: Crown, 1946.

"The Russian People, " adapted by Odets from the play by Konstantin Simonov, in Seven Soviet Plays. Ed. Henry Wadsworth Longfellow Dana. New York: Macmillan, 1946.

Secondary Sources

A. BOOKS

Aaron, Daniel. Writers on the Left. New York: Harcourt, Brace & World, 1961.

Abramson, Doris E. Negro Playwrights in the American Theater, 1925-1959. New York: Columbia Univ. Press, 1969.

Agee, James. Agee on Film. Vol. I. New York: Mc-Dowell, Obolensky, 1958.

Allen, Frederick Lewis. Since Yesterday, 1929-1939. New York: Harper, 1940.

Behrman, S. N. People in a Diary: A Memoir. Boston: Little, Brown, 1972.

Bentley, Eric. The Playwright as Thinker. New York: Harcourt, Brace, 1955.

_____. "Poetry of the Theater," in What Is Theater? New York: Atheneum, 1968.

Bergson, Henri. "Laughter," in Comedy: Plays, Theory, and Criticism. Ed. Marvin Felheim. New York: Harcourt, Brace & World, 1962.

Bernstein, Irving. The Lean Years: A History of the American Worker, 1920-1933. 1960; rpt. Baltimore: Penguin, 1966.

_____. The Turbulent Years: A History of the American Worker, 1933-1941. New York: Houghton Mifflin, 1970.

Bird, Caroline. The Invisible Scar. New York: McKay, 1966.

Block, Anita. The Changing World in Plays and Theatre. Boston: Little, Brown, 1939.

Block, Haskell M., and Robert G. Shedd, eds. Masters of Modern Drama. New York: Random House, 1967.

Brown, John Mason. Seeing Things. New York: McGraw-Hill, 1946.

_____. Two on the Aisle. New York: Norton, 1938.

Burke, Kenneth. The Philosophy of Literary Form. Baton Rouge: Louisiana State Univ. Press, 1941.

Burnett, Whit, ed. This Is My Best. New York: Dial, 1942.

Clay, James H., and Daniel Krempel. The Theatrical Image. New York: McGraw-Hill, 1967.

Clurman, Harold. All People Are Famous. New York: Harcourt Brace, Jovanovich, 1974.

_____, ed. Famous American Plays of the 1930's. 1959; rpt. New York: Dell, 1968.

_____. The Fervent Years. 1945; rpt. New York: Hill and Wang, 1957.

_____. Lies Like Truth. New York: Macmillan, 1958.

_____. The Naked Image. New York: Macmillan, 1966.

_____. On Directing. New York: Macmillan, 1972.

Cohn, Ruby. Dialogue in American Drama. Bloomington: Indiana Univ. Press, 1971.

Cowley, Malcolm. Think Back on Us ... Carbondale: Southern Illinois Univ. Press, 1967.

Downer, Alan S. Fifty Years of American Drama. Chicago: Regnery, 1951.

Dusenbury, Winifred L. The Theme of Loneliness in Modern American Drama. Gainesville: Univ. of Florida Press, 1960.

Farmer, Frances. Will There Really Be a Morning? New York: Putnam's, 1972.

Fiedler, Leslie. "The Two Memories: Reflections on Writers and Writing in the Thirties," in Proletarian Writers of the Thirties. Ed. David Madden. Carbondale: Southern Illinois Univ. Press, 1968.

218 / Clifford Odets

_____. _Waiting for the End._ New York: Stein and Day, 1964.

Flanagan, Hallie. _Arena: The History of the Federal Theatre._ 1940; rpt. New York: Blom, 1965.

Flexner, Eleanor. _American Playwrights, 1918-1938._ New York: Simon & Schuster, 1938.

Freedman, Morris. _American Drama in Social Context._ Carbondale: Southern Illinois Univ. Press, 1971.

_____. _The Moral Impulse: Modern Drama from Ibsen to the Present._ Carbondale: Southern Illinois Univ. Press, 1967.

Freud, Sigmund. "Wit and Its Relation to the Unconscious," in _Comedy: Plays, Theory, and Criticism._ Ed. Marvin Felheim. New York: Harcourt, Brace & World, 1962.

Gagey, Edmond M. _Revolution in American Drama._ New York: Columbia Univ. Press, 1947.

Gassner, John. _Masters of the Drama._ 3rd. rev. ed. New York: Dover, 1954.

_____. _Theatre at the Crossroads._ New York: Holt, Rinehart and Winston, 1960.

_____. _The Theatre in Our Times._ New York: Crown, 1954.

Gibson, William. Introduction to _Golden Boy_ (musical version). New York: Bantam, 1966.

Goldstein, Malcolm. "Clifford Odets and the Found Generation," in _American Drama and Its Critics._ Ed. Alan S. Downer. Chicago: Univ. of Chicago Press, 1965.

_____. "The Playwrights of the 1930's," in _The American Theater Today._ Ed. Alan S. Downer. New York: Basic, 1967.

_____. _The Political Stage: American Drama and Theater of the Great Depression._ New York: Oxford Univ. Press, 1974.

Gorelik, Mordecai. New Theatres for Old. 1940; rpt. New York: Dutton, 1962.

Griffin, Robert J. "On the Love Songs of Clifford Odets," in The Thirties: Fiction, Poetry, Drama. Ed. Warren French. DeLand, Fla.: Everett/Edwards, 1967.

Gurko, Leo. The Angry Decade. New York: Dodd, Mead, 1947.

Himelstein, Morgan Y. Drama Was a Weapon. New Brunswick, N. J.: Rutgers Univ. Press, 1963.

Kachuk, Rhoda Silver. "The Portrayal of the Jew in American Drama Since 1920. " Unpublished Ph. D. dissertation, Univ. of Southern California, 1971.

Kanfer, Stefan. A Journal of the Plague Years. New York: Atheneum, 1973.

Kazin, Alfred. Bright Book of Life. Boston: Little, Brown, 1973.

_____. Starting Out in the Thirties. Boston: Atlantic, Little, Brown, 1965.

_____. A Walker in the City. 1951; rpt. New York: Grove, 1958.

_____ and Daniel Aaron, eds. Emerson. New York: Dell, 1958.

Kempton, Murray. Part of Our Time. 1955; rpt. New York: Dell, 1967.

Krutch, Joseph Wood. The American Drama Since 1918. Rev. ed. New York: Braziller, 1957.

Langner, Lawrence. The Magic Curtain. New York: Dutton, 1951.

Lawson, John Howard. Success Story. New York: Farrar & Rinehart, 1932.

_____. Theory and Technique of Playwriting and Screenwriting. 1936; rpt. New York: Hill and Wang, 1960.

Levant, Oscar. The Memoirs of an Amnesiac. New York: Putnam's, 1965.

Lewis, Allan. American Plays and Playwrights of the Contemporary Theatre. New York: Crown, 1965.

Lifson, David S. The Yiddish Theatre in America. New York: Yoseloff, 1965.

Lumley, Frederick. New Trends in 20th Century Drama. 3rd rev. ed. New York: Oxford Univ. Press, 1967.

McCarthy, Mary. On the Contrary. New York: Farrar, Straus & Cudahy, 1961.

_____. Sights and Spectacles. New York: Farrar, Straus, 1956.

McGraw-Hill Encyclopedia of World Drama. Vol. III. New York: McGraw-Hill, 1972.

Mangione, Jerre. The Dream and the Deal: The Federal Writers' Project, 1935-1943. Boston: Little, Brown, 1972.

Mantle, Burns. Contemporary American Playwrights. New York: Dodd, Mead, 1939.

Mendelsohn, Michael J. "Clifford Odets: The Artist's Commitment," in Literature and Society. Lincoln: Univ. of Nebraska Press, 1964.

_____. Clifford Odets: Humane Dramatist. DeLand, Fla.: Everett/Edwards, 1969.

Mersand, Joseph. The American Drama, 1930-1940. New York: Modern Chapbooks, 1949.

Meserve, Walter J. "Drama," in American Literary Scholarship, 1969. Ed. J. Albert Robbins. Durham: Duke Univ. Press, 1971.

Miller, Arthur. Arthur Miller's Collected Plays. 1957; rpt. New York: Viking, 1973.

Morris, Lloyd. Postscript to Yesterday. New York: Random House, 1947.

Murray, Edward. Clifford Odets: The Thirties and After. New York: Ungar, 1968.

Nathan, George Jean. Encyclopedia of the Theatre. New York: Knopf, 1940.

O'Hara, Frank H. Today in American Drama. Chicago: Univ. of Chicago Press, 1939.

Pells, Richard H. Radical Visions and American Dreams: Culture and Social Thought in the Depression Years. New York: Harper & Row, 1973.

Rabkin, Gerald. Drama and Commitment. Bloomington: Univ. of Indiana Press, 1964.

Rideout, Walter. The Radical Novel in the United States, 1900-1954. 1956; rpt. Cambridge: Harvard Univ. Press, 1965.

Rosten, Leo. The Joys of Yiddish. New York: McGraw-Hill, 1968.

Rougemont, Denis de. "Religion and the Mission of the Artist," in Spiritual Problems in Contemporary Literature. Ed. Stanley Romaine Hopper. 1952; rpt. Gloucester, Mass.: Smith, 1969.

Rowe, Kenneth Thorpe. A Theatre in Your Head. New York: Funk & Wagnalls, 1961.

Salzman, Jack, and Barry Wallenstein, eds. Years of Protest. New York: Pegasus, 1967.

Shannon, David A. The Great Depression. Englewood Cliffs, N. J.: Prentice-Hall, 1960.

Shuman, R. Baird. Clifford Odets. New York: Twayne, 1962.

_____. "Clifford Odets: From Influence to Affluence," in Modern American Drama: Essays in Criticism. Ed. William W. Taylor. DeLand, Fla.: Everett/Edwards, 1968.

Sievers, W. David. Freud on Broadway. New York: Hermitage House, 1955.

222 / Clifford Odets

Slochower, Harry. No Voice Is Wholly Lost. Toronto: Mc-
Clelland and Stewart, 1945.

Smiley, Sam. The Drama of Attack: Didactic Plays of the
American Depression. Columbia: Univ. of Missouri
Press, 1972.

Susman, Warren I. "The Thirties," in The Development of
an American Culture. Ed. Stanley Coben and Lorman Ratner. Englewood Cliffs, N. J.: Prentice-Hall,
1970.

Swados, Harvey, ed. The American Writer and the Great
Depression. Indianapolis: Bobbs-Merrill, 1966.

Teller, Judd L. Strangers and Natives: The Evolution of
the American Jew from 1921 to the Present. New
York: Delacorte, 1968.

Terkel, Studs. Hard Times: An Oral History of the Great
Depression. New York: Pantheon, 1970.

Thomas, Bob. King Cohn: The Life and Times of Harry
Cohn. New York: Putnam's, 1967.

Tynan, Kenneth. Curtains. New York: Atheneum, 1961.

Warshow, Robert. The Immediate Experience. New York:
Doubleday, 1962.

Weales, Gerald. American Drama Since World War II. New
York: Harcourt, Brace & World, 1962.

_____. Clifford Odets: Playwright. New York: Bobbs-
Merrill, 1971.

_____. "The Group Theatre and Its Plays," in American
Theatre. (Stratford-upon-Avon Studies 10.) New
York: St. Martin's, 1967.

Wecter, Dixon. The Age of the Great Depression. New
York: Macmillan, 1948.

Williams, Jay. Stage Left. New York: Scribner's, 1974.

Wilson, Edmund. The American Earthquake. 1958; rpt.
Garden City: Anchor, 1964.

B. ARTICLES

Atkinson, Brooks. "Odets Not a Failure. " New York Times,
3 Sept. 1963, p. 30.

_____. "A Review of The Country Girl. " New York
Times, 11 Nov. 1950, p. 10.

_____. Review of Golden Boy. New York Times, 21 Nov.
1937, Sec. 11, p. 1.

Aulicino, Armand. "How The Country Girl Came About. "
Theatre Arts, 36 (May 1952), 54-57.

Becker, William. "Reflections on Three New Plays. " Hudson Review, 8 (Summer 1955), 263-68.

Berch, Barbara. "Going Their Way Now?" New York Times,
27 Aug. 1944, Sec. 2, p. 3.

Brown, John Mason. Review of The Big Knife. "Biting
the Hand. " Saturday Review, 32 (19 Mar. 1949), 34-
35.

_____. Review of The Flowering Peach. "On the Crest
of Waves. " Saturday Review, 38 (15 Jan. 1955), 30.

Brustein, Robert. "America's New Culture Hero. " Commentary, 25 (Feb. 1958), 123-29.

Burt, David J. "Odets' Awake and Sing!" Explicator, 27
(1968), Item 29.

"Clifford Odets, Playwright, Dies. " New York Times, 16
Aug. 1963, p. 27.

Clurman, Harold. "Around Night Music. " New Republic,
124 (30 Apr. 1951), 22.

_____. "Clifford Odets. " Saturday Review, 46 (14 Sept.
1963), 10.

_____. "Clifford Odets' Ideals. " New York Times, 25
Aug. 1963, Sec. 2, p. 1.

_____. Review of The Country Girl. "The First Fifteen
Years. " New Republic, 123 (11 Dec. 1950), 29-30.

224 / Clifford Odets

_____. "Sins of Clifford Odets. " New Republic, 120 (14 Mar. 1949), 28-29.

Cowley, Malcolm. "The 1930's Were an Age of Faith. " New York Times Book Review, 13 Dec. 1964, Sec. 7, pp. 4-5, 14-17.

_____. "A Remembrance of the Red Romance. " Esquire, 61 (Mar. 1964), 124-30.

_____. "While They Waited for Lefty. " Saturday Review, 47 (6 June 1964), 16-19, 61.

"Credo of a Wrong-Living Man. " Time, 80 (14 Dec. 1962), 40.

Fagin, N. B. "In Search of an American Cherry Orchard. " Texas Quarterly, 1 (Summer-Autumn 1958), 132-41.

Farrell, James T. Review of Paradise Lost. Partisan Review and Anvil, 3 (Feb. 1936), 28-29.

Ferguson, Otis. "Pay-off on Odets. " New Republic, 100 (27 Sept. 1939), 216-17; (4 Oct. 1939), 242-43.

Fiedler, Leslie. "The Search for the 30's. " Commentary, 20 (Sept. 1955), 285-89.

"'55 Pulitzer Jury Chose Odets Play. " New York Times, 18 Aug. 1963, Sec. 1, p. 80.

Gassner, John. "The Long Journey of a Talent. " Theatre Arts, 33 (July 1949), 24-30.

_____. "Playwrights of the Period. " Theatre Arts, 44 (Sept. 1960), 19-22, 69-71.

Gibbs, Wolcott. "A Review of The Country Girl. " New Yorker, 26 (18 Nov. 1950), 77-79.

_____. Review of Golden Boy. "The Ring and the Bow. " New Yorker, 28 (22 Mar. 1952), 54.

Gilder, Rosamond. Review of Clash by Night. Theatre Arts, 26 (Mar. 1942), 150-52.

_____. Review of Rocket to the Moon. Theatre Arts, 23 (Jan. 1939), 12-13.

Goldstone, Richard H. "The Making of Americans: Clifford Odets' Implicit Theme." Proceedings of the IVth Congress of the International Comparative Literature Association, 1966, 654-60.

Gorelik, Mordecai. "Legacy of the New Deal Drama." Drama Survey, 4 (Spring 1965), 38-43.

————. "Social vs. Irrational Theatre." Players, 46 (1971), 208-10.

Hart-Davis, Rupert. Review of Awake and Sing! Spectator, 160 (25 Feb. 1938), 311.

Hartley, Anthony. Review of The Big Knife. Spectator, 192 (29 May 1942), 507.

Haslam, G. W. "Odets' Use of Yiddish-English in Awake and Sing." Research Studies of Washington State University, 34 (1966), 161-64.

Hayes, Richard. "The Flowering Peach." Commonweal, 61 (11 Feb. 1955), 502-3.

Hewes, Henry. "American Playwrights Self-Appraised." Saturday Review, 38 (3 Sept. 1955), 18-19.

Hughes, Catharine. "Odets: The Price of Success." Commonweal, 78 (20 Sept. 1963), 558-60.

Hunt, Albert. "Only Soft-Centred Left." Encore, 8 (May-June 1961), 5-12.

Hyams, Barry. "Twenty Years on a Tightrope." Theatre Arts, 39 (Apr. 1955), 68-70, 86.

Isaacs, Edith J. R. "Clifford Odets, First Chapters." Theatre Arts, 23 (Apr. 1939), 257-64.

Kaplan, Charles. "Two Depression Plays and Broadway's Popular Idealism." American Quarterly, 15 (Winter 1963), 579-85.

Kauffmann, Stanley. "Is Artistic Integrity Enough?" New Republic, 142 (8 Feb. 1960), 22.

Kerr, Walter. "Night Music." Commonweal, 54 (27 Apr. 1951), 58-59.

Krutch, Joseph Wood. Review of The Big Knife. Nation, 168 (19 Mar. 1949), 340-41.

_____. Review of Clash by Night. Nation, 154 (10 Jan. 1942), 45-46.

_____. Review of Golden Boy. Nation, 145 (13 Nov. 1937), 540.

_____. Review of Night Music. Nation, 150 (2 Mar. 1940), 316-17.

_____. Review of Waiting for Lefty and Till the Day I Die. "Mr. Odets Speaks His Mind." Nation, 140 (10 Apr. 1935), 427-28.

Lawson, John Howard. Review of Waiting for Lefty. New Masses, 2 July 1935, p. 39.

Lerner, Max. "My Friend Clifford Odets." San Francisco Examiner, 29 Aug. 1963.

McCarten, John. "Revolution's Number One Boy." New Yorker, 13 (22 Jan. 1938), 21-27.

Marshall, Margaret. Review of The Country Girl. Nation, 171 (25 Nov. 1950), 493.

Mendelsohn, Michael J. "Clifford Odets and the American Family." Drama Survey, 3 (Fall 1963), 238-43.

_____. "Odets at Center Stage: A Talk with Michael J. Mendelsohn." Theatre Arts, 147 (May 1963), 16-19, 74-76; (June 1963), 28-30, 78-80.

_____. "The Social Critics On Stage." Modern Drama, 6 (Dec. 1963), 277-85.

Miller, Arthur. "The Family in American Drama." Atlantic, 197 (Apr. 1956), 35-42.

"Mr. Odets Is Acclimated." New York Times, 3 May 1936, Sec. 10, p. 4.

Mitgang, Herbert. "Odets Goes to Genesis." New York Times, 26 Dec. 1954, Sec. 2, pp. 1, 3.

Mottram, Eric. "Living Mythically: The Thirties." American Studies 6, 3 (1972), 267-87.

Nathan, George Jean. Review of Night Music. "The White Hope Gets Paler." Newsweek, 15 (4 Mar. 1940), 42.

Norton, Elliot, "Clifford Odets Sans Message." New York Times, 5 Nov. 1950, Sec. 2, p. 3.

"Odets and the Comrades." Newsweek, 39 (2 June 1952), 23.

O'Hara, John. Review of The Big Knife. "Desire Under the Rose." Newsweek, 19 (12 Jan. 1942), 46.

Pearce, Richard. "Pylon, Awake and Sing! and The Apocalyptic Imagination of the 30's." Criticism, 13 (1971), 131-41.

Peck, Ira. "The Theater Did Not Want Clifford Odets." New York Times, 18 Oct. 1964, Sec. 2, p. 3.

Peck, Seymour. "An Angry Man from Hollywood." New York Times, 20 Feb. 1949, Sec. 2, pp. 1, 3.

Phelan, Kappo. Review of The Big Knife. Commonweal, 49 (25 Mar. 1949), 590-91.

Phillips, William. "What Happened in the 30's." Commentary, 34 (Sept. 1962), 204-12.

Potter, Vilma. "Baldwin and Odets: The High Cost of 'Crossing.'" California English Journal, 1 (1965), iii, 37-41.

Rahv, Philip. "Proletarian Literature: A Political Autopsy." Southern Review (Winter 1939), pp. 616-28.

Schumach, Murray. "Hollywood Gets Unusual Praise." New York Times, 1 Oct. 1959, p. 39.

Shuman, R. Baird. "Clifford Odets: A Playwright and His Jewish Background." South Atlantic Quarterly, 71 (1972), 225-33.

_____. "Thematic Consistency in Odets' Early Plays." Revue des Langues Vivantes, 35 (1969), 415-20.

_____. "Waiting for Lefty: A Problem of Structure. " Revue des Langues Vivantes, 28 (Nov. -Dec. 1962), 521-26.

Sugrue, Thomas. "Mr. Odets Regrets. " American Magazine, 122 (Oct. 1936), 42-43, 106-8.

Sullivan, Dan. Review of Waiting for Lefty. New York Times, 17 Dec. 1967, p. 58.

Vernon, Grenville. "Mr. Odets' Plays are Jewish. " Commonweal, 29 (16 Dec. 1938), 215.

Wagner, Arthur. "How a Playwright Triumphs. " Harper's, 233 (Sept. 1966), 64-70.

Weiler, A. H. "'Niger' Will Flow on Film. " New York Times, 27 May 1973, Sec. 2, p. 11.

Whitehead, Robert. "Odets' Tale for Today, and Our Time." Theatre Arts, 38 (Oct. 1954), 24-25.

"White Hope. " Time, 32 (5 Dec. 1938), 44-47.

Willett, Ralph. "Clifford Odets and Popular Culture. " South Atlantic Quarterly, 69 (1970), 68-78.

Wilson Library Bulletin, 11 (Feb. 1937), 374.

Worsley, T. C. Review of The Big Knife. New Statesman, 47 (9 Jan. 1954), 40.

Wright, Basil. Review of Awake and Sing! Spectator, 192 (8 Jan. 1954), 37.

Young, Stark. Review of Awake and Sing! "Awake and Whistle at Least. " New Republic, 82 (13 Mar. 1935), 134.

_____. Review of Waiting for Lefty and Till the Day I Die. "Lefty and Nazi. " New Republic, 82 (10 Apr. 1935), 247.

_____. "New Talent. " New Republic, 83 (29 May 1935), 78.

C. MISCELLANY

"Communist Infiltration of the Hollywood Motion-Picture Industry, Part 8." House Committee on Un-American Activities. Hearings, May 19-21, 1952, pp. 3453-3512.

"The Sum and Substance: A Dialogue on Contemporary Values." Telecast, Burbank, Calif., 1963. Interview of Clifford Odets by Dr. Herman Harvey.